D0179118

Cliff Goodwin has worked as a reporter, feature writer and sub-editor for various newspapers and magazines. His coverage of the 1988 Lockerbie air crash earned him a regional press award and he has published in over 200 newspapers and magazines worldwide. *Evil Spirits* is one of Cliff's four bestselling biographies, which include *To Be A Lady: The Story of Catherine Cookson* and *When the Wind Changed: The Life and Death of Tony Hancock*. He has recently also revised and updated his biography of Sid James to coincide in 2001 with the twenty-fifth anniversary of the death of the *Carry On* star.

EVIL SPIRITS

The Life of Oliver Reed

Cliff Goodwin

To Sarah: my beautiful companion and my friend.
Thank you for saving my life.

This paperback edition first published in 2001 by
Virgin Books Ltd
Thames Wharf Studios
Rainville Road
London W6 9HA

First published in hardback in Great Britain in 2000 by
Virgin Publishing Ltd

Reprinted 2001 (three times), 2002 (three times)

A catalogue record for this book is available from the British Library.

ISBN 0 7535 0519 3

Typeset by TW Typesetting, Plymouth, Devon
Printed and bound in Great Britain by Mackays of Chatham PLC

On Monday, when the sun is hot
I wonder to myself a lot:
'Now is it true, or is it not,
'That what is which and which is what?'

Prologue

Richard Burton was hitting the bottle with Jimmy Hurt the night before his death. He knew it was going to kill him, but he did not stop. I don't have a drink problem. But if that was the case and doctors told me I would have to stop, I'd like to think I would be brave enough to drink myself into the grave.

Sunday, 2 May 1999

OLIVER REED IS FINISHING his seventh bottle of German beer. He waves the empty at Paul Cremona. The Maltese bar owner keeps hold of the next bottle, forcing the actor to lean across the bar. 'You are like a bird freed from a cage,' he whispers in Oliver's ear. 'No drink for a week and on Sunday you go mad.'

Oliver takes the bottle and winks. 'Don't worry,' says Cremona. 'You are my best customer.'

At the far end of the bar Josephine Reed is showing Cremona's wife the gold bracelet Oliver gave her two days earlier. It was a special present for her 35th birthday, secretly designed and made by a Valletta jeweller. The older woman makes approving noises. 'I think he loves you very much,' she says.

I saw an old movie of mine on television the other night and I thought, 'God, Almighty!' I didn't realise how bad I was.

Oliver has been in Malta for five weeks. For his part in *Gladiator* he has let his grey hair grow long. He is suntanned

1

and looking surprisingly healthy and determined to enjoy his last week on the Mediterranean island and his last Sunday lunchtime at The Pub.

Turning his back to the bar Oliver looks around the room. It is small, no bigger than twenty-foot square. Down each wall are wooden bench seats. Five round tables. Few chairs. At the far end, in keeping with The Pub's mock-English decor, the single window is divided into squares like a Dickensian sweet shop. Outside, Valletta's Archbishop Street is bright and hot.

Warren, the Cremonas' son, has finished sorting bottles in the cellar. He shakes hands with Oliver and says he is going home to watch the San Marino Grand Prix on television. Warren is a lifelong Ferrari fan. Oliver supports McLaren. The two men trade friendly insults and Oliver promises to say goodbye before he flies home to Ireland.

As Warren leaves, a party of Royal Navy ratings fill The Pub. On their cap band is the name of their ship, HMS *Cumberland*. They recognise Oliver, who opens his arms and pulls two of the sailors toward him. 'Lets have a drink,' he announces. 'Black rum all round.'

If I went round constantly kissing babies in prams, saying I believe in the Church and doing good, the public wouldn't be interested. That's not what the public expects from Oliver Reed. They want him to fall off the edge of a dustbin, get into fights and get drunk and do all the things you read in the papers.

By two thirty Oliver has downed twelve double measures of Captain Morgan's Jamaica rum – not his favourite spirit – and is back to his usual doubles of Famous Grouse whisky. His bar bill that lunch time alone has already reached 270 Maltese lira, almost £450.

One by one the sailors leave. After signing autographs, Oliver's shoulders and arms are aching. He ignores the pain. Too much arm wrestling. He smiles at his wife and takes his drink and sits on the floor between the door and the jukebox. A few minutes later he is snoring loudly and apparently in a deep sleep.

The snoring stops. Oliver's head has fallen forward, as if he were thoughtfully studying something in his glass of whisky. In the half-light Josephine notices her husband's lips are darkening. When she reaches him it is obvious something is badly wrong.

I regret not having made love to every woman on earth, I regret having not kissed the wet nose of every dog on earth, I regret having not been into every bar on earth, but that doesn't make me a hell raiser. If somebody punches me on the nose, I will punch them back; if somebody buys me a drink, I will buy them one back.

Neriku Farrugia is the first to reach her side. The Maltese seaman first met Oliver while working as an extra on the film *Cutthroat Island*. 'Help him,' Josephine says. 'Please help him.' As Farrugia lifts his friend on to one of the bench seats Oliver grits his teeth and hisses: 'Lay down. Lay down.'

Oliver's breathing is shallow and rapid. His fists are clenched. Beside the bench, and level with his head, is a wooden table. His right hand comes up and begins punching the underside of the table. Each time his fist makes contact it lifts the table clear of the floor. He is desperately, painfully sucking in air, his lips grotesquely dark against his suntanned face and the white stubble of his beard.

Someone – Farrugia doesn't know who – is shouting for an ambulance. The men in the bar lift Oliver's body on to the floor. Farrugia cannot find a pulse. Pulling back the 61-year-old actor's head, he starts mouth-to-mouth resuscitation, desperately punching at his chest.

I am only an actor – not a priest beyond reproach. I'm not a villain, I have never hurt anyone. I am just a tawdry character who explodes now and again.

The ambulance arrives a few minutes later. As the paramedics work on Oliver the seaman moves back and sits on a stool in front of the bar. Josephine is quite calm. She is shaking her head gently from side to side.

From Archbishop Street the ambulance turns right into St Ursula Street. A car is blocking the corner into Castille Place. Bumping the kerb the driver looks over his shoulder into the back of the ambulance. His colleague has stopped giving heart massage and is feeling for a heartbeat. There is none.

Inside a casualty bay at St Luke's Hospital the doctors work for thirteen minutes to revive the actor. It is too late.

Oliver Reed is dead.

Chapter One

'My fear is what is going to happen to my body when life has left it.'

THERE WAS A SENSE OF URGENCY as the young man in the trench coat and hat and sensible beige-coloured shoes hurried across Coombe Lane and away from Raynes Park station. The mid-afternoon train from Waterloo – not his usual train – was half full and on time.

Already 26, he was still lean and never filled out the way his mother had wanted him to. He was terribly shy. He was frightened of people. Sport was the only thing he cared about, and horse racing in particular. He could talk to people about horses and handicaps and how the going at Fontwell or Sandown affected the chances of the second favourite, but the world in general frightened him. And at this moment he was extremely apprehensive.

He turned into Durrington Park Road and saw the doctor's car parked outside his house. Like most of the properties in this middle-class Wimbledon side street No. 9 was a detached house with a small front garden enclosed by a wooden fence and overgrown privet. It was mid-February and smoke was rising from the chimney. Inside he found his mother reassuringly sipping tea in the bay-windowed front room. Above him he could hear the doctor and midwife walking back and forth on the bare floorboards of the master bedroom. There was also the sound of his wife giving birth to their second child.

The house was his mother's. Beatrice May Reed had bought and taken possession of No. 9 Durrington Park Road in 1915. She was upright and polite and with the soft vowels peculiar to someone born and educated on the Isle of Thanet.

Her neighbours attributed the absence, and eventual non-appearance, of a 'Mr Reed' to the war raging across most of Europe. With Mrs Reed had come an assortment of children: Robin, Guy, Carol, Juliet and Peter. At four years old, Peter was the youngest.

By 1934 Peter Reed had realised his teenage ambition to become a racing journalist and was contributing to the sports pages of a national newspaper. He had also fallen in love. Marcia Beryl Andrews was the daughter of a City business-man and a caring but pretentious mother who, despite their misgivings, soon realised they could do nothing to divert their energetic daughter's intention to marry a young man who appeared to possess no ambition whatsoever. The couple married and moved to a small but adequate house in Cobham Road, Fetcham, just south of Leatherhead. Orchard Cottage was also a short taxi ride from Tattenham Corner racecourse and the stables of Epsom Downs. It was here, on 7 February 1936, that Marcia gave birth to the couple's first child. They christened the boy David Anthony Reed.

Finances were tight. Even with the little extra Peter made from betting on the horses he wrote about and tipped, it was soon evident a journalist's salary could not support his family and sustain his wife's apparently endless extravagances. When, less than fifteen months after the birth of their son, Marcia announced she was once again pregnant, Peter swallowed his pride and sought his mother's help. Sometime in the autumn of 1937 they moved back to the Wimbledon house in which Peter Reed had grown and lived for the majority of his life.

On 13 February 1938 – just six days after David Reed's second birthday – and after a long and painful confinement Marcia gave birth to her second son. The arrival sparked an immediate and bitter quarrel between husband and wife and opened the first irreparable crack in their marriage. Marcia wanted to call the baby Launcelot after her father, a sugges-tion Peter did not like and a name frowned upon by the child's grandmother. Why not call him Robert after one of his father's own relatives? Marcia, who suddenly found herself besieged and outvoted in a house that was not her own, attempted a compromise: her youngest son would be called

Oliver, in deference to her own mother Olive. The disagreement was still smouldering when Peter Reed visited Wimbledon register office on 4 March to record his son's birth. The registrar, Alfred Good, was informed the parents had still not settled on a name and left the appropriate column blank; it would be another eighteen years before the entry was officially completed. To a world of doctors and schoolteachers and other petty administrators the boy would grow up as Robert Oliver Reed. To his family and friends – and to his mother's satisfaction – he would be called Oliver Reed.

As the only male resident of No. 9 Durrington Park Road, Peter Reed's name now replaced his mother's on local authority roles as head of the household. Although her mother-in-law still employed and paid the wages of a cook, maid and butler it was Marcia Reed who effectively oversaw the domestic affairs.

Within days Marcia had visited a large store that catered for the needs of domestic staff and, armed with the relevant measurements, demanded to be shown a selection of uniforms. Unswayed by the latest colours and styles favoured by the nobility, Marcia was far more likely to choose something to match the curtains. The cook, who seldom left the kitchen except to go to her top-floor bedroom, always wore grey with a very large apron. Daisy the maid was inevitably in some shade of green with a small and elegant apron. And George the butler wore a traditional black suit and mirror-polished black shoes.

For Marcia Reed motherhood was never a profession, more a part-time hobby. One of her first demands was for a nanny to look after her young family. With such a small staff the nanny occupied top slot in the domestic hierarchy, sometimes eating with the staff in the kitchen and sometimes with Peter and Marcia in the dining room. Most of her time was spent with her two charges.

Childhood, for the latest addition to the Reed family, was a collection of images and colours. The nanny wore a grey uniform to which she added, whenever she went outside, a white cap and stiff white cuffs. At home Oliver's memory stored flashes of . . . 'A burning fire grate . . . A potty overturned on a linoleum floor . . . The taste of cold urine . . .

A world of legs – table legs, chair legs, sideboard legs, human legs'. Like his brother Oliver was allowed, even encouraged, to call all adults by their Christian names. Kisses, too, even between adults and maiden aunts should be delivered full on the lips.

On 27 April 1939, the government announced the military call-up of all men aged between 20 and 41. Should war come, and Peter was convinced it would, it would be only a matter of months before the upper age limit was increased. He informed, first his mother and then his wife, his intention to register as a conscientious objector. 'Wars start because politicians want them to,' Peter explained to a colleague. 'The thought of ordinary decent men killing each other, no matter what country they are from, is barbaric.'

It was an argument Marcia thought cowardly and futile. Bitter rows turned the Durrington Park Road house into a battle zone. Married to a husband she no longer respected – and certainly did not love – Marcia secretly plotted her escape. Long before Britain and France declared war on Germany, the private war between Peter and Marcia was over.

Early in September Marcia and her younger son were driven to an aunt living in Berkshire, far enough from London to escape the feared bombing. David, due to start preparatory school early the next year, would remain in Wimbledon with his father. As the Phoney War dragged through the winter she relented and allowed Oliver to return to Peter in south London. Marcia had another reason for remaining in the country: she had fallen in love with an RAF officer.

On 2 July 1940, the first German bombs fell on London. A month later a Luftwaffe bomber was shot down over the capital. The Blitz had started. Marcia returned to Wimbledon, scooped up her younger son and followed her lover to his new posting in Buckinghamshire. She left no note and did not tell Peter's mother where she would be living. The new home to which Marcia brought two-year-old Oliver was her lover's thatched cottage on the outskirts of Bledlow, near Princes Risborough. The rented house was stone-floored and smelled of wood smoke and warm hay and was ruled over by Nanny Morgy, an elderly cook devoted to her employer.

Bledlow was a quiet village, one of a score of hamlets tucked beneath the wooded scarp of the Chiltern Hills. The only strangers it attracted were cyclists and ramblers exploring the Buckinghamshire countryside or Roman historians walking the nearby Icknield Way. For any stranger, let alone a child too young to read, the lanes approaching Bledlow gave no clues to journey or destination, for the signposts to such places as Christmas Common, Park Corner and Russell's Water had all been dismantled or destroyed in the fear of invasion.

Her son wasn't the only possession Marcia transported to Buckinghamshire. Crammed beside him on the back seat of the car had been a tall metal cage containing Ockey, an African parrot. Each evening after dinner Marcia would switch on 'the Murphy', a brown Bakelite wireless, and waltz in great swoops around the cottage sitting room. Snatching up the parrot's cage, she would deposit it on the radio, commanding Ockey to 'dancey-dancey-dancey', to which the bird would stiffen its bright green tail feathers and strut about in time to the music. To a three-year-old there was only one way to compete. Oliver would clamber on to the coffee table and shuffle and stamp his feet. It was, he claimed many years later, his first public performance.

Sometimes there would be air raids. Nanny Morgy would grab the toddler from his bedroom-cum-nursery and they would huddle together under the Morrison shelter in the kitchen. The shelter, which doubled as a table, was made of steel and had wire-mesh sides to protect the occupants from falling masonry and bomb debris. The floor was padded with cushions and pillows and Morgy, smelling of flour and cloth and wax, would read stories from *Winnie-the-Pooh* as the Bofors guns crump-crumped in the distance.

Here is Edward Bear, coming downstairs now, bump, bump, bump, on the back of his head, behind Christopher Robin. It is, as far as he knows, the only way of coming downstairs, but sometimes he feels that there really is another way, if only he could stop bumping for a moment and think of it. And then he feels that perhaps there isn't. Anyhow, here he is at the bottom, and ready to be introduced to you. Winnie-the-Pooh.

Through the eyes of an inquisitive and sensitive child Oliver's brief existence had so far little to do with reality. He had no recollection of his father, nor of his older brother. His mother rarely spoke of Wimbledon. And his world focused more on the blue-uniformed men who visited the cottage or sang and staggered out of the Red Lions or mysteriously and silently disappeared overnight.

One day between the wail of the siren and the thump-thump of the bombs Nanny Morgy and her charge heard a different sound. From under the table it sounded like hundreds of popguns being fired in quick succession. As the pop guns got faster and faster the sound got louder and louder until Morgy, pricked into action by a sense of impending doom, grabbed the boy and dragged him through the open back door.

The pair emerged into the sunlight just in time to see an aircraft with both its engines ablaze dipping toward the cottage.

BANG!!!???***!!!

Piglet lay there, wondering what had happened. At first he thought that the whole world had blown up; and then he thought that perhaps only the Forest part of it had; and then he thought that perhaps only he had, and he was now alone in the moon or somewhere, and would never see Christopher Robin or Pooh or Eeyore again.

The Messerschmitt had skimmed the top of the cottage, ripping off the ridge thatch and setting light to the rest. By the time Morgy and Oliver picked themselves up, the bomber had crash-landed two fields away. The RAF firemen from a nearby base soon had the blazing roof under control and the inquisitive Oliver wandered away to look at the wreckage.

From a grassy bank he could see the plane embedded in a ploughed field. On what remained of the tail was a swastika and on the fuselage a black and white Luftwaffe cross. Looking down through the scattered windscreen the boy could see the pilot, his eyes still open and his head slumped to one side. A trickle of bright red blood ran from the corner of his mouth.

It was the first dead body Oliver had seen. Wrapping his arms around himself he began to cry. He was still crying when Nanny Morgy found him an hour later.

Sugar, butter and bacon were the first foodstuffs to be rationed after Britain's declaration of war. Whether by deceit or out of genuine motives, Marcia registered her youngest son with the Ministry of Food as a vegetarian. Non-meat-eaters were allowed an extra ration of eggs and cheese and Nanny Morgy put them to good use, supplementing the produce from the garden allotment and the daily bunches of carrots donated by a neighbouring retired French general with an obsession for root vegetables.

One morning, not long after Oliver's fourth birthday, a letter arrived at the Bledlow cottage. It was from Peter Reed's London solicitor and informed Marcia, in the polite but threatening language employed by lawyers, that her days in hiding were over.

It had not been too hard for Peter to trace his wife's whereabouts through the family's ration book. The only surprise is that he took so long. He made no threats or demands. He simply wanted his wife, whom he still loved and was prepared to forgive, to know that he knew where she was living and, with both ends of the bridge now established, it was up to Marcia to make the return journey.

Life at Bledlow was far too gay for Marcia to consider any kind of reconciliation. The men her lover invited to the cottage were young and intelligent and desperately virile. On special days her son was allowed to stay up late, pushing his way through a sea of blue-serge trousers to deliver the drinks or plates of sandwiches Nanny Morgy made in the kitchen. For the adult Oliver, the memory was sprinkled with a dusting of childish romance. 'During the war I used to be a cocktail barman at my mother's lover's cocktail parties,' said Oliver. 'And the guests were from fighter and bomber command and the parties used to get smaller and smaller and the laughter got less and less as the men I had seen would go off to war and die drunk.'

To a young boy's knee-high view of the war – even the fringes of it – the people and places survived more as childhood whimsy than adult wisdom. There were no 'bombers coughing at the end of the garden' nor did they taxi 'down the field and onto the runway where they roared off and sailed away like unflapping bats into the red evening sky'.

Its position tight under the Chiltern scarp made Bledlow an impossible location for an airfield. Of the twelve RAF bases in wartime Buckinghamshire the closest to the village was at Haddenham, near Thame, five miles to the northeast. Consisting of little more than a grass aerodrome, served by a hangar and three billet huts, RAF Detachment Thame was the brief home of the pioneering Glider Training Squadron. The twelve Army pilots – wearing khaki and not blue uniforms – moved on to the base in December 1940, and flew out the last of the prototype gliders two years later. It is more likely, therefore, that Marcia's lover – 'who never wore wings' – was a senior officer stationed at one of the nearby RAF training bases.

Buckinghamshire was never a front-line county in the air war: more than half the county's air bases were primarily concerned with pilot training or the selection of bomber crews, although Bomber Command headquarters at Naphill outside High Wycombe was one of the exceptions. There were no fighter squadrons stationed in Buckinghamshire and, from 1942, the only active-service squadrons were B-17 crews of the United States Army Air Force based at Bovingdon and Cheddington.

Cutting through the lanes, it would take Marcia's lover less than twenty minutes to drive north from the Bledlow cottage to No.11 Operational Training Unit at Westcott. From squadrons and selection bases around Britain pilots and navigators and engineers and air gunners would descend on Westcott, and its satellite at nearby Oakley, to be trained as bomber crews. Many of the pilots had seen action during the Battle of Britain. 'They had names like Pip and smoked pipes and wore white ribbons beneath their wings with diagonal purple strips,' recalled Oliver years later. 'They were young and full of extravagance, indulgence, elegance and arrogance and I felt exhilarated by their rowdy bonhomie.' When the faces disappeared it was because the crews had been posted to Lancaster and Halifax squadrons around Britain.

It was on the River Thame, south of Westcott, that the crews were tested on their sea survival techniques. Dressed in full flying gear and with their bright yellow Mae Wests inflated, they would hurl themselves from a bridge and into the water to be assessed by a squadron leader 'with a face like a badger's bum'. One day, claims Oliver, he was allowed to watch:

> It was there I first met Lovely Gravy. The other pilots jumped into the river two at a time with a rubber dinghy held between them, but he jumped over the parapet of the bridge with his dinghy tied to his head and shouted out 'Lovely Gravy' before hitting the water flat on his back. I thought it was the most wonderful thing I had ever seen. So I climbed on the parapet and old Badger's Bum looked up, startled, and pointed his finger. I thought it was my signal. I jumped and my mouth filled with water and I couldn't swim. Lovely Gravy pulled me out and turned me upside down to empty the water out of my wellingtons.

Some evenings, when the wind was from the south and when the weather was warm enough to leave his bedroom window open, Oliver thought he could hear the distant rumble of thunder. When he asked Nanny Morgy what it was, she explained it was the German bombs falling on London.

In 1940, soon after his wife's disappearance, Peter Reed had moved out of his mother's house and into an apartment overlooking Wimbledon Common. The board that examined his claim to be a conscientious objector had restricted his movements and ordered him to contribute to the war effort; Peter volunteered as an ambulance driver. The raids had kept him constantly busy and exhausted. Eventually, Peter decided it was time for Marcia to look after their elder son.

Returning to the cottage one afternoon Oliver was confronted by a fair-haired boy he did not recognise. 'Hello, Ollie,' said the boy, offering his hand.

David Reed was two years older and two inches taller than his brother. To a boy whose brief memory could recall little else than the kindness of two or three females and the rowdy camaraderie of a largely male population, the sudden appearance of this 'polite but determined' rival was unnerving. Oliver's immediate recreation was to stomp his way to the top of the stairs and hurl his toy dog Fizzy over the banister. 'I really didn't mind him that much,' admitted Oliver many years later. 'Most small boys got babies for brothers and mine arrived grown up, with a school cap, stiff leather gloves and a Mickey Mouse gas mask case'.

The youngest and most inquisitive member of the Reed family was a long way from making the connection between his ancestry and his own compulsive behaviour. It was, for a five-year-old boy, nothing more than instinct, a flux of rootless inquisition and innocence.

He did not know why, but somewhere, deep inside the child, the tight green jumpers of the Land Army girls and the pleasing creases of their khaki breeches produced as unsettling excitement. And when Nanny Morgy caught him listening to the breathless giggles from beneath the camouflage-draped gun emplacements beyond the garden fence it lit a fascination and force within Oliver Reed that burned for the rest of his life.

Chapter Two

'I wish I could have written a book or a film about the love story of Herbert and May.'

I N LITHUANIA IN THE LATE MIDDLE AGES: the Prussian princes who once invaded the Baltic state were now established as land-owning aristocrats; German was the approved language and, for a merchant, adopting a Germanic name would almost certainly have attracted the approval of the ruling establishment, if not more custom. It was not long before the Beerbohm family firm was one of the biggest and busiest timber importers and traders on the Baltic coast.

In modern terms it would have been hailed a supreme example of 'public imaging'. As a corruption of *Birnbaum*, the German for pear tree, it linked the family with its trade. There could, however, have been a deeper, and more personal, meaning. A popular German saying of the time included the phrase *'der Apfel fällt nicht weit vom Birnbaum'*. A loose, but acceptable, translation would be 'like father, like son' – an admirable sentiment for a business employing two or even three generations.

When the Beerbohms helped Frederick the Great finance a minor conflict they were rewarded with an estate called Bernsteinbruch and, from their humble beginnings, were now highly regarded and welcome confidants of the Prussian royal family. Ernst Beerbohm, Oliver's great-great-grandfather, had married Amalie Henrietta Radke. She was a beautiful and independent woman.

Like all the Beerbohms, Ernst and Amalie produced a large and surprisingly healthy family. The youngest of their twelve children was Julius. Sometime in the 1820s Julius decided his fortune lay outside his native Lithuania and persuaded his father to finance an extended education in France. It was while studying commerce in Paris that Julius earned the nicknamed 'Monsieur Superbe-Homme', a sarcastic swipe at his bearing and fashionable clothes. In 1830, just as a revolutionary fervour was once again sweeping the French capital, Oliver Reed's great-grandfather boarded a packet and set sail for England.

Trading corn from the City of London proved as lucrative and time consuming as Baltic timber. It was not until Julius reached his early forties that he wooed and then married Constantia Draper, an Englishwoman little more than half his age yet who shared his passion for Dickens and languages; her husband could speak six fluently.

Constantia fell pregnant within the year and the couple moved to a large house at No. 2 Pembridge Villas, Kensington. It was here, despite her ever-declining health, that Constantia gave birth to three boys and a girl in yearly succession before collapsing and dying at the age of 32. Herbert Beerbohm – Oliver's paternal grandfather – was born on 28 January 1852.[1]

Throughout her confinements and ill health the Kensington house was kept by Constantia's younger sister Eliza, not an uncommon arrangement in Victorian society. Within a month of his wife's death, and apparently ignoring the conventions of mourning, the businessman proposed to his sister-in-law. English law in the 1850s refused to allow a widower to marry his dead wife's sister. Julius, a calm and unimaginative man, promptly whisked Eliza off to Switzerland, where they married before returning to London to start a family of their own. The new marriage produced five more children and a confused set of relationships. Julius's youngest child was Max Beerbohm – the future artist – who, as well as being Herbert Beerbohm's half-brother, was also his cousin.

By the age of seventeen Herbert had already joined and performed with several amateur dramatic clubs. He was a tall

---

[1] Officials at Somerset House mistakenly recorded Herbert Beerbohm's year of birth as 1853; the error was later corrected.

and slim youth whose carroty red hair contrasted sharply with his turquoise-green eyes, and his 'foreign' profile and good looks seem to have placed him in constant demand as villain or scoundrel. His announcement that he wanted to earn his living on the stage found little favour with his elderly father. Julius Beerbohm had already lost his eldest and youngest sons to dubious adventures – Ernest was in the Cape Colony and Julius Jnr in Patagonia – and he was not about to lose another. The family corn business badly needed an infusion of new blood and Herbert was ordered to stay.

His sense of duty lasted eight years. During the day Herbert mollified his father by playing the role of corn merchant. Each evening he left the Kensington house to perform impressions of Henry Irving and JL Toole and other leading actors at smoking parties and Bohemian clubs.

By 1876 Julius Beerbohm relented. 'Possibly Herbert's lack of aptitude for business, total boredom with figures of any kind, an infinite capacity for taking no pains at all with the corn business, were additional reasons for his father being in the end willing to go,' says Madeleine Bingham in her biography *The Great Lover: The Life and Art of Herbert Beerbohm Tree*. 'By this time Julius had other sons and possibly they would be drawn to the city.'

Allowing his 24-year-old son to leave the family firm, the patriarch advised Herbert to work hard and aim for the pinnacle of his profession. Legend has it that Herbert informed his father that the 'top of the tree' was where he was going and, as a constant reminder, he would adopt the name 'Tree'. Herbert Beerbohm Tree was now a professional actor.

After two years of poverty and mounting debts, Herbert had still not secured a full-time engagement. In 1878 he was invited to play Grimaldi in a Globe Theatre charity perform-ance of *The Life of an Actress*. Following the show he was called aside and invited to join the Bijou Theatre Company on its forthcoming provincial tour. The run would start at Folkestone Town Hall on Monday, 20 May, and to advertise the company's latest addition its posters announced:

Besides the well known members of the Company, the management have much pleasure in announcing that they have secured the services of Mr. H. Beerbohm Tree who will appear during the week in various pieces and on Wednesday and Friday will give (by special desire) his inimitable Dramatic and Mimictic Recitals. Stalls (price three shillings) are to be obtained at Goulden's Library, Folkestone.

Unlike his father, who despite being a passionate husband was rarely passionate about sex, Herbert was physically attractive and attracted to women. To his friends Herbert admitted several actresses had been 'good' to him on tour, 'good' being a late-nineteenth-century euphemism for physical love. He was, nevertheless, committed to marriage. In late 1881 Herbert met the woman he was eventually to marry. At eighteen Maud Holt was eleven years his junior, a flighty young woman determined to become an actress and marry an actor, and equally determined to make him suffer in the process.

Within three months Herbert Beerbohm Tree and Maud Holt were engaged. Their future son-in-law appalled the Holt family: Herbert had arrived for lunch in frayed shirt cuffs and talked of nothing but the theatre. A remonstration from Maud flaired into an argument and the engagement was off. Reconciliations were inevitably followed by further tearful separations until, the following summer, Maud finally agreed to set a date for their wedding. Herbert and Maud were married on 16 September 1882.

One of Tree's greatest achievements was the building of Her Majesty's Theatre – later renamed His Majesty's – to his own specifications. It was the fourth building on the same Haymarket site since Vanbrugh's original New Opera House and cost £30,000. In 1705 Vanbrugh's Queen's was still surrounded by farms, the acoustics were appalling and performances were frequently punctuated by animal noises. Almost two centuries later Tree's luxury theatre offered a new dimension in sound and comfort for both performers and audience.

Her Majesty's was opened in 1897, Queen Victoria's Diamond Jubilee year, by the Prince of Wales and not without incident. As he arrived, Prince Edward was dismayed to see that Beerbohm Tree had dressed his white-wigged doorman in replica uniforms to those worn by Buckingham Palace servants. Seconds later, as the prince entered the foyer, the electricity failed, plunging the building into darkness. But the irritations were minor and, within a year, Beerbohm Tree received a knighthood.

Beerbohm Tree was driven as much by instinct and inspiration as perspiration. His few errors of judgement were spectacular and legendary. One of his friends was JM Barrie. Sitting in his domed living room the author started to read the script of his new children's play. After just two acts the actor-manager begged his friend to stop. 'You must be mad,' Beerbohm Tree informed Barrie. 'It will never be popular . . . especially with a name like *Peter Pan*.'

Like royalty, Beerbohm Tree rarely carried cash. Most days he was forced to pay off his cab by borrowing five shillings or half-a-crown from the box office. And during the sumptuous receptions in the living quarters built into the dome of the theatre – the main room was fifty feet long – he would often disappear without explanation. Bored with the official function, he had slipped out to a nearby cabbies' shelter, where he played dominoes until dawn.

Just when or how Beerbohm Tree met Beatrice May Pinney is a mystery. The daughter of a music professor, Beatrice May was born on 23 May 1871 in Ramsgate, a resort often frequented by the Tree family. She was a gentle and good-natured young woman who much preferred to be called by her middle name, and her ancestry was as long as and still more distinguished than that of her future lover.

Professor William Pinney was a direct descendant of John Pinney, the architect and builder. Another relative was Charles Pinney, a mayor of Bristol, who nearly lost his life in the 1831 Bristol Riot. But it was William Pinney's wife, Henrietta, whose family would eventually add a splash of intrigue to the Reed bloodline and, according to Oliver, be responsible for much of his excessive behaviour. As a Rowlatt, Henrietta was the daughter of Canon Rowlatt of Exeter, whose family was founded by a bastard child of Peter the Great. On her mother's side there were several royal connections, including a direct line to Charlemagne, the eight-foot King of the Franks and the founder of the Holy Roman Empire.

The rebellious and reforming Peter fascinated Oliver, who related his ancestor's achievements and infamy with equal enthusiasm and never failed to point out the parallels in their characters.

In 1689 the sixteen-year-old Peter mounted a coup to force his half-sister Sophia, the regent, to resign and retire to a convent. The teenager feared that his half-brother Ivan, with whom he had ostensibly been sharing power, was about to have him killed. After the takeover Peter appointed his mother to effectively rule Russia as regent until he reached adulthood.

The new tsar was determined to modernise and improve his country, founding its future more on military and commercial strength than traditional and inflexible politics. Less than ten years after coming to power, and still in his mid-twenties, Peter became the first tsar in history to cross the Russian border except on a military campaign. He equipped and financed a 250-strong 'travelling embassy' – including priests, officials, dwarfs and bodyguards – and began roving around Europe, to learn the techniques and crafts he wanted his people to adopt. During his three-month stay in London he worked as a Deptford shipyard carpenter wielding a saw or hammer or adze with common labourers.

Throughout his 36-year reign he remained a political and social enigma. He trained and equipped a formidable army of 200,000 men and possessed one of the strongest navies in Europe. Yet his far-sighted and far-reaching social reforms changed old Russia for ever. He remodelled the calendar, simplified the alphabet and founded the first Russian news-paper. He abolished the *duma* of the Moscow aristocracy, reorganised the government and introduced a poll tax. He forced the practice of shaven chins and short, Western coats – anyone arriving at the gates of a city wearing a long Russian robe was made to kneel while the coat was cut to knee length. But his most dazzling reform was saved for the military and civil service. With the introduction of Peter's 'Table of Ranks' any commoner could rise on merit to the highest positions.

A barrel-chested man standing six feet nine inches tall, Peter passed on to his descendant far more than a loose physical resemblance. Two and a half centuries later Oliver Reed would find himself walking through a genetic hall of mirrors, unwittingly trapped in a congenital maze. Two of his relatives inherited the Romanoff withered hand, a deformity shared by Kaiser Willhelm II. Oliver the actor thankfully grew up with less violent traits of his monstrous great-great-grandfather.

During his three-month stay in London the tsar and fifteen of his retinue lodged at Sayes Court, the elegant and beautiful Deptford home of the diarist and landscape gardener John Evelyn. Within days Peter had transformed his residence into one of the bawdiest and rowdiest houses in England. Royals and aristocrats were quick to accept his invitation to dinner. Once inside, they discovered Peter had posted guards on the doors with orders not to let anyone out until they had drunk at least four bottles of wine. Trials of strength left every brass lock shattered and more than three hundred panes of glass broken. One drunken party ended when the kitchen was destroyed by an explosion.

Outside the 'Zarrish Majestie' decimated Evelyn's prize gardens and bowling green by staging wrestling and boxing bouts. One contest netted him five hundred guineas when he matched one of his bodyguards with an English knuckle fighter. When the Russians left it cost £250 to repair the damage to the house and grounds.

Peter sought anonymity by frequently swapping identities with one of his party and insisting he be always accompanied by a group of fools and dwarfs. Anyone – man or woman – who poked fun at Peter's size or his nervous facial twitch, an affliction he developed in his teens, was promptly knocked flat.

'The young Peter, drunk, pop-eyed, making dreadful faces, roaring, slashing about at random with his sword, was a fearsome host,' recorded the historian Stephen Graham. 'Any man he liked he kissed, any woman he unlaced. Anyone who enraged him he struck a fearful buffet. His head had a very unpleasant nervous shake. His eyes were roaming, flashing, audacious, full of inventiveness and wild humour, or else full of adventurous cruelty, vengeful, implacable. His "cats' whiskers" bristled over a full sensual mouth of extraordinary coarseness. His giant frame brooded over his guests at table like a vulture among lesser birds. But he did not brood over his wine. No one knew what would be his next action. All learned to be apprehensive.'

During the summer of 1698 Peter and his mistress travelled to Portsmouth to inspect the royal dockyard. The couple were accompanied by eleven members of his 'aristocracy of mirth' and eight servants. During an overnight stop at Godalming the party consumed 'five ribs of beef weighing three stone, one sheep weighing fifty-six pounds, three-quarters of a lamb, a shoulder roasted and a loin of veal trussed with bacon, eight pullets, four couple of rabbits, three dozen of sack [white wine], one dozen of claret and bread and beer proportional'.

Peter was not attracted by, or attractive to, women. 'He handled them very roughly and if he commonly slept with one it was because he was terrified of sleeping alone,' claims his descendant with a degree of admission.

Seduced by Beerbohm Tree's charm and charisma as their affair continued, May gave birth to their first child, Claude, in her late twenties. In 1903 when Robin was born, Tree decided to install his lover closer to his own London home and bought Daisyfield, a house on the borders of Putney and Wandsworth and verging on Wimbledon Common. There were stipulations. If May couldn't have respectability she at least wanted a family of her own and changed her surname to Reed because 'I am but a broken Reed at the foot of a mighty Tree'.

In her biography, *The Great Lover: The Life and Art of Herbert Beerbohm Tree*, Madeleine Bingham wonders:

The question that poses itself was what Beatrice May Pinney (Mrs Reed by deed poll) told her children? It was an age when children were not expected to know anything about the lives of the godlike adults who surrounded them. Secrets were easy to keep. Did Herbert pose as the inevitable 'uncle' or 'guardian' of so many stories of the period? Did Mrs Reed invent some exotic occupation for the man of her choice. When registering the births of his children it was stated that Herbert Reed was 'of independent means', a nice gentlemanly phrase which could cover a multitude of sins and omissions. Did Mrs Reed tell the neighbours that Mr Reed (of independent means) was an intrepid traveller who spent much of his time abroad? How did she explain his constant comings, and equally swift goings? Or did she live a quiet domestic suburban life keeping herself to herself, as it was possible to do in those days, with a faithful servant or two to keep her secrets and help her bring up her fathered, but fatherless brood.

In 1905, eighteen months after the Reed family had moved to Daisyfield, May gave birth to her third son, Guy. By 1911 there were three more children: Carol, whose work as a film director would earn him a knighthood; Juliet, her only daughter; and Peter, the youngest.

Tree – like the majority of his ancestors and descendants – was a sexual animal, fathering three legitimate daughters and half a dozen illegitimate children during his twenty-year affair with Beatrice May Pinney. Maud, Lady Tree, knew exactly what was going on. When an acquaintance noticed that her husband was paying fulsome compliments to an actress, she remarked, 'The trouble with Herbert's compliments is that they are usually followed by confinements.'

Peter Reed – Oliver's father – was just six years old when his own father died suddenly on 2 July 1917. Beerbohm Tree's family moved swiftly to protect his name, not only as a great actor-manager but also as a loyal husband and father. They searched his personal papers and all documents and references to May Reed and his illegitimate children were destroyed or removed. In death Tree had already moved to treat both his 'wives' equally. Half his £105,000 estate went to his long-suffering and faithful lover.

Oliver was, at least for the second half of his life, a dedicated but undisciplined disciple of Gregor Mendel, the nineteenth-century Austrian-born monk and botanist. His experiments, largely with peas, led to the discovery of the basic principles of heredity and subsequently laid the foundation of the science of genetics. Mendel theorised that certain physical features and characteristics were passed on through paired units of heredity, now known as genes. Oliver Reed was convinced that not only had he inherited a smattering of his ancestors' physical attributes, but that their character and mental outlook had also somehow survived the centuries.

For Herbert Beerbohm Tree, his actor-manager grand-father, Oliver claimed not only a genetic and temperamental bloodline but a direct psychic circuit. At times of stress or confronted by a career crossroads Oliver would talk over the problem with his long-dead forefather. There were other, more tangible, similarities to both their lives. Oliver Reed and Herbert Beerbohm Tree both claimed they were born old, and grew younger and younger; both were uninterested and vague at school and floated through their academic years; both men were pernickety about the word 'actor', insisting it was pronounced 'act-tor'; both had numerous affairs with leading ladies in their productions; both manipulated and managed the press to further their careers – Herbert was the first British actor to hand out publicity photographs; both men gave the impression they were less astute than they really were. And, from childhood to manhood, grandfather and grandson found boredom a constant and irritating curse.

It was a process for which Oliver developed his own hybrid theory. Never afraid of death – more afraid he would not be given the Hemingway option of dying 'like a man' – Oliver passionately believed in a transference of personality from one living ancestor to another. In his autobiography, *Reed All About Me,* he explains:

> I believe very strongly that we don't disappear forever but return through the living. Not reincarnation in the sense generally believed by many, as a new baby and a brand new soul, but living on through the living. I know that my grandfather lives on through me, and as I take a great joy in nature, the trees and the birds and the way the wind blows, just as my grandmother did, I know that a part of her also lives on through me. It is because of this that I will never grow old.

Chapter Three

'I have a pride in my family; with all their eccentricities and gentleness and madness and genius and backwardness and greatness and nothingness.'

THINGS WERE STARTING TO GO WRONG at Bledlow. The tantrums and petty flirtations that heralded the destruction of Marcia's marriage now looked as though they would end her three-year affair.

There were new and fascinating guests at the cottage cocktail parties. By 1943 the American 8th Army Air Force had established its headquarters at Wycombe Abbey School and USAAF staff officers were regular visitors to RAF Westcott. One of Marcia's 'lovers' was Captain Wilbur T Hannigan, an Irish American pilot from Brooklyn. Five years older than most of his fellow bomber pilots, Hannigan arrived in England late in July 1943. 'Two days later I was being introduced to this stunning woman I assumed was the wife of an RAF officer,' he remembers. 'She was charming and elegant and had this wonderful knack of making you feel as though you were the most important person in the room. I was smitten.'

Hannigan, who cannot recall seeing any young children at Bledlow, eagerly accepted Marcia's invitation to visit the cottage whenever he was not flying. 'Marcia was too fond of men – and the excitement of men – to remain faithful,' adds the retired Miami lawyer. 'I certainly wasn't her only American visitor.'

One evening Marcia's lover announced he was being posted to a bomber base in Yorkshire. Marcia exploded in a whirlwind of anger and frustration. She refused even to consider moving north; and then there were the boys to consider: a new school had to be found for David, and Oliver had not yet started his education. Offers of marriage and adoption failed to calm her. Like her marriage, the affair was over.

Launcelot Andrews was an Edinburgh-born businessman who spoke with a soft Lowland accent. His experiences as a World War One officer with the King's Own Scottish Borderers left him with a slight limp, a fear of gas and a rabid hatred of the German nation. By the early 1920s he had secured a managerial position with Fyffes, the fruit importer and distributor, and was earning enough to move his wife and young family to the south London suburb of Wimbledon. Each morning Andrews dressed in a conservative grey suit, retrieved his umbrella from the hat stand in the hall of No. 74 Marryat Road and set off to catch the Tube to his City office.

Around the house Andrews resembled a rotund, balding Buddha with a mischievous smile frozen at the corner of his mouth as if he were inwardly laughing at some secret joke. He may never have dared pinch the maid's bottom, but there was no doubt he thought about it. At weekends and partly to relieve the boredom he drank himself into a frenzy of national pride, marching round the house and gardens waving a Union Flag and singing 'Rule Britannia' in a loud and lively voice.

As the daughter of a Sussex farmer, Olive Andrews had grown accustomed to her husband's exuberant ways. She was snobbishly houseproud and ruled her detached domain with unforgiving pride: the yards of mahogany were polished daily and the antimacassars changed whenever a chair or over-stuffed coach was used. When Marcia telephoned to say she was coming home to Wimbledon it was Olive who readily forgave her daughter's behaviour, but Launcelot who forbade her from returning to her husband.

Olive's deliberate speech and high-pitched voice often gave the impression that her mind, if not her body, was some-where else. She also had the habit of addressing everyone as 'darling'. Almost as soon as he could speak David Reed mimicked the habit and began calling his grandmother

'Dardin'. He could not remember her, but young Oliver was about to be reunited with his Granny Dardin.

If they could not keep the war from their grandchildren the Andrewses at least attempted a semblance of normality within their extended family. While Launcelot dispensed an endless – and apparently illegal – supply of rationed toffees his wife recited poems extolling the virtues of domestic harmony:

One cries and says I love you,
The other smiles and says I know.

Outside the Marryat Road house they waged a relentless and vicious campaign against their 'cowardly' son-in-law. In the street Launcelot Andrews refused to acknowledge his presence and left any local shop that Peter entered. While his own son, Marcia's younger brother, was enslaved as a Japanese prisoner of war working on the Burma Road Launcelot refused to allow 'that bloody conchie' across the threshold. Olive, meanwhile, publicly and loudly presented her wife's estranged husband with a white feather whenever their paths crossed.

The smog of hatred and disrespect that surrounded his father's very existence began to permeate the six-year-old Oliver as deeply as the smell of Launcelot Andrews's pipe. The kitchen whispers and mumbled sarcasm forever over-shadowed Peter Reed's kindnesses and love for his son. 'Oliver came to hate his father,' admitted a friend. 'As far as he was concerned his father's decision not to fight in the war reflected on him personally and Oliver spent the rest of his life carrying the guilt. It was something you could not shake him on, his father had been a coward and Oliver detested that part of his life.'

Less than a week after their return from Buckinghamshire Marcia enrolled her younger son at Wimbledon Common Preparatory School. Opened in 1919 as a prep school for the sons of local gentry, it originally occupied the ground floor and basement of No. 47 High Street, just around the corner from Marryat Road. Three years later the school's founding principal – a 'sweet and charming' middle-aged woman called

Miss Whiting – sold the establishment to her teaching assistant. It was under Miss GCB Holland that the school and its reputation continued to grow, forcing a move to new and larger premises at No. 20 Homefield Road.

It was to Homefield Road one Monday morning that Marcia led the young Oliver, dressed in his grey uniform with its yellow, white and silver piping. The badge on his blazer incorporated a squirrel – allegedly inspired by the red squirrels that inhabited Wimbledon Common – and the motto, 'Industry with Cheerfulness'.

Originally built as a private house, The Squirrels was far less imposing than it appeared to the newest of the school's forty pupils: there was a basement storeroom, a ground-floor office and two classrooms on each of the two upper storeys. As a Froebel-trained teacher, Miss Holland insisted on continuing the discipline that a pupil's freedom is a vital part of the learning process.

For the next ten months Oliver made unimpressive progress at The Squirrels. 'His academic achievements were far less outstanding than his personality and charisma,' recalls Barry Turner, current assistant head at the school, whose mother took over as principal a few years after the departure of its most famous pupil.

By the following spring it was evident that the two-year gap between Oliver and his older brother was widening by the term. Each day Marcia would stand her younger son in the middle of the morning-room carpet and order him to recite his lessons. Spelling was always a painful experience.

'Spell "are",' commanded Marcia.

Her son examined his shuffling feet. 'A-r-e-r.'

'No, no, Oliver, Not "a-r-e-r". "A-r-e" spells "are".'

'I can't.'

'Try "you" then,' said Marcia. 'You know you can spell "you".'

The boy caught sight of his grandmother entering the morning room. 'Y-o-o-u.'

'He's impossible,' tutted Dardin. 'What can we do with the boy?'

The answer – if anyone at Marryat Road had bothered to look – was as much in the book Nanny Morgy had given him on his departure from Bledlow as it was in his head.

Underneath the knocker there was a notice which said:

PLES RING IF AN RESER IS REQIRD

Underneath the bell-pull there was a notice which said:

PLES CNOKE IF AN RESR IS NOT REQID

These notices had been written by Christopher Robin, who was the only one in the forest who could spell.

The Squirrels' teachers could report one positive response: their six-year-old charge was already showing a remarkable and deepening love of animals. Breaking his journey home, Oliver would cross Homefield Road to his headmistress's house to pet and help feed the dozens of stray cats Miss Holland had rescued from the bombsites and ruins of south London.

Years later, after his younger brother Simon and son Mark Reed both became pupils, Oliver Reed would arrive unannounced at 'Squirrel' sports days wearing his old school cap and scarf. 'He was always excessively polite to my mother,' adds Barry Turner, 'and usually sober.'

On 13 June 1944 – while Oliver was sitting in his classroom at The Squirrels – dockers on both banks of the Thames at Tilbury and Gravesend looked up into the clear blue sky. The tiny aircraft was easy to spot. The yellow-red flame and the deep, throaty crackle from its engine suddenly died and the plane stalled and nose-dived; as it hit the ground a huge explosion rattled windows for more than a mile. Hitler's first *Vergeltung* (retribution) weapon had landed on wasteland near Swanscombe in Kent. Within a week, and with the Allied invasion pinned down along a loosely connected seventy-mile Normandy front, more than a hundred V-1 flying bombs a day were falling on London and the south of England.

Dubbed 'Doodlebugs' by the press, the V-1 blitz was nerve-racking and deadly. Launched from the Pas de Calais, the small pilotless aircraft were set on a predetermined course and carried a one-ton high-explosive warhead. When the measured amount of fuel ran out they plunged indiscriminately to earth. Whether by fate or some fluke of physics Wimbledon and south London was getting more than its fair share of destruction. Early in July a Doodlebug exploded on the playing field of King's College School, forcing an abrupt end to the summer term. Three weeks later another fell closer to the town centre. Launcelot Andrews had just left a bank when the blast hurled his body across the street.

Returning from her father's funeral, to which Peter Reed was not invited, Marcia informed her estranged husband that she wanted her sons removed from Wimbledon as quickly as possible. For once Peter agreed. Within the month both parents had deposited David and Oliver on the gravel forecourt of an Old Woking school. It was only a short drive down the A3 from Wimbledon, but far enough from London for Marcia to consider it safe.

Hoe Place Preparatory School occupied an impressive former private residence surrounded by twenty acres of woodland and playing fields. Its academic role was 'to afford a sound general education' for its pupils and 'to prepare boys for public school and the Royal Navy'. Examining the prospectus, Peter Reed may well have recieved the impression that the staff were more concerned with their charges' health than scholastic development. 'The District Medical Officer speaks of Woking as an exceptionally healthy locality . . . The climate is mild and bracing and is recommended by medical men as particularly suited to children.'

None of which influenced Peter Reed's decision to choose Hoe Place for his sons. Fees were £40 per term per boy – 'Special terms for the sons of clergymen, Naval and Military officers' – and Peter was more interested in the discount being offered for brothers attending at the same time. He certainly could not stretch to paying the extra guinea a term for out-of-hours instruction in carpentry or boxing or shooting.

Hoe Place, which took full and weekday boarders, agreed to enrol the boys, but only after a direct appeal from one of Peter's older brothers. Guy Reed was a quiet and sensitive man who spent a disproportionate amount of his income on buying paintings and antiques to fill his small cottage in Old Woking High Street. He was also a close friend of Captain W Sinker, the appropriately named former Royal Navy officer who now owned and ran Hoe Place school.

It was Sinker, his hands smelling of powdered chalk and his breath of whisky, who greeted his new intake of pupils.

Young Oliver watched with increasing alarm as his luggage was unloaded and his parents drove away. Once they were out of sight he let rip with an animal howl which, over the next few days, dribbled first into a continuous stream of choking sobs and then into lonely and muffled tears – 'I cried in the lavatory and the rhododendron bushes.'

Like the boys' late grandfather, Sinker viewed patriotism as a duty and selected his teaching staff almost exclusively from the ranks of Great War veterans and younger disabled servicemen. He insisted the walls of his establishment be decorated with posters and newspaper cuttings of heroes and military adventures and maps of the British Empire. David Reed, however, quickly found an unofficial use for one of his school maps. Marcia was, by now, earning a living as an actress and the highlights of her infrequent visits were the descriptions of the towns and theatres in which she performed. David marked each location on a map of the British Isles.

Each evening and twice on Sundays the headmaster, predictably nicknamed 'Stinker' by the boys, would marshal his pink-capped and gaberdine-coated pupils and march them stiffly to the chapel on the far side of the cricket ground. These daily appeals to God had as much lasting effect on Oliver Reed as did the class lessons, but almost fifty years later he wrote to the local newspaper protesting at plans to convert the chapel, with its impressive fifteenth-century perpendicular tracery windows, into extra classrooms.

In this new environment the six-year-old flourished as a character while simultaneously floundering as a pupil.

Invariably deposited in the back row of a class, Oliver floated through most lessons in a puzzling blur of boredom and frustration. Mathematics, sums, numbers became a life-long mystery. English, grammar, literature, words intrigued but confused him. History, dates, battles, adventures ignited his imagination and sent it cartwheeling out of control. 'When the Romans came to Britain, I was riding wheel cap to wheel cap with my pagan Queen and I was with Drake and his admirals when we knelt before another Queen with the spoils of the Spanish Main.'

Fighting shoulder to shoulder with William the Conqueror or Robin Hood or hacking his way through the jungle in search of Livingstone elevated Oliver, at least in his own imaginings, to a childish peerage. 'I was a prince,' he admitted years later. 'Deep within me, my genes, like silicon chips, keep giving out mind flashes of previous existences and I felt a certain contempt for the common lot I played and rubbed shoulders with.'

The household arrangements at Hoe Place were overseen by Mrs Sinker, whom the boys addressed as 'Matron'. During his first and only winter at Hoe Place, Oliver developed a dry, hacking cough and raised brownish-pink spots behind his ears and across his chest. To Mrs Sinker, who by now was experienced at diagnosing the catalogue of illnesses that swept the school dormitories, it was obvious Reed Minor was Hoe Place's latest measles victim. The infection was so severe it damaged the sight in one eye and, despite regular visits to an orthoptist, left Oliver with a permanent squint.

Out of the sick bay and back in class Oliver once again sank to the bottom. After the initial shock of being swiped by the flat of a teacher's ruler or having his hand reddened by a slipper, he soon found his antics were at least winning him a desperate notoriety. 'I was starting to feel a personality creeping up and I was beginning to wear my dunce's cap like a crown,' he recalled.

His first caning came when he paid a fellow junior his entire week's pocket money to push him into the river at the bottom of the school grounds. A few days later he and David were called to the headmaster's office and informed they would be leaving Hoe Place. 'I thought it was because of the swimming incident,' added Oliver. The truth was the money had run out. Peter Reed could no longer afford a private education for his two sons.

Times were hard for Peter Reed. As a conscientious objector, the restrictions on his movements – under penalty of imprisonment – had made it almost impossible for him to earn a living. His savings were gone and he was surviving on his mother's allowance. In 1940, when May Reed had exchanged the Durrington Park Road house for a smaller Wimbledon property, her son had moved to No. 7 North View, a flat in a large house overlooking the common. His mother's excess furniture and servants had gone with him. And now, as if to complicate matters, he had fallen in love.

Kathleen Mary Cannon – Kay to her family and friends – was a widow employed as a senior secretary by the London-based fashion chain, Wallis. Intelligent and smartly dressed, she dedicated herself to coping with the war as well as she could. Clothes, like most necessities, were still rationed and Kay spent her evenings running up skirts and dresses from material remnants. Unlike Marcia, who arrived at Hoe Place with treats and unbelievable stories, Kay proudly unwrapped brown-paper parcels of hand-knitted socks and scarves.

Ever the pragmatist, Kay accepted Peter's precarious financial situation – and the bailiff's visits – with characteristic calm. Britain, she reasoned, would soon rediscover its prewar enthusiasm for horse racing. In the meantime there was Peter's ambition to write novels. He would write and she would earn and manage the money and David and Oliver would spend the final term of the academic year in Southend with Peter's elderly and long-retired Nanny Laidlaw.

The war in Europe officially ended on 8 May. Like every other town and village in Britain, the Essex resort was festooned with Union Flags and red, white and blue streamers. The celebrations and street parties went on for weeks. But not for the 'extra-ordinary and quite eccentric' Laidlaw.

To Laidlaw the world was a poisonous and lethal place. Given the unexpected yet welcome opportunity of nurturing a new generation of Reeds, she saw it as her duty to protect them from further contamination; from tea with milk and white sugar; from white bread and margarine; from jam and honey; from sweets; in fact, from just about everything young boys could be expected to enjoy. Convinced the cold slimy mud of the Thames estuary held some remedial and elixir-like power, Laidlaw would march the boys down to the foreshore and refuse to allow them home until they buried each other up to the neck in mud.

What was left of the summer term was disorganised and disrupted and spent, much to Marcia's disapproval, in a single-storey village school not far from Laidlaw's Essex home. It was the first – and last – state school Oliver and his brother would attend. 'It was bedlam,' remembered Oliver. 'Hundreds of screeching children. Big boots. Big knees full of scabs. Girls with red elbows laughing and pushing one another. Boys with torn vests fighting in heaps and playing football with a tennis ball against goal posts on the wall.'

By late July the boys were back at Marryat Road. A week or so later Oliver crossed Wimbledon High Street and the Causeway and walked the length of a narrow bridle path before cutting back across the common to his father's North View apartment. He found Peter Reed lying on a mattress in the garden; beside him there was a collection of toilet-roll tubes. 'Sit down, Oliver,' he said, handing his son one of the cardboard tubes. 'We're going to play telephones. You like Kay, don't you, Oliver?' The seven-year-old boy nodded. 'Through the tube, Oliver. Through the tube.'

'Yes.'

'And you know I like her a lot?'

'Yes.'

'And you know she likes you and David a lot?'

'Yes, Peter.'

'Well, soon, very soon, we're all going to live together in a new house.'

'In Wimbledon?'

'No, not in Wimbledon. At a place called Tunbridge Wells. In the country. You'll like it, Oliver, I'm sure you will.'

When Peter finished his 'telephone' call the pair went inside for tea. The flat was stripped almost bare – what the bailiffs had refused to take was being packed into a collection of wooden tea chests. In the kitchen Daisy the maid and George the butler were sitting on a large table. There were no chairs.

Farnham Farm House was a rambling, near-derelict property west of Tunbridge Wells and less than four miles from where Peter's father, Herbert Beerbohm Tree, attended prep school. Halfway between the villages of Langton and Rusthall a steep lane ran up to the house. It was so overgrown with wild roses and brambles that Peter was forced to leave the family's ageing Austin Seven at the bottom and hack his way up with a pair of borrowed shears.

Built in the 1700s, the original house was used as a smugglers' den before being owned and enlarged by a wealthy landowner. By the time Peter bought it the farmhouse had been abandoned for several years and was barely inhabitable; it was draughty and dirty, the floorboards and doors creaked and the rooms were crisscrossed with dusty cobwebs. To the boys it was 'Dracula's Castle'.

With the war over Peter was free to travel and return to work. His first job was as a public relations officer with a large firm of on-course bookmakers. His first priority was to marry Kay. Returning to Kent as the new Mrs Reed, Kay was greeted by her two stepsons. 'Hello,' said Oliver, shaking her hand. 'Are you our new mummy?'

The days at Farnham Farm House settled into an orderly routine. Peter and Kay Reed spent each week at a new flat they had bought on the Bushey Road, just southwest of Wimbledon. The country house and the boys, when not at school, were left in the care of a housekeeper paid for by a succession of lodgers. Each weekend the couple would drive the forty miles to Tunbridge in time for Friday night supper. Early the next morning Peter would climb the five flights of stairs to the attic room he had converted to an office. For two days the sound of his typing echoed around the house: long, uninterrupted sessions meant he was working on his latest novel; short, quick bursts his features for racing newspapers. Money from his columns financed his betting and his betting subsidised his two homes and his sons' education. It was a tiring balancing act, but Peter had another incentive – his wife had just discovered she was expecting their first child.

The second winter of peace proved to be one of the coldest for decades. By late January, after a mild, frostless Christmas, the temperature plunged and snow began to fall. For the next two months Kent, and most of Britain, was paralysed.

Living at 'Dracula's Castle' became a child's paradise. There was no school and, recalled Oliver, 'Icicles drooped from the roof and left the windows as sightless as cracked spectacles. It was so cold that the homemade bottles of lemonade turned to ice in the stone pantry and exploded. The old pipes that groaned in agony for a decent plumber in summer were frozen solid without their overcoats of sack lagging. Snow starched the trees and everything outside was as silent as a Christmas postcard. At the back of the house, the steep cowfield was as flat as the side of a tent, and perfect for our toboggan which we pushed up and down until the snow became black glass and the run so slippery that we could throw ourselves on to it without the sledge and finish up spinning about like swaddled Eskimos on the frozen stream.'

The winter was not without its dangers. Water for washing and baths needed to be boiled on the kitchen range and then carried in saucepans and buckets to the top-floor bathroom. To save time Peter Reed suggested heating the bathroom cold pipe with a blowlamp. All went well until the flame strayed on to one of the ancient wooden beams. The house was saved only by the ingenuity of one of the lodgers, who organised a snow-chain and, while Peter telephoned the fire brigade, pelted the smouldering woodwork with snowballs.

As her pregnancy advanced Kay Reed spent more of her time at Farnham Farm House. Early on 5 August 1947 Peter collected his wife and drove her to Cedar Court Nursing Home at Sutton, where she gave birth to his third son. The day before she left the private Surrey hospital she recorded her baby's details with a visiting registrar. The boy would simply be called Peter after his father. Kay, who gave her own address as Farnham Farm House, informed the official her husband was a journalist living at No. 125 Merton Mansions, Merton.

It was the middle of the summer holidays and to mark Kay's return and his stepbrother's arrival Oliver was allowed to cook and decorate a cake. Excited and happy, nine-year-old Oliver greeted his parents at the bottom of the lane and was allowed to carry his new brother back to the house in a wicker Moses basket. Inside, Peter and Kay announced they had decided to christen the boy Peter Simon Reed. Like his older brother – Robert Oliver Reed – Simon would grow up never using his first name.

Although Kay's confinement was still several months away, Peter had decided in early December 1946, after a particularly lucrative session at the racetrack, that it was time to hire a nanny to look after the imminent addition to the family.

Ingmar was a lusty, well-built girl of Swedish descent who spoke with a comic-book Scandinavian accent. She and her parents had escaped to Britain during the early years of the war, at the conclusion of which the teenage Ingmar drove a lorry through London in the VE parade. On her nights off she overcame the shortage of stockings by painting her legs with dilute cocoa before marching down the lane to the nearest pub.

Her sexual frustrations remained unquenched. Then one cold night she arrived in the boys' room with a thermometer – 'Just to zee if you are varm enough.'

Ingmar's idea of raising the temperature included removing her nightdress and sliding into bed with her eleven- and nine-year-old charges. 'Had Ingmar been a man and we little girls she would have been locked up as a child molester,' admits Oliver of his first sexual encounter.

Back at school Oliver became increasingly unruly and downgrading him to a lower stream produced no improvement in his work. When he failed to hold his own among boys of his own age he was downgraded once again, this time to the first year; he was a boy of nine who spent his days practising his letters or reciting the two-times table. There had to be another reason for his 'extremely poor standard of work'. His teachers, the majority of whom had only just qualified after half a decade in the forces, needed an excuse for their pupil's poor concentration: they blamed his eyesight.

The severe bout of measles Oliver contracted at Hoe Place had left him with a cast in one eye. A local optician explained to Peter Reed the dangers of leaving the squint untreated. It was quite possible his son was seeing double and could eventually lose the sight in his 'lazy' eye. Wearing a pair of National Health glasses with brown paper across one lens produced more taunts than it did improvement in Oliver's classwork and, after one violent outburst, Peter Reed was asked to look for a new school.

At first a London specialist offered a more practical solution. Each week Peter drove his son from Tunbridge to an orthoptist's surgery in the capital. For an hour at a time Oliver peered through a variety of lenses into a 3-D 'magic box' and exercised his damaged eye by placing matching letters and numbers on top of each other. But no matter how hard he concentrated the '6' always seemed to land on the '9' and the 'B' on the 'D' or the 'P'. The treatment was not a success.

While David went off to Neville House School near Eastbourne, his younger brother found himself the only child in a men's surgical ward in Tunbridge Wells Hospital. There was little surgery could do for their son's eyesight, Peter and Kay Reed were informed, but a cosmetic operation would realign the squint and prevent further damage. When the couple returned to the boy's bedside after his operation they were horrified to see both his eyes surrounded by purple and black bruises and his nose encrusted with dried blood.

Oliver returned to London for his weekly eye exercises, hampering his education still further. This time the orthoptist – with the unlikely name of Miss Wodge – tried something different: aeroplanes slid easily into hangars, horses into stables and cars into garages. The only blindness her young patient suffered was word 'blindness', pronounced Miss Wodge.

More schools followed, although never the thirteen Oliver once claimed. At one school a caning led inevitably to expulsion. Most took the easy way out and gave up on a boy they branded 'backward, a slow developer or plain stupid'. In his autobiography Oliver relives the experience: 'In every school I sank to the bottom of the class in a bubblehead of day dreams. I was always the cuckoo in the nest as I struggled to decipher the hieroglyphics of letters and numbers. I could never get them in the correct order or the right way up or the right way round.'

There were the occasional successes. For the first time Oliver was being taught by a woman teacher who seemed to be giving the 'great lump of a boy' in her class the extra attention he deserved. At the end of one English lesson Oliver handed his teacher a scribbled, almost illegible, poem. His reward was two gold stars.

From a hen to a wren
To a witch's eye,
I bring you enchantment
From the sky.
Raindrops fall which
Birdies drink,
Wormies like to roll and turn,
Birdies like to peck and nest,
Chickens lay,
Bankers pay,
While all the while the witches watched.

By the spring of 1949 the Reeds had all but abandoned Farnham Farm House. Since turning thirteen David had lived with his father to allow him to attend King's College School in Wimbledon. His younger brother was still away at boarding school and with no lodgers since before Christmas the upkeep of the old house and the wage of a housekeeper-cum-cook were expenses the couple could ill afford. 'It was a lovely home,' Peter confessed to a fellow journalist, 'but never the right one for us.' In July the Kent property was sold and Marcia and young Simon moved permanently back to No. 7 Merton Mansions, a larger and more spacious apartment in the same building as before.

During the summer, and ever hopeful of improving his second son's academic outlook, Peter added his name to the King's College School enrolment list. Oliver would join the school soon after his thirteenth birthday in 1951. In the meantime he needed a good preparatory establishment to allow him to pass the common entrance examination. On 4 September 1949, Oliver Reed attended his first class at Rokeby School.

Still occupying the Downs house to which it had moved in 1879 – and less than half a mile from the Durrington Park Road house in which Oliver was born – Rokeby was being run and managed by joint headmasters, HV Fisher and his brother-in-law JA Olive. To his delight the new pupil discovered Olive had spent four years of the war as a Royal Air Force officer and that one of its old boys, Squadron Leader Ian Bazalgette, was awarded a posthumous Victoria Cross in

August 1945. All of which fired Oliver's imagination but, like the inclusion of the poet Robert Graves on the school's roll of honour, did little to capture his classroom attention.

In December Peter received a letter from Rokeby informing him that, 'As the standard demanded by public schools is at present very high, we think it right to warn you that we do not consider your son has a reasonable chance of entry at the age of thirteen at any of the better known public schools.' After just one term Peter Reed was being asked to find his son a new school. A few days before Christmas one of the headmasters added a one-line note to his ex-pupil's record card: 'Not up to standard – leaves at my suggestion.'

Lessons from a private tutor also failed and in September 1951 Peter once again deposited his troublesome son at the entrance of a boarding school. This time it was Ewell Castle School, an establishment in the Surrey countryside which attempted to salvage the education of common-entrance-exam failures.

As a Ewell Castle boarder Oliver was relatively content. His size and strength and determination quickly singled him out as a class bully – 'No boy in the school dared take the Mickey.' In class he was making steady, if not spectacular, progress – 'I still couldn't spell, but somehow the words on the written page were beginning to take shape.' And, for the first time in his life, he found a hero-teacher – 'I would have been sacked if it had not been for my housemaster Geoff Coles.'

Unlike Oliver's previous teachers, Coles possessed the talent and persistence not only to identify and understand his pupil's weaknesses but to encourage his strengths. At Ewell and under Coles's guidance Oliver stopped being a victim. In his first year he learned to play chess. In year two he volunteered for special reading classes and soon discovered the pleasure of reading and reciting poetry. By his final year, and enraptured by his housemaster's animated reading of the *Biggles* stories, Oliver regularly outmarked his classmates in English literature. His spelling remained doubtful.

Somewhere in Simon Reed's memory between childhood experience and family legend is the first recollection of his older brother. It was, as ever, a clash between father and son.

Complaining about his fifteen-year-old son's academic failings, Peter Reed challenged him to spell 'hippopotamus'. When the teenager failed his father announced, 'Right, you're not leaving this house until you can spell it correctly.'

At five, and ten years younger than his brother, Simon Reed was a self-confessed 'competitive smart arse'. Retreating to his bedroom, he practised spelling 'hippopotamus' until he was letter-perfect and then returned to perform the feat in front of his family.

But it was as a sports master that Geoff Coles won his pupil's lifelong devotion. Oliver's defective eyesight ruled him out of any sport involving fast-moving objects, but athletics, which relied on stamina and determination, was deemed safe.

Oliver entered his final year at Ewell Castle as Captain of Athletics, a title that dismayed Peter Reed. During the winter Oliver came third in the All England Cross Country Championships. And when, the following summer, Oliver announced he had entered every event in the school sports day, Peter began a relentless and unsuccessful campaign to persuade his son to withdraw from half the races: entering everything was nothing more than showing off; when he won nothing he would be disappointed; he would injure himself. Peter even telephoned the school to try to get Coles to scratch his son from the events.

Oliver swept the board. On his way home to show his seven cups and trophies to his Granny May he was stopped by the police, who assumed he had stolen them. Peter Reed arrived at Merton police station to retrieve his sixteen-year-old son heated and irrational. 'You're no better than a gorilla,' he told Oliver.

The freedom and kudos Oliver enjoyed at Ewell disappeared the moment he left school and returned to Merton Mansions; he did not fully understand why but just walking through the door made him angry and on edge. His resentment needed a victim and Kay Reed inevitably found herself the target of her stepson's misguided repression: she was not his real mother; she had no right to order him about; she did not love him. Oliver was verbally scalding and physically intimidating. When she could no longer stand the pressure

Kay fled to the garden, picking stones from the path and hurling them at the wall.

'If you think of the most difficult teenager coping with an exaggerated chip on his shoulder, you have just a fraction of what it was like for my parents trying to live with Oliver,' recalls Simon Reed. 'He was impossible to control. My father threw him out so many times, but each time he would come back. The peace would last for about a week and then there would be another enormous row and he was gone again.'

Like most teenagers Oliver found himself on a confusing but highly exhilarating emotional seesaw: he rejected his father and his home as worthless and inconsequential, yet soon became homesick and lonely; he was convinced of his stupidity by not being able to spell or add up, yet found no difficulty in attracting the prettiest girls; he was belligerent and scratchy and easy to provoke, yet felt shame more quickly and more deeply than most boys his age.

Each time Oliver fled to Marryat Road and Granny Dardin's he returned defiant and more self-assured than ever. Peter Reed was losing respect and losing control. There was only one person to blame for his son's cruel rebelliousness, he ranted. Oliver had inherited Marcia's bad blood and her Mediterranean complexion. The end finally came in 1955 when Oliver ignored his father's 9 p.m. curfew and returned home late. The argument spilled from room to room, Oliver once again attempting to shift the blame to Kay Reed. 'Go to your room,' Peter ordered his seventeen-year-old son. 'And write out, "I must not be rude to my mother. I have been insolent and must not do it again".'

The front door slammed. Oliver was on his bicycle and pedalling away down Bushey Road. By the time the teenager passed Wimbledon Chase railway station Peter was beside him in his Rover car. 'Come back, gypsy boy,' he screamed at his son. 'You'll end up the same as your mother. Come back gypsy boy.' The chase ended when Oliver slipped through some bollards and rode away across Wimbledon Common. He would not see or talk to his father for another five years.

Word that his paternal grandmother was dying reached Oliver one weekend not long after his departure from Merton Mansions. Early in the war May Reed had sold her Durrington Park Road home and moved to a smaller, less demanding house in nearby Lingfield Road. Now, approaching her mid-eighties, she spent most of her time propped up in bed and looked after by a loyal but equally ageing Irish maid. The walls of her bedroom were lined with photographs of her children and grandchildren. She was, Oliver confessed, the 'only one who understood me, listened to me, encouraged and kissed me'.

As he was about to leave, his grandmother said, 'I'm quite tall, Oliver. I hope they make the coffin long enough.' That night Beatrice May Reed died. Her grandson, too proud to make up with his father, hid in the rhododendron bushes at the bottom of the garden and cried as he watched the coffin being carried from the house.

His hair growing long and his pockets almost always empty, Oliver spent his afternoons and evenings haunting the courts and alleys of Soho. 'I went around staring at everything and being accosted by everyone,' he recalled. The Salvation Army workers thought he was out of work and homeless and gave him free tea and sandwiches and the prostitutes and old men in grubby coats offered him sex. When he eventually saved up enough money and courage to buy himself into a St Anne's Court strip club he walked into the middle of a fight between rival football fans – and into a job.

The basement club was just off Dean Street and owned by an Italian-born 'gangster' called Jacko, who claimed to have run a Chicago speakeasy during the prohibition. Jacko's most treasured possession – after his chain of Soho strip clubs and brothels – was a pair of yellow leather gloves worn and given to him by his hero, Edward G Robinson. He kept the gloves wrapped in tissue paper in the top drawer of his desk, bringing them out to impress his new employees.

Jacko handed Oliver two one-pound notes and told him to buy himself a suit and come back the next afternoon. He could keep the change. The pay, at five shillings a week, was less extravagant but the work was easy and from his place at the door Oliver could just see the 'skinny bums' of the girls as they clambered on and off the stage. When his eight-hour shift as doorman was over Oliver would walk through the deserted streets to Covent Garden, chatting to the market porters while he ate a stand-up breakfast from a coffee stall.

The job lasted less than a month. When the club was raided by police Oliver smashed a toilet window and escaped into the crowds of Soho. He went back a few days later to discover the club locked and barred. Jacko and the girls had disappeared.

His next job lasted a little longer, but ended just as abruptly. Signing on at Wimbledon labour exchange, Oliver was told there was a vacancy for a junior warehouseman at a Raynes Park seed merchant's. It paid £2 15s a week – less pension contribution – and involved weighing and packing Carter's Tested Seeds into sixpenny packets. The work was excruciatingly boring; on a good day he was allowed to open the mail. Not even Granny Dardin was surprised when he stayed in bed one morning and refused to go back.

There was plenty of unskilled work about but Oliver was, by now, formulating his own plans for the future. His older brother David was already in the army completing his National Service and Oliver's call-up was only months away. They had both talked about trying their luck as film extras. That wasn't good enough for Oliver: if he was going into films he was going to be a star. In the meantime, he collected another buff-coloured interview card from the man at the labour exchange and reported for work at St Helier Hospital, Carshalton.

Rumours of a film crew's arrival quickly spread through the hospital and reached Oliver as he was taking a tea break in the porter's lodge. 'I was half expecting Uncle Carol to come through the door followed by a camera and sound equipment.' Oliver was sharing his shift in the casualty department with Pete Sanders, another porter using his job at the hospital to support his hopes of a show-business career. After work the pair went to watch the filming in the hospital grounds.

Sanders was shocked to see his friend marching towards a duffle-coated man holding a clipboard. 'A few minutes later he came back and announced we had got a part in a crowd scene,' recalls Sanders. 'It wasn't much. All we had to do was stand and watch the action, something we were already doing from the other side of the road. We never got paid.'

The film was a romantic farce called *Value for Money* and told the undistinguished story of a North Country businessman who, determined to broaden his outlook on life, ends up falling in love with a London showgirl. Equally predictable for a mid-fifties Rank production, it featured two of the company's biggest stars, John Gregson and Diana Dors.

On 13 February 1956 – Oliver's eighteenth birthday – the postman delivered a brown manila envelope to Marryat Road. It was time, the War Office decided, for him to start his National Service. Two weeks later Oliver reported to a local drill hall for his medical.

In July, and while he was still working as a porter at St Helier Hospital, a second printed letter arrived informing Oliver he had passed and that he would be drafted into the Royal Army Medical Corps. With the letter was his first day's pay of five shillings and a list of personal effects he was expected to bring with him: a yellow duster, boot polish, Brasso. Accepting the first day's pay had a more sinister meaning: although recruits still had a month of civilian life they were officially in the army and subject to army law. Anyone failing to report could be charged and face a court martial.

The money was also expected to pay for a pre-enlistment haircut. During his next lunch break Oliver visited a barber's shop opposite the ABC restaurant in Carshalton and demanded a *short* back and sides.

Chapter Four

'It took me a little while to discover the wisdom of the old Army adage: "if you can't beat the bastards, join 'em".'

THE TRAIN FROM WATERLOO WAS CRAMMED with bricklayers, carpenters, carpet fitters, engineers, farmers, mechanics, milkmen, musicians, painters, plumbers, salesmen, shop assistants and welders. By the perverse law of army logic Oliver was one of the few Royal Army Medical Corps recruits who had any kind of medical experience – as a hospital porter.

At Fleet the recruits and their assortment of cases and brown-paper parcels were bundled unceremoniously into a convoy of Bedford lorries and driven a mile and a half through the Hampshire countryside to the Queen Elizabeth Barracks at Church Crookham. Every recruit was passed from company to company as his ten-week basic training progressed. The first fourteen days were spent in B Company: kit was issued; documentation completed; inoculations given; housekeeping skills such as ironing and polishing taught; and basic drill mastered.

Not long after his arrival Oliver discovered that his own documentation was surprisingly inaccurate. Each recruit was expected to arrive with a copy of his birth certificate. With the pain of his departure from Merton Mansions still raw, Oliver refused to make contact with his father or stepmother. The army applied for a copy of his birth certificate, only to discover that his forenames, Robert Oliver, had never officially been registered at Somerset House. On 26 September eighteen-year-old Oliver officially added his names to the record of his birth.

For Private Reed, army discipline was little different from the institutionalised regime of his boarding schools. Oliver listened to his companions' barrack-room complaints with contempt. 'At that moment in time they resented their loss of liberty,' said Oliver. 'The freedom to watch telly whenever they wanted, to eat fish and chips out of newspapers, ride the whip at fun fairs and be cosseted by their mothers who scurried home from work with a tin of spaghetti for tea.'

From B Company the RAMC's latest intake was divided into 25-man squads and spent eight weeks attached to D, E and F Companies. On the parade ground they were taught to march and in the camp classrooms sat through lessons in first aid, nursing and hygiene. The medical corps' colours were cherry red, royal blue and gold. As noncombatants its orderlies wore red lanyards on their right shoulders, the opposite arm to fighting units and, according to army tradition, to show the enemy they were not firing a rifle on the battlefield. Under the Geneva Convention front-line medics could handle a rifle only to make a casualty's weapon safe and to defend a wounded soldier from attack. Rifle drill was kept to a minimum. When Oliver reported for all-night guard duty protecting the depot armoury from IRA attack the only weapon he was allowed to carry was a pickaxe handle.

During the first week in October, and with his basic training over, Oliver was ordered to report to the camp's Personnel Selection Officer. Even though his initial request to follow David into the Royal Military Police had been ignored his public school education would almost certainly have qualified him for a commission. Within a few days his commanding officer had rubber-stamped his application and Oliver was told to report to a War Office selection board at Barton Stacey, not far from Andover. Oliver was, recalls one of his RAMC friends, born officer material. 'He was word-perfect, his speech was pronounced and deliberate and he even swaggered like an officer.'

It was a different world from the bullshit and bawling at Church Crookham. For the first time in months Oliver was addressed as 'sir', NCOs and privates opened doors for him and jovial pipe-smoking captains and lieutenants complimented him on being a 'jolly good chap' and a 'fine fellow'.

His courage on the assault course and manners in the mess met with obvious approval – 'pips were already beginning to grow on 23324533's shoulders'.

On the final day of the week-long course he was told to write an essay on 'the role of the modern army'. The result was a scribbled and disjointed muddle: his arguments were sound but his handwriting and vocabulary belonged to a thirteen-year-old. No one, least of all Oliver, had informed the army of his dyslexia.

There could be only one answer, assumed his examiners: he had no desire to join the officer ranks and was using the written test to vent his juvenile sarcasm. As ever the military needed a reason for its failure and Oliver was ordered back to Aldershot for a session with the command psychiatrist, a 'nervous and silly' man who asked him whether he had wet the bed as a child or stolen money from his parents. When Oliver confessed he came from a broken home the officer tutted and scribbled enthusiastically in his notebook.

If the army wouldn't make him an officer, Oliver would climb the ladder himself, or at least as high as he could in two years. One way was to remain at Queen Elizabeth Barracks as a squad instructor. After four weeks on a Potential Depot Staff course he was given his first stripe and promoted to lance corporal. The youngest NCO at Church Crookham, he had not yet been assigned a company. One recruit remembers Oliver standing in for a sick NCO and informing his class, 'You know what it's like to get out of civilian clothes, now I am going to teach you to be a soldier.' By January he had been made up to full corporal and attached permanently to D Company.

As a £2-a-week squad instructor he now had his own room at the end of the barrack block. Perhaps his closest friend at that time was Barry Balmayne, an F Company NCO who shared Oliver's interest in show business and went on to become a stage performer and appear in 26 episodes of the 1970s soap *Crossroads*. Until Balmayne visited Oliver's room he was unaware of his family connections. Slipped into the frame of a mirror was a photograph of Oliver standing in what appeared to be a circus ring with his arms around Gina Lollobrigida and Burt Lancaster. It was taken on the set of

Trapeze, a film his Uncle Carol was directing a few weeks before his nephew joined the army.

Balmayne's locker and walls were covered with pictures of Yana, the London-born singer discovered by the comedian Dave King who, by the late 1950s, had her own show on BBC television. Oliver's pin-up was the blonde French actress Brigitte Bardot. 'We would swap pictures and talk about what we would do after National Service,' recalls Balmayne. 'There was no doubt where Oliver was going – he wanted to be a film star.'

It was over a cup of tea in the NAAFI that Oliver first suggested celebrating his squad's graduation with a concert party. Each company had its own recreation room complete with stage. As 'producer', he trawled his latest intake for talent, wrote the script, scrounged and improvised costumes, directed rehearsals and even devised and performed his own act. Following Balmayne's debut as a stand-up comic, Oliver shuffled on stage as 'Mexican Pete, the Mexican Peddler'. Disguised under a shaggy wig and drooping moustache and with a string round his neck holding up a street hawker's tray, he would 'sing in this most amazing Mexican accent', recalls the NCO.

Balmayne not only witnessed Oliver's stage debut, he also watched the future actor down his first ever pint of beer.

Opposite the Church Crookham camp was the army-owned Tweezledown racecourse. Twice a month during the winter it was used to stage point-to-point meetings. Safety regulations demanded medical orderlies at each jump and the pair discovered they could supplement their pay by volunteering to make up a stretcher party. 'Nobody ever fell off and we just sat in the ditch beside the fence watching them go by,' says Balmayne.

For Oliver the attraction of the extra pound he received for an afternoon's work was soon tarnished by the boredom. Each of the eighteen fences was numbered. During races Oliver would swap the numbers around to confuse the riders. One Saturday he turned up with something under his jacket – Balmayne looked up to see his friend changing their fence number for a café sign.

The RAMC depot was surrounded by a string of country pubs: the Windmill at Ewshot, the Horns at Crondall and the Wyvern in Church Crookham itself. Beside the Tweezledown course was a fourth inn called the North Horns. On their way back to camp Balmayne suggested they change and return for a drink. To his surprise, Oliver, whom he had never seen drink anything stronger than orange juice, ordered a beer. It wouldn't be his last. Late one night he returned drunk to his billet and insisted one of his squad members get out of bed to play jazz clarinet. Forgiving his corporal's midnight demand for music, Peter Hudson also found Oliver's attempts to transform himself into a parade-ground warrior 'hilarious – he acted the stereotypical corporal and could be quite terrifying even though he was actually very kind and funny'.

On duty Oliver was just as popular and equally cavalier as his Mexican alter ego. He was repeatedly on checks and charges for minor misdemeanours, and his disregard of army regulations earned him a grudging respect from one of his superiors. At least once a week he would sleep through reveille and miss his squad's nine o'clock inspection parade. Other corporals would have lost a stripe, but his company sergeant major was a mild-mannered Welshman with whom Oliver shared a mutual respect. Sergeant Major 'Taff' Morris had recently returned from fighting Malayan insurgents with a Military Medal and a beautiful Malay wife – two factors that won him Oliver's instant approval.

Taff Morris was a physically small man who had earned his rank through bravery, not bullshit. And, claims one of his squad corporals, he was more than a little frightened of Oliver. 'Standing to attention for a dressing down, Ollie could look serious and stern and then the corners of his mouth would move into the meanest of smiles and you could see the mischief creeping across his face,' remembers the National Serviceman. 'He was a rogue and Taff Morris knew it. He was never quite sure what Ollie would get up to next.' Morris didn't have long to wait.

Each Thursday evening there was a dance in one of Church Crookham's three giant gymnasiums. To get there from the billets the men had to cross the camp's red gravel parade square. Even though they were off duty anyone crossing the square had to march – arms shoulder high at the front, belt high at the back. One Thursday late in March 1957 Oliver was leading some of his men to the dance. He was using his cane as a baton and singing 'The Yellow Rose of Texas'. The second his foot hit the square a voice bellowed through the darkness: 'Corporal Reed . . . *shun!*'

The regimental sergeant major – a six-foot-seven-inch former Welsh rugby international with a voice as big as his frame – had been waiting in the shadows of a nearby hut. RSM 'Di' Rowlands was the only man on the camp who could down a gallon bucket of beer in one go and took equal pride in stamping on what he called 'bolshie part-time soldiers'.

If Oliver's behaviour as an NCO was questionable, his performance as an instructor was second to none. His commanding officer, however, was duty bound to make an example of an errant NCO, especially one brought to his attention by the regimental sergeant major. Oliver was dealt the 'paper punishment' only the services could devise or sanction. For disregarding the parade square he was reduced to the rank of private. But while he was in the CO's office, he was informed, he might like to apply for a posting to a field ambulance unit – one that needed a corporal.

Oliver travelled to Hong Kong on the HMS *Oxfordshire*. The troop ship, like every other vessel bound for the Far East, was forced to make the thirty-five-day passage around the Cape of Good Hope, making the journey a long and tedious event.

On docking, clutching their shore-leave passes, the entire draft poured on to the streets of Hong Kong intent on consuming as much beer as possible and spending their back pay in as many brothels as their stamina allowed.

The colony was hot and damp and Oliver spent the afternoon drinking Tiger beer with a group of Scots soldiers. As darkness fell one of them asked him, 'What about a woman?'

'OK,' said Oliver, holding out a handful of loose change and unsure how much it would cost.

'That's all right,' said a kilted sergeant. 'Over here you can get laid for two-and-six.'

The only privates and NCOs allowed into Hong Kong's Wanchai district were Red Caps. Guided through the labyrinth of narrow streets by his Scottish companions, Oliver was beginning to regret his drunken boast. Contracting a venereal disease was deemed a self-inflicted injury and a chargeable offence under army regulations. Propelled into what seemed like a giant tin shack, he was greeted by rows of beds, each creaking under the weight of a bouncing white bottom.

'Two dollars for a fuck. One dollar for a wank,' announced a round and sweaty Chinese woman.

Pleading poverty, Oliver opted for 1s 3d worth of relief and was led away by an octogenarian woman whose appearance and clammy hand were so frightening he was unable to manage an erection. 'Tommy have too much beer,' she hissed in disgust before waddling off. Oliver, still a virgin, was left to pull up his trousers and gingerly return to his mates.

In 1898 the New Territories of Hong Kong were leased by China to Britain for 99 years. By 1957, only four years after the end of the Korean War, there were growing fears that communist China might attempt to retake the colony. To forestall any invasion a series of mainland bases were set up and reinforced, each supported by an RAMC field ambulance unit. The day after the *Oxfordshire* arrived in Hong Kong Oliver was informed he was being posted to 18th Field Ambulance at Taipo, twenty miles north of Kowloon.

Taipo was just four miles south of the communist border and was little more than a collection of olive-green camouflaged tents and corrugated-iron huts. By the summer 18th Field Ambulance transferred to a former Royal Air Force base near the shanty village of Sek-Kong. The unit moved into brick-built barracks and a purpose-built hospital. The camp was surrounded by steep green hills and reached by a single winding road. One member of Oliver's Hut 34 squad remembers that 'he was fairly shy and certainly wasn't much of a drinker'. Joining Bernard Davies in the NAAFI, Oliver never drank more than two or three bottles of beer.

Returning to the billet, Oliver would frequently treat Davies and his fellow privates to an impromptu concert party. Sooting his hands in the hut's stove he would black his face and shuffle and sing his own version of *The Black and White Minstrels Show*. The late-night performances could last anything up to an hour with Oliver cracking jokes and delivering 'Mammy' and 'Chantilly Lace' in a variety of voices. His other bedtime entertainment was making up and acting out a series of spine-chilling ghost stories. 'He was so good,' recalls another of Hut 34's residents, 'some of the younger lads used to pull their sheets over their heads. If he could have written them down he would have earned a fortune.'

As an NCO whose flexing of the rules had resulted in his overseas posting, Oliver could be surprisingly rigid. Taking one drill session he overheard Davies chatting to his neighbour and delivered a vicious and humiliating dressing down. Back in the billet Oliver put his arm round the shell-shocked friend. 'When you're on duty it's Private Davies and I'm Corporal Reed,' he explained. 'In here you're Barney and I'm Ollie.'

Davies remembers: 'Off duty he was a very likable and sincere person. The kind of person you felt completely at ease with and with whom you could have an open conversation.'

Years later while dictating his autobiography Oliver claimed that as an NCO he had been ostracised and snubbed by his squad. 'They hated my guts,' he wrote; 'this hurt me a bit because I wanted to be popular when I was off duty, but they shunned me when I tried to make friends. They refused to forgive me for doing my job properly. I pushed them so hard they came top in everything, but they didn't thank me for it so I went off to the NAAFI and drank on my own.' It was a strange repayment for what others saw as an honest day-to-day friendship. A smoker with the habit of apparently never possessing a packet of cigarettes, Oliver would scrounge odd fags throughout the week. After pay parade on Thursday he would buy a pack of two hundred from the NAAFI and place the opened carton on the top of his locker. Anyone he owed cigarettes to could help themselves.

There was no gymnasium at Sek-Kong. To keep himself fit Oliver ran most mornings and entered every sporting and inter-unit athletic event, winning a trophy for a three-mile race. Always competitive, Oliver would hire a fleet of Kowloon rickshaws and challenge his friends to race from bar to bar downing a beer in each.

One day Oliver was informed by Captain Dodds, the 18th's administration officer, that as the unit's most enthusiastic sportsman he was being 'promoted' to Rugby Officer. Rugby was a game Oliver had never played at boarding school and knew nothing about. His attempts to organise a tournament ended in failure when his own team, dubbed the Stove Pipe Stompers, were ignominiously beaten into submission by an infantry regiment. There were perks, however: as rugby co-ordinator he was allowed a Jeep and driver to ferry him between meetings. And as every Far East officer seemed to be followed by his own dog it was only right, reasoned Oliver, that Sek-Kong's newest 'officer' should also have a pet. He spent days driving from village to village until he found a suitably forlorn and needy animal.

The majority of National Servicemen were quite willing to resume their civilian jobs or use their army training to start new careers. With a single brief appearance in *Value for Money*, Oliver soon convinced his colleagues he was destined for film stardom. Films, remembers Bernard Davies, were his corporal's obsession. 'Physically he was strikingly good-looking and it didn't take much to imagine him as a star,' says Davies. 'His physique was impressive but his eyes were his real feature – so blue and expressive, his eyes said everything.'

Hidden in the bottom of Oliver's kitbag were several dog-eared copies of the *Tatler*. Whenever he felt homesick he would retrieve the magazines and thumb through the illustrated features on country houses and society weddings. 'I used to study the smart suits the quack-quack set was wearing,' he remembered. 'I didn't want to be a hospital porter or a labourer when I got back to civvie street. I had no training or qualifications, so I decided I would have to marry a rich girl if I was going to make something of myself. It was obvious I was going to need a wardrobe of quack-quack clothes.'

After ripping a feature on men's fashion from one *Tatler*, he set off to Hong Kong intent on emptying his Post Office savings book and investing the cash in half a dozen new suits. The tailor nodded approvingly each time Oliver pointed at one of the photographs and promised to copy each outfit exactly. Two days later his six suits, folded and wrapped in paper, were ready. His new wardrobe had cost him just under £60, the equivalent of eight weeks' pay.

Back in England he wondered why people were giving him strange glances. He knew the magazines were two years out of date, but the suits were brand-new and immaculately tailored. It was only when he reread the *Tatler* pages that he discovered the feature was about men's clothes in the 1930s.

Chapter Five

'I've got a face like a dustbin, but people are learning that if you kick a dustbin over and rhododendrons drop out, it's glorious.'

OLIVER REED WAS BACK IN LONDON. Two years in the army had left him with less than £100 in savings, six dated suits, a healthy sun tan, a taste for alcohol and the ability to pepper his speech with the word 'fuck' in a way so natural as to be inoffensive.

The capital was awash with would-be actors and actresses, most of whom lived within walking distance of the film-company and casting-agency offices in and around Soho. By early September Oliver had moved out of the first-floor bedroom offered by his Granny Dardin – 'There was no way I was ever going to live with my father again' – and into a flat in Redcliffe Square, just across the road from Brompton Cemetery. Living in the room at the top of the next landing was another would-be actor called Jack Burke.

The Irishman, who had won a prewar Jaguar in a poker game but never earned enough money as a film extra to pay for any petrol, was impressed with Oliver's brief appearance in *Value for Money*. Becoming a star was, recalls the Irishman, the last thing on his new friend's mind. 'Ollie was desperate for sex,' says Burke. 'He had somehow come through the army a virgin and as a red-blooded male that bothered him.' The problem was solved when the pair were invited to a party two hundred yards across the square, in a flat occupied by six women schoolteachers.

A twenty-year-old actor without an agent and with just one film under his belt needed three things to find work:

experience, luck and a membership card for the Film Artists' Association, the extras' trade union. Oliver obtained the third of these from another Irishman called Ned Lynch who, as an FAA official, seemed to spend more time in the Earl's Court and Brompton Road pubs than he ever did on a film set. The others he manufactured from a combination of sex and lies.

It was obvious, Oliver soon realised, that it was not the directors and casting agents he needed to impress. It was their secretaries. After finding out which studio office was hiring extras, he would start collecting background gossip on a director's secretary.

Aware he would never be allowed in to see a director, Oliver would call at a studio's London office asking for an interview. A few minutes of charm and chat was usually all he needed. That night, after a few drinks and a fish-and-chip supper, Oliver would ask his date if she minded stopping off at his flat to collect something. The visit to Redcliffe Square ended in the bedroom and the 'something' turned out to be Oliver's acting résumé and photograph.

'It wasn't unexpected, but it was certainly original,' admits Cherry Dearing who, at 21, was one of the youngest executive secretaries at Regal Films. Pretty soon she would also have the dubious distinction of losing her virginity to a young actor called Oliver Reed. 'I agreed to go out with him because he was incredibly good-looking and had this amazingly seductive voice. When he spoke, he looked at you as if you were the only person in the room.'

The Redcliffe Square flat was crowded and noisy, so Dearing agreed to go out again the following night. This time they went to the cinema before returning to the secretary's own ground-floor rooms near the river at Pimlico. As Oliver was dressing he propped a photograph against the bedroom clock. 'He didn't need to tell me what to do with it,' admits Dearing. 'By nine o'clock it was on the top of the extras file.'

Called for an audition at Twickenham Studios, the twenty-year-old actor, still tanned from his months in the Far East, informed the director Sidney Smith he had recently returned from touring South Africa with a repertory company. Smith, however, remembered he was more impressed by Oliver's 'hungry face'.

'What does your father do?' asked Smith.

'He's a journalist,' Oliver answered. 'A sports writer.'

'Good,' said the director. 'You can be a press photographer.'

On his way out Oliver was told to report to the costume department for a fitting. The wardrobe assistant was obviously having a bad day. 'Journalist,' she grunted, before diving into the rack of costumes and emerging with a neatly pressed camel-hair top coat. 'That night,' admitted Oliver, 'I telephoned my father and got him to lend me his journalist's mac.' It was a brief and convenient truce in their estrangement. Father and son had not spoken for more than three years; it would be another three before they could face each other in the same room.

Three years – and 12,000 miles – after making his first screen appearance, Oliver arrived at London Airport North to sign on for his second film.

Hello London starred Sonja Henie and Michael Wilding. The Norwegian-born ice skater had won the women's world amateur figure-skating championship ten times and three Olympic gold medals between 1927 and 1936, mainly by introducing ballet movements into her routines. After the war Henie toured the world with sell-out ice shows built around her exhibition displays before starring in several films. Supported by a clutch of British guest stars, including Stanley Holloway, Dennis Price, Roy Castle and Dora Bryan, the plot of the skater's latest musical involves a flying visit to London where she is persuaded to give a charity performance.

Oliver was handed a Voigtlander plate camera and told to join a gaggle of photographers sent to cover the star's 'arrival' at London Airport. As Henie stepped from the plane Oliver elbowed his way to the front of the press pack. 'I put everything I had into that first part,' he recalled. 'And I was determined to get myself noticed.'

It worked. As the crew packed up Oliver was approached by the assistant director. 'Have you got a change of clothes?' he asked. Oliver nodded. He was wearing one of his Hong Kong suits under his father's coat. For the rest of the afternoon Oliver danced his way around the capital on the top deck of a red London bus.

Walking back to Redcliffe Square with £14 in his pocket – £7 for each 'appearance' – Oliver felt strangely ambivalent towards the film's stars. The 46-year-old actress and dancer had done little for her unnoticed extra. 'Her legs were muscle-bound and unattractive,' commented a disappointed Oliver. 'What I noticed most about Michael Wilding was the extraordinary way he walked, so that the toes of his shoes scraped along the ground.'

The system held true. By the end of 1958 Oliver bedded his way into four more films. *The Square Peg* was an 89-minute Rank comedy and one of a series starring Norman Wisdom. In *Life is a Circus* he found himself dressed as a cowboy being chased down Windsor High Street by the Crazy Gang. And for *The Captain's Table* – issued the following year – he became a passenger sunning himself on the deck of a back-lot 'liner' at Pinewood Studios. When Oliver arrived at Twickenham Studios for a walk-on part in *The Four Just Men*, a cinema spin-off from the popular television series, he was recognised by the assistant director from his first film. An actor had been taken ill and they needed someone to shout from the crowd. Clutching a piece of paper on which were scribbled his lines, Oliver delivered his first eleven words on screen.

The work may have been enjoyable and regular, but it was never self-supporting. Including the £12 he received for his impromptu speaking part in *The Four Just Men*, Oliver had so far earned just £56 from his acting. It was barely enough to cover the £6-a-week rent on his West Brompton rooms, and never left enough to scratch away at the arrears.

Oliver searched the pockets of his spare trousers. One shilling. He put the coin in the gas meter and relit the fire. His army savings were running out as fast as the gas. It was time, he conceded, to visit his Uncle Carol.

It was a cold December afternoon. Oliver turned left into the King's Road. By the time he reached Carol Reed's upright and impressive Chelsea home it had started to rain. For his nephew it was like stepping into a comfortable but slightly musty Edwardian dream. Warmed by a blazing fire and a glass of whisky, Oliver detailed his list of credits since they had last spoken. Two years earlier, in 1956, Carol Reed was about to direct the circus drama *Trapeze* when Oliver asked to be taken on as an extra. His uncle refused.

Oliver had since proved his determination to become an actor – 'Something the family, if not Oliver, had known for years,' recalled Carol Reed. He now had to learn the mechanics and disciplines of acting. If he refused to consider the Royal Academy of Dramatic Art – founded by Oliver's grandfather Herbert Beerbohm Tree in 1904 – he should at least join a repertory company. It was not the advice Oliver wanted to hear – 'I didn't give a damn about the theatre, films is where I wanted to be.'

Both men were conscious of – and determined to avoid – any suggestion of nepotism, yet the older Reed remained convinced that meeting the right people in the right places was as good as any place to launch an acting career. 'Put yourself about a bit at the Ritz Grill,' he suggested, sublimely ignorant of the fact his nephew neither knew where The Ritz was nor had enough money to patronise it if he did. 'What about joining a few good clubs?' The younger Reed shook his head a second time.

Cashing in on the family pedigree was another possibility. 'Seek out the people that can help you and pitch a tent outside their front doors,' suggested the director, 'and every morning when they come out, step out of your tent and say, "Excuse me, I'm Oliver Reed, I would like you to give me a job." '

As his nephew was leaving, Carol Reed offered the final suggestion of the afternoon. 'Spend as much time as possible at the cinema,' he said. 'If you think a film is bad, watch it over and over again until you're convinced you know why it is bad. The same with good films: only when you are convinced you know the reason a film is good should you try to emulate those finished performances.'

His uncle's advice only confirmed what Oliver had already decided. Bawling at a squad of shuffling recruits on the far side of a parade ground was equal, he reasoned, to anything an ageing thespian could teach him. 'I had seen enough of drama and dressing up and flag culture and petty conformity and puking men and hurt men and social schools,' he confessed several years later.

In the late 1950s cinema programmes included a full-length feature and a shorter 'B' movie, interspersed with the *Pathé News* and Pearl and Dean adverts, and running in sequence from early afternoon until late evening. For just sixpence a day Oliver bought himself a place at his 'university' of the cinema. 'People were making films about the North and the mills and the untapped areas of England and about people who sweated and farted – and so those were the parts I studied the hardest.'

Not long into the New Year Oliver was watching *Ben-Hur* in a cinema near the Baron's Court flat he was now sharing with a girlfriend when he noticed his neck was sore and painful. The daylight outside hurt his eyes and gave him an instant and blinding headache. Next morning his temperature was over a hundred and a purplish rash covered his chest and upper arms. He reluctantly agreed to call a doctor who, taking one look at his patient, called an ambulance. The lethargy and irritability Oliver thought were nothing more than the start of a bad case of influenza were the first signs of bacterial meningitis – easily treatable with antibiotics, but still requiring hospital treatment and plenty of bed rest. Something his career – and bank balance – could do without.

Marcia Reed had by now remarried into what her son disparagingly called the 'quack-quack' society. From a single factory near Liverpool docks the Sulis family fortune had grown by supplying ropes and hawsers to every port and shipping company in Britain. The Sulises now lived in an impressive mansion in the Cheshire countryside, which, Marcia decided, was the ideal place for her youngest son to convalesce and get to know his new stepfather. To Oliver's delight Bill Sulis possessed even less respect for military discipline. Dismissed from the Royal Air Force when he wrote off a fighter by attempting to hedge-hop upside down, he spent the rest of the war with a cavalry regiment, where his adventures were only slightly less expensive.

It was now three months since Oliver had appeared in a film. Back in London he discovered he had some unexpected competition. David Reed, whose National Service was spent as an officer with the Royal Military Police, was out of work and hoping to launch an acting career of his own. The pair made the daily rounds of casting offices and advertising agencies, handing out glossy photographs and attempting to make contacts, with little success. For David the competition was always one-sided. 'In his early twenties Oliver was extraordinarily good-looking,' says the older Reed. 'His eyes were just fantastic.' There were other things about his brother's appearance equally as memorable.

Opposite Chelsea Football Club's Stamford Bridge ground on the Fulham Road was a coffee bar. The drinks were cheap and the dubious but friendly Italian owner appreciated the value of serving the stars of the future. 'When you are famous, I am famous. I put up a sign to say you eat here.' When David Reed informed his new girlfriend and future wife she was about to meet his brother nothing prepared her for the 'thing' that walked through the coffee bar door. Mickie Reed will always remember her first sight of her future in-law: 'Oliver was wearing a skull hanging from a chain around his neck, a white shirt tied in a knot above his bare waist and the tightest jeans you have ever seen in your life.'

The next week Oliver was scouring *The Stage* when he spotted a bottom-of-the-page advertisement for a new children's series. Pressing the best of his Hong Kong suits he set off for the BBC studios at Shepherd's Bush. 'What auditions?' the receptionist said, eyeing him suspiciously.

'For *The Golden Spur*,' said Oliver. 'It's a new television series.'

The woman lifted a telephone. 'You've come to the wrong address,' she told him smugly. Oliver had misread the advert. When he got to the corporation's rehearsal rooms in Gower Street half the students from RADA next door had already been auditioned and the other half were queuing in the corridor. A female production assistant was handing out a single page of script. Inside the office the producer was sitting cross-legged on the top of his desk, his neck and his eyelids drooping. At least he had had enough time to learn his lines. With the assistant reading the other parts Oliver acted his own. 'OK, OK,' said the producer, whose eyes were now firmly shut. 'You've got the part of Richard of Gloucester.'

His performance in *The Golden Spur* – screened during the early summer as a seven-part weekly series – was impressive enough to attract the attention of an agent. Signed on a guaranteed £5-a-week 'wage', Oliver reported to Pat Larthe's office each morning to be handed a list of auditions; most were for television advertisements whose makers needed somebody with features less 'continental'.

The makers of a popular brand of margarine needed a constant supply of 'customers' for their supermarket challenge commercials; a shopper was stopped and asked, 'Can you tell Stork from butter?' No one ever could. At the same Oxford Street audition, and on the same agent's books, was a slim, red-headed young woman with a wide confident smile. 'Did you get the job?' Oliver asked.

'I'm afraid not,' she said, 'They told me I was too beautiful for the girl next door.' Oliver had to agree.

When he looked round she was gone. 'Listen,' he said, bursting through the rehearsal room door. 'You've got to audition me next because a wonderful girl has just left this office and I want to go after her.'

'You're not the sort,' said one of the producers.

'How do you know I'm not her sort?' demanded Oliver.

'No for the part. You're not a boy-next-door type.'

He had almost given up when he caught sight of the redhead emerging from a nearby department store. 'Hello, again,' he panted. 'My name's Oliver Reed.'

Kate Byrne was an eighteen-year-old whose ambition to succeed as a model was surpassed only by her determination to marry. Over coffee they held hands and shared secrets. She was, she admitted, already engaged to a jealous and violent man. On her finger was an enormous diamond engagement ring. The one thing Oliver omitted to tell her was that he was having a passionate and exceptionally physical affair with an older woman called Tina. The solution was simple – 'I shuffled my dates and had an affair with both of them at the same time.'

His six-week double-cross ended when he was readmitted to hospital. A blood test proved that a second bout of meningitis was nothing more than German measles, but not before both young women decided to visit his sickbed – on the same afternoon. They arrived from opposite ends of the ward and the realisation was instant and humiliating and

Oliver found himself on the sharp end of a very angry triangle. First Kate deposited the contents of a box of a hundred cigarettes over his head. Then Tina hurled a pound of grapes at him.

'You can't have us both,' screamed Kate.

'You'll have to choose,' demanded Tina. 'And right now.'

Oliver chose Kate.

On 14 October 1959, Oliver picked up an evening newspaper left on the bar in which he was drinking. The red ink of the front-page stop-press column caught his eye. There was a single headline in bold type, each word on a new line: ERROL FLYNN DIES. His film hero was dead – 'The star I most wanted to be, the man who played all the parts I wanted to play, was gone.' Oliver ordered another Guinness and stood to attention as he downed the pint in a single swallow.

Walk-on parts were beginning to clock up. *The League of Gentlemen* was a rousing crime caper from the Allied Film Makers company, with most of its founder members – producer Michael Relph, director Basil Dearden, screenwriter Bryan Forbes and actors Jack Hawkins and Richard Attenborough – making solid contributions to its first feature film. Hawkins, having recruited his band of cashiered army officers, has hired a room at the New Gate Theatre Club, ostensibly for a play reading. He is about to unveil his plan for the perfect bank robbery when a flouncy Oliver bursts in – 'This isn't *Babes in the Wood* then?' – stamps his foot and leaves.

It was a twenty-second appearance that marked the start of a remarkable year. Not only would Oliver make more films in 1960 than in any other year of his five-decade career. He would also have the dubious distinction of rising from a brief sixteen-word appearance as a disgruntled homosexual to playing his first lead as a flesh-eating werewolf.

Two weeks before Christmas 1959 Oliver was summoned to an audition at Hammer's Bray Studios in the Berkshire countryside between Windsor and Maidenhead. No one had warned him it was impossible to reach the studios by bus and when he arrived at Windsor's Riverside railway station he had to spend most of his spare cash on a taxi.

To wait for his screen test, Oliver was taken to the studio canteen, where he discovered the 'best bread-and-butter pudding since my gran used to make it'. His audition, in what appeared to the 21-year-old actor little more than the side room of a half-derelict country house, took less than fifteen minutes. He was introduced to a snub-nosed young woman and given one line to recite, first to camera and then acting to his silent partner: 'Virginia, I love you. I know I turn into a monster at night, but I love you.'

Not knowing if he had got the part, Oliver trudged the four miles back to Windsor and his Waterloo train despondently picking leaves off the roadside hedgerows and trying to decide what he was going to tell Kate. The next day a secretary from Hammer's London office telephoned his Carlyle Mansions flat to offer Oliver a day's work on a film that would begin shooting early in the New Year. It was called *The Two Faces of Dr Jekyll*.

Hammer Productions Ltd was formed in November 1934 by William Hinds, a music-hall comedian who performed under the stage name William Hammer. A year later he joined forces with Enrique Carreras, who had set up a distribution company called Exclusive Films Ltd. Although effectively sister companies, both firms exploited different prewar markets, Hammer making original films and Exclusive reissuing more profitable London Films and British Lion features. By the late 1940s Hammer had been incorporated as Exclusive's production division. Within a decade Hammer – by now under the directorship of the founder's descendants – had turned its back on low-budget musicals and comedies to concentrate almost exclusively on Gothic horror.

Unlike other production companies Hammer never owned a traditional studio. Overheads were kept to a minimum by hiring other studios or making films in a succession of large country houses: the first was Dial Close at Maidenhead, then Oakley Court a few miles away near the village of Bray, then Gilston Park, a former Harlow, Essex, country club, and finally Down Place, once again at Bray.

At Hammer Oliver found a company and studio crew that matched both his personal and professional philosophy: his sense of urgency; his frenetic energy; his belief in teamwork; his need to improve his craft; but above all his dedication to earn money.

Freddie Francis was an early Hammer director who went on to win two cinematography Oscars. 'I don't think Hammer was ever interested in making films,' Francis admits. 'It was simply a wonderful business organisation. Hammer could have been making anything it wanted. They would say to Jimmy Sangster, "Write a script". Jimmy would write the script in no time, and they would come to somebody like me and say, "Get directing it!" And in about two weeks we were off and running. It was rather annoying, however, to go in as a director and find that all the sets, and even the make-up designs, had been okayed before you were hired. On Hammer's schedules and budgets there was never any time to change these things.'

With his toe, if not his foot, in the Hammer door Oliver at last gave in to Kate's Irish persistence on the question of marriage. At twenty, Kate still needed her father's consent to marry. Patrick Byrne may have begrudgingly admired Oliver's ambition, but he certainly didn't consider him a suitable match for a good Catholic girl who had survived the poverty of Dublin's Canal Street and who needed the stability of a hard-working husband. A bigger problem was Oliver's ancestry. 'Ollie may have been able to hold his own in an Irish pub, but he was still an English toff,' admits a friend of the family. Predicting her father's reaction, Kate forged his signature on the wedding form. Oliver, too, was worried how his father might react to the announcement.

The couple kept their secret through the Christmas holiday but Oliver's agent was not going to let the publicity slip through her client's fingers. On 2 January 1960 – not New Year's Day as Oliver frequently claimed – the couple arrived at Kensington register office to be confronted by a Press pack sent to cover the wedding of the film director Carol Reed's actor nephew.

Inside, the ceremony was brief and formal. The bride gave her full name as Catherine Elizabeth Byrne and declared she was a freelance model living at No. 19 Thring House, Stockwell, SW9. Oliver gave his profession as 'actor' and his address as No. 10 Carlyle Mansions, Kensington Mall, W8. The witnesses were recorded as David Reed, the only member of both families the couple dared invite, and John Harrison.

There was no reception and no honeymoon. Instead the newlyweds made their first married argument last a week. David had given the couple an unwanted Christmas present: a voucher that could be exchanged for a long-play record or a night at the Talk of the Town, the 'steak-and-one-frozen-veg' theatre restaurant converted from the former Leicester Square Hippodrome. Kate wanted the LP. Oliver wanted the night out. The argument rumbled and sparked into the night. Cornered by his bride's Celtic temper, Oliver suddenly announced he was already regretting the marriage. 'Not half as much as I regret marrying you,' Kate snapped back. The next morning Oliver set off 'tired and sex-less' to make the first of nine films for Hammer.

'Everyone told me not to do horror films,' Oliver would later admit. 'But all I wanted to do was act.' His first acting contract for Hammer lasted a single day and involved playing a tough nightclub bouncer – something he had personal experience of – in *The Two Faces of Dr Jekyll*, yet another reworking of the Robert Louis Stevenson classic.

On the way out Oliver called at the Bray cashier's office and signed for his £25 fee – the money would be sent direct to his agent – and caught the train and tube back to Kate and the Ladbroke Grove flat they were 'borrowing' from his Aunt Juliet. Born in April 1910, Juliet Reed was the only daughter of Herbert Beerbohm Tree and 'Mrs' Reed and was only a year older than her younger brother, Peter Reed. By 1961 Oliver's Aunt Juliet and her husband owned several properties, including a six-room apartment in Ladbroke Grove, west London. The house had been built on the embankment of the main railway line between Paddington and the West Country and within shunting distance of the Old Oak Common sidings. Each time an express went through, the building 'trembled dramatically'. To keep an eye on both her property and her newly married nephew, Aunt Juliet installed an elderly army colonel.

For the first time in his life Oliver was relying on a woman to keep him afloat and subsidise his drinking. It would not last. Although she had not yet told her husband, Kate was sure she was pregnant. If her calculations were correct, their first child was due sometime in January or February. In the meantime she had to keep working. At twenty and with her figure intact she was still in demand as a photographic and catwalk model. Each morning Kate would give her husband his daily pocket money and leave for work. By lunchtime Oliver had given up waiting for the telephone to ring and resumed his studies at the 'Odeon University'.

The tenancy of the Ladbroke Grove flat lasted less than three months. It was now obvious, at least to the newly married David Reed, that the acting talent in the family had passed exclusively to his younger brother. For David, supporting his new wife needed a steady income and could never be the hit-and-miss business Oliver Reed appeared so philosophically to accept. 'I was also a little short of Ollie's dedication and ambition,' adds David, leaving his half-brother Simon to explain: 'Ollie was never in love with acting. He wanted to be a star and he was going to be a star no matter what it took.' Part of David's plan was to invite his brother and sister-in-law to share the Kensington Mall flat. Soon after St Patrick's Day 1960 Oliver and Kate moved in only to be informed that David had decided to rejoin the Army and the lease on the property was fast running out.

Paddy Byrne was a hard-drinking, hard-working Irishman who, no matter how deep the hurt over his daughter's deceit, was not about to allow her to suffer the indignity of homelessness. This prospect was hardly likely given Oliver's family connections and the fact that Olive Andrews had rooms to spare in the Marryat Road house, but Oliver was still at odds with his father and had something to prove to his Wimbledon relatives. So, borrowing a Bedford lorry from the garage where he worked as a fitter, Byrne loaded up his daughter and son-in-law's suitcases and possessions – a bed, an oil heater, an iron and ironing board – and transported them south across the river to the Byrnes' council flat in Thring House, Stockwell.

By early May he could stand it no longer. A card in a nearby newsagent's was advertising for a door-to-door vacuum-cleaner salesman. Oliver rang the number and was told to go straight round.

'You're a good-looking boy,' said a man in a Max Miller suit and a loud bow tie, eyeing the young man standing nervously in front of his desk.

'I'm an act-or,' Oliver replied, splitting the final word into two distinct syllables.

The man sucked at his teeth. 'I suppose you know what this job entails?'

'Selling vacuum cleaners?' suggested Oliver.

'This job is all about persuasion,' said the man, adjusting his bow tie. 'You demonstrate the equipment to the wife during the day and then go back and talk to the husband in the evening.'

'So my job is really to persuade the husband?'

'No, it's the wife you have to work on.' The man winked at Oliver. 'As I said, you're a good-looking boy and I'm sure you're a man of the world. Mind you, some of these housewives aren't too pretty though. You can start on Monday.'

Oliver trudged the three miles back to Stockwell. He was depressed and angry and itching for an argument. Kate was still at work. Her mother would have to do. 'By the way,' said Mrs Byrne before Oliver could open his mouth. 'Your agent called. He wants you to ring him.'

On 19 May 1960 Oliver flew to Dublin from the airport where he had launched his acting career two years earlier. Shooting for *The Sword of Sherwood Forest* would start the next day. Hammer had hired Ardmore Studios, south of Dublin. By coincidence the nearest town was also called Bray. The film's star was Richard Greene who, for four years, found weekly fame as Robin Hood on television. For contractual reasons Greene was the only actor hired for the cinema spin-off.

It had taken Oliver ten films to earn himself a character credit with more than just a few lines of dialogue. Dressed as the treacherous thirteenth-century nobleman Melton, he slays the Sheriff of Nottingham, played by the veteran Hammer star Peter Cushing. The front cover of *The Sword of Sherwood Forest*'s publicity campaign book, issued to cinema managers on the film's release, includes a still of Oliver stabbing his victim.

For Oliver the days filming in the County Wicklow forests and foothills were a childhood fantasy come true. For the first time in his two-year film career he was being paid to slash and thrust and cut his way through his own whimsy – 'It was hide-and-seek with swords; it was goodies and baddies and damsels in distress and I was Errol Flynn and every other hero I had watched at the cinema.'

And when the day's make-believe was over Oliver found pleasure in the reality of illicit sex. Less than a week after leaving his pregnant wife he plunged into a passionate nightly affair with a 'beautiful blonde' Irish woman. His account of their meeting was probably accurate: 'She screamed down the road at 150 miles an hour in her sports car and screeched to a halt a few hundred yards from where I was sitting outside a pub. Somebody introduced us and I invited her out to dinner.' His denial of consummating the affair was certainly a lie: 'It was a long time to be without a woman, but I was only just married and I wanted to stay faithful to Kate so I contented myself, and amazed myself, with just being with her.'

Forty years later Oliver's Irish lover has, for the first time, spoken publicly about their affair. 'Sex was not a major thing with Ollie,' she admits. 'He rushed the act, the same way he hurried through everything else in his life at that time. I got the impression he was only interested in the big event; what led up to it was of minor interest. Having an affair and cheating on his wife was far more important to him than actually having a physical relationship.' It was, she felt, the same with Oliver's career. 'Acting, helping to make a film, was only of passing interest. Being seen as part of the finished product, having his name among the credits, was the only thing that mattered.'

When he returned to London a new kind of reality confronted him. A keen-eyed photographer had spotted Kate's ever-growing waistline and confronted her about her pregnancy. The modelling assignments dried up. In a stew of frustration and desperation Kate tried modelling clothes for expectant mothers for mail-order catalogues. Once again the jobs ran out. Not this time because she was pregnant but because she looked too young. In the opening months of the Swinging Sixties it was deemed unseemly for a teenager to flaunt her condition.

It was time, Oliver announced, for them to move back to Wimbledon. 'Roots are very important in the insecure world of acting and Wimbledon was where my roots were. I thought that if I went back to my birthplace, everything would be more secure.' In the summer of 1961 the couple moved to a cramped and musty flat at No. 29 Woodside, Wimbledon. Most of the money from Oliver's month in Ireland disappeared on rent and second-hand furniture and did little to improve the depressing shabbiness of their first home together. Only yards from Wimbledon railway station, the windows and teacups would rattle each time a train arrived. Shades of Ladbroke Grove.

It was a testing year in which his earnings kept pace with his self-confidence – rising from tearful frustration to inflated aggression.

Although far from happy about his client's abilities, Oliver's agent was at least optimistic enough to put the 22-year-old actor up for speaking parts. A small part in the Jose Quintero-directed *The Roman Spring of Mrs Stone* failed to materialise. After another audition Oliver was told to report to Elstree Studios, north of London, where the country's top comedy star was making his second film.

Written by Ray Galton and Alan Simpson, *The Rebel* was to be Tony Hancock's escape from what he saw as the 'death cell' of No. 23 Railway Cuttings, East Cheam. The comedian had already made his last *Hancock's Half Hour* for BBC radio and television and was determined to establish himself as an international star. In many ways *The Rebel*'s plot was a mirror image of Hancock's own plight.

Frustrated by his nine-to-five city routine and his landlady's hostility towards his painting and sculpting, Hancock decides to move to Paris. Soon after his arrival in the French capital he shuffles into a Left Bank café and eavesdrops on a discussion by a group of scruffy young artists. One of them delivers a pompous one-line condemnation of what he describes as 'chocolate-box art'. For some reason he kept fluffing the line. Hancock, who was not in the shot, remained patient but still he couldn't get it right. The director Robert Day took Oliver aside and delivered a whispered ultimatum. The next take was perfect.

'He offered to drive me home after the day's shooting,' recalls Sandor Eles, another actor in the same scene. 'Not far from Elstree he pulled his car into a lay-by and started crying like a baby. Oliver was convinced he was an awful actor and would never be asked to do a film again.' Unaware that Oliver had spoken to his uncle four years earlier, Eles suggested his friend should approach Carol. Oliver seemed horrified – 'At that time he had a bigger fear of nepotism than he did of failure.'

The Rebel was a major success in Britain. It became one of the most popular 'star comic' films of the postwar era, out-grossing the established high earners of British cinema such as the year's two *Carry On* films – *Constable* and *Regardless* – and the latest additions to the *Doctor* and *St Trinian's* series.

Oliver filled the days between films and waiting for his agent to telephone by widening his circle of friends and discovering still more places to drink. Michael Monks was stage manager to a repertory company based at the Wimbledon Theatre. The actors and stage hands drank in a pub next door called the South Wimbledon Club. One afternoon Oliver arrived with a group of friends and invited Monks to join them at a 'secret drinking hideout'.

The Woodland Wives was an off-licence run by a quietly spoken but large man introduced to Monks as Big Jim. Following his newfound cohorts, Monks entered the premises by the front door and left by a storeroom door at the back. Sitting on beer crates and wine boxes, the group would drink and chat their way through the afternoon, shushed into silence each time the doorbell went and a customer entered the shop.

In the pub on sunny afternoons Oliver would become visibly twitchy. Everyone knew what was coming. 'Right, piss-nicks.' Seconds later the group had cleared the bar and scattered in opposite directions – one descending on the baker's to buy bread and rolls, another sweeping through the local delicatessen for cheese and ham, a third heading for the Woodland Wives – to rendezvous on Wimbledon Common for a boozy picnic.

Another Oliver invention was the 'Wimbledon Eight', a high-speed pub crawl around the eight public houses and drinking clubs that skirted the common. Supping in the Dog and Fox or the Rose and Crown or the Green Man, Oliver would slam his empty glass on the counter and announce: 'Right lads, Wimbledon Eight.'

The rules were as simple as they were lethal: each member of the party was allowed fifteen minutes to down a pint of beer in each establishment before the two-minute dash to the next, a consumption of eight pints in just under two hours. Arriving back at the original bar Oliver invariably decided to 'go again' and, despite protests of poverty and intoxication, goaded his companions into a second lap. 'We would be halfway round and stop and Ollie, being Ollie, would insist on carrying on alone,' recalls Monks. 'He only managed the sixteen once.'

At least once or twice a week Kate would join her husband for a night out. His first impression of this 'fabulous, exciting' women never left Michael Monks. Accompanied by an equally attractive friend called Claire and both dressed in denim jeans, leather jackets and high leather boots, the pair were, claims Monks, light years ahead of the fashion and the competition. 'Kate and Claire would match anyone drink for drink and, when it was their round, thought nothing of going to the bar to pay for it.' Still a dubious practice for most young women in the infant sixties.

To a fellow drinker, John Plackett, the Reeds seemed deeply in love and ideally matched. 'Kate was a great communicator. She loved meeting and talking to people and was always very bubbly and happy,' recalls the sign maker. 'It was the perfect life really: drinking, parties and occasionally Ollie would go off and earn some money acting.'

Only one of Reed's closest friends was married. It was Mick Friar's shared marital status or, far more likely, the confusion he sowed and delighted in that made him Oliver's favoured companion. To casual acquaintances, Friar – known to Oliver as Mickus – described himself as 'an artist in burnt clay'. To his friends he was a bricklayer. A brilliantly funny and articulate man, he was better-looking and always better dressed; taking Friar to be the actor and the grubby, T-shirted Oliver the building-site worker was a common mistake.

Staggering home from the pub, Oliver devised a unique and dangerous method for testing his best friend's loyalty –

and bravery. The pair would hold hands and spread-eagle themselves in the road. Unfazed and uncowed by the blaring horns and the drivers' abuse Oliver and Friar would hold hands, ignoring the screech of brakes, until the very last minute. Whoever let go first was chicken. 'Mickus and I have shared death,' Oliver would proudly boast.

Chapter Six

'Everyday life is my favourite theatre. People are my favourite actors.'

O N MONDAY, 5 SEPTEMBER 1960, ANTHONY NELSON KEYS sat behind his desk in his Wardour Street office and began dictating letters. As Falcon Films' general manager he had the task of hiring the team of specialists needed for each new Hammer production.

The last letter of the afternoon was addressed to Roy Ashton at his Surbiton, Surrey, home confirming the quietly spoken Australian as head of make-up for Hammer's fourth film of the year, *The Curse of the Werewolf.* It would, unknown to Keys, give Oliver Reed his first leading role.

Ashton had learned his make-up skills before the war as an apprentice with the Gaumont British Film Corporation at its Shepherd's Bush studio. In 1957, with 25 films on his list of credits, Ashton was invited to work on *The Curse of Franken-stein* at Bray. *Werewolf* would be his sixth film for Hammer in little over two years.

The 51-year-old make-up artist got wind of the latest Falcon production earlier that summer and drove the twenty miles from his Surbiton home to the studios, now known as Bray Court, to scrounge a copy of the script. The next day he set off for London to photograph and sketch stuffed wolves in the Natural History Museum.

By August Ashton, hired for each Hammer project as a film-by-film freelance, was ready to pitch his werewolf concept. 'The hardest thing was to find out exactly what the producers wanted,' recalled Ashton.

The producer, Tony Hinds, liked the initial designs and agreed Ashton should develop them further. 'To create the wolflike appearance on an actor meant setting up a full-sized model and adapting its appearance to a human head.' Hinds, however, had still not settled on who should play the part of Leon, the lycanthropic youth.

For Ashton there was only one suitable actor on the Hammer books. 'I suggested Oliver Reed. He was exactly right: his powerful bone structure was just right for the appearance and his gifts as an actor were perfect for the part. In addition, he resembled a wolf when he was angry.'

Ashton, who had still not been officially offered the job as the film's head of make-up, telephoned Oliver at his Wimbledon flat and invited him to Bray. 'He was most co-operative,' Ashton said in his unpublished memoirs. 'He was very ambitious at the time and nothing was too much trouble, after all this film was his big chance. As a professional artist goes, I think he was marvellous.'

Shooting for *The Curse of the Werewolf* started on 12 September. There were still a few days for Ashton to perfect his latest creation. More than anything, he was unhappy with the werewolf's fangs. One morning Oliver arrived at the Thameside studios with a friend. In the make-up room he introduced Ashton to a fellow Australian, Phil Rasmussen. It was soon apparent to Rasmussen, a dental surgeon, where the make-up man was going wrong. 'He was attempting to make the werewolf's fangs by taking impressions of real teeth,' said Rasmussen. 'It was an impossible task and I suggested he design his own from scratch.'

For Oliver the application of the werewolf's make-up was a tedious – and sometimes painful – experience. Each morning he would arrive at Bray by seven and sit patiently for up to two hours as Ashton and one of his assistants glued pieces of the monster mask on to the actor's face, laying hair over the joins and his own skin. Ashton recalls:

I made an appliance which fitted underneath his eyes and went right over the top of his head and over his ears. I pushed out his nostrils with a pair of candles. I used walnuts first of all. You cut a walnut in half, punch a hole through the shell, and stick it up the nostril. It's a bit uncomfortable. But if you take a candle and draw the wick out of it, then that leaves you with a sort of hollow cylinder. I cut sections off of that and stick them up the artist's nose and the warmth of the nose adjusts the shape of the candle to the shape of the nostrils. Then you can breathe easily and it doesn't irritate the nose.

I made the eyebrows up a little more massively as well. Then you have got to make teeth and heaven only knows what and at the back of the neck a dog makes some very characteristic movements which needed to be reproduced on this wolf-like person. I made a series of beards which fastened around the neck so that they just slipped around there when the artist moved. A succession of hair falls, rather like overlapping sheathes, were fitted to the back of the neck and towards the shoulders. His main trunk was fitted with a leotard and yak hair was put all over this to simulate the coat of a wolf.

The hands were covered on the back with coarse hair. The fingernails were extended to suggest claws. Contact lenses were inserted for extreme close shots. Teeth were extended – canines made and fitted. It was quite a complicated job. It took about an hour and a half to two hours. I was hardly ever off the set where Oliver Reed's make-up was concerned.

Oliver's on-screen transformation into the werewolf caused more problems, this time for the director and camera crews. Ashton came up with a solution:

I suggested the wolfman's transformation by only showing his hands. To do this we had to lock the cameras off in the same position for each shot of the stop-motion photography: I prepared a cast out of plaster with their imprints, so that, every time they stopped the camera, we could take Oliver away to apply more hair and to make the nails a little longer. When he came back he put his hands in the cast again, as it had been before. Roughly speaking, this is what it was: the whole treatment took about two hours.

To the actor's mischievous sense of humour Ashton's handiwork brought an unexpected bonus. 'No one would sit next to me in the studio canteen,' recalled Oliver. 'Even the waitress used to eye me strangely and keep me at a distance.'

Oliver's work on *Werewolf* officially terminated on 2 November. He had earned around £1,000 for eight weeks' work and moved, for the time being at least, into the pantheon of leading men. Years later he would remember the promotion as his first real test as an actor. 'As an extra an actor gets his first half-dozen films for free – you are basically playing yourself in a variety of different surroundings. And then the present moment catches up with you and you have to use your imagination to create a character. That's when your acting career really starts.'

For devoted Hammer fans the film ranks as one of Bray Studio's better efforts. At its best it is an earnest attempt to understand and interpret Iberian folklore – sometimes too closely. The Spanish government was so upset by *Werewolf*'s portrayal of eighteenth-century Spain that it refused to allow the Hammer horror to be screened in any Spanish cinema for more than fifteen years.

The plot of *Werewolf* is classic Hammer. After rejecting the advances of a lecherous old marquis, a deaf-mute servant girl is thrown into the dungeons where she is raped by a fanged and unkempt fellow prisoner. She later dies while giving birth and her son is eventually adopted by the kindly professor, Don Alfredo Carido, played by Clifford Evans. Despite the mutilation of numerous goats and kittens, few people suspect Leon – played by Oliver – has inherited the werewolf genes of his father. Only with a full moon does Leon revert to his lycanthropic state and Carido is forced to kill him with a silver bullet.

Verdicts on the Terence Fisher-directed film remain unanimously bleak. 'Even by Hammer standards,' reported the *British Film Institute Bulletin*, 'this is a singularly repellent job of slaughter-house horror ... Surely the time has come when a film like this should be turned over to the alienists for comment; as entertainment its stolid acting, writing, presentation and direction could hardly be more preclusive.'

There was a glimmer of hope for 22-year-old Oliver. One lone critic described his performance as 'mesmerising'.

On 21 January 1961 – 23 days before Oliver's 23rd birthday – Kate gave birth to their first and only child. The boy, born at Nelson Hospital, Merton, was named Mark Thurloe Reed and registered at the town's register office on 1 March – only four days within the legal time limit set for recording a birth.

Guessing Oliver's profession was almost impossible. Already a Hammer leading man, he found that there were few, if any, visible benefits to his increasing status as an actor. Enquiries about his latest film or contract were ignored or swept politely aside. Names were never dropped. Work was work and play was play. As a stage manager with acting ambitions of his own, Michael Monks was always amazed how his friend found time to prepare for a part: 'Not once did I see him with a script in his hand. Not once did he say he couldn't come out because he was learning his lines or rehearsing.'

But Oliver *was* working. He may have moved on from stealing from Kate's purse or begging money from Dardin to pay for an afternoon at the cinema, but every public and saloon bar he visited and every pint he bought was an investment. 'Provided I could make my drink last out, I had the whole lesson from the best teacher on earth – the genuine original,' he explained. If a part demanded a rough, loud-mouthed navvy Oliver would trawl the workingmen's clubs until he found a character to fit, watching every mannerism, every faltering action, every slurred and mumbled expression. For upper-class 'piss artists' he homed in on London's drinking clubs. 'I studied them as they came in with their pinstripes, stiff collars and bowler hats and watched the whisky get hold of them until the tie became crooked, the voice got louder and by the end of the evening they would be calling their wives whores.'

Summer Saturday afternoons brought a family duty Oliver never forgot, no matter how much his younger brother wished he had. An enthusiastic all-round sportsman, Simon was developing into an exceptional cricketer, a talent his masters at King's College School had already predicted would assure him a career as a county professional. 'I would be in the middle of a key home match,' recalls Simon, 'and precisely fifteen minutes after the pubs closed there would be a roar down the lane and Ollie and his mates would turn up.

Everything would turn raucous and I would try to pretend he wasn't there because it was so embarrassing. But the masters loved it because it brought a new dimension to the cricket.' Celebration or consolation pints were invariably on Oliver.

By the end of 1961 cinema audiences were treated to their third dose of Oliver as a Hammer baddie: his role as Brocaire in *Pirates of Blood River* had been brief yet competent.

For *The Damned*, based on the HL Lawrence novel *The Children of Light*, Oliver swaps his fur and fangs for a tweed jacket and black tie and exploits the latest social neurosis of petty violence and radiation. His performance would also inspire one of the seminal novels of the 1960s.

For once Oliver is cast in a role superbly suited to his limited experience and brooding defiance. His entrance – a portent of his work for Ken Russell – is equally symbolic and menacing. Oliver and his motorcycle gang roar on to the scene to beat up and rob an American tourist to the off-screen chant of the rock anthem 'Black Leather'. Looking down on his bleeding victim, Oliver asks his black-leathered girlfriend, played by Shirley Ann Field, 'Are you happy in your work, Joanie?'

It was, according to the film critic and writer Tim Lucas, the actor's first major performance. 'Oliver gives a brooding, oedipal performance of dash and subtlety, his nursery rhyme taunting of Simple Simon tracing his misanthropy to an embittered childhood. No common thug, King [Reed] oversees rather than participates in his gang's attacks; indeed, his anger is so repressed that his only outburst in the film is triggered by the sculptures of a woman artist (Viveca Lindfors) – the symbols of a free and guiltless expression.'

Anthony Burgess would later admit it was Oliver's portrayal of King, the leader of a predatory teenage gang, that inspired him to write *A Clockwork Orange*. The novel was adapted for the cinema and, in response to a spate of attacks copying scenes from the film, its director Stanley Kubrick took the unique step in 1973 of ordering a lifetime ban on its screening. It was finally released in the UK again on 17 March 2000 after Kubrick's death in March 1999.

Alan Freeman had founded his own record label, Polygon, in the early 1950s and his first two signings were Petula Clark and Jimmy Young. In 1954 Polygon merged with Pye Records and Freeman was appointed an executive producer. With Pye's financial clout and reputation, it was easy for him to follow his taste and enthusiasm and build a catalogue of comedy records. The majority of Freeman's productions were long- or extended-play discs. Late in 1962 he decided to take a chance on a comedy single with a skit on Mike Sarne and Wendy Richard's best-selling hit, 'Come Outside'. Pye's tongue-in-cheek offering would be the classic duet 'Baby, It's Cold Outside' with the inspired – if bizarre – pairing of Joyce Blair, sister and television dance partner of Lionel Blair, and Oliver Reed. The record flopped and was reported to be Pye's lowest seller of the decade.

The fortune – and the fame – failed to materialise. Oliver could at least afford a new home for his wife and eighteen-month-old son. From Woodside the family moved up Wimbledon Hill Road to a spacious flat in a converted Victorian house at No. 1 Homefield Road, only ten properties away from where Oliver had attended The Squirrels.

In the join between the 1950s and 1960s a new type of actor was emerging to interest British film directors. The fake-elegant officer-gentlemen whose trademark was the tapping of a cigarette on a monogrammed case were being replaced by the rough trade. Brash and physical young men whose personal ineptitudes – drunkenness, weight and a constantly shot-off mouth – were more in tune with the public about to enter a third decade of peace.

Oliver has since developed his own theory. 'At one time, when I first started going to the pictures, it was matinée idols with perfect features who were all the rage,' he offered. 'They were eclipsed by the stiff-upper-lipped granite boys. Then came the working-class "lad next door" type of face. By the time I started getting parts the uglies were in vogue.'

In 1963 Oliver was hired to portray one of his 'uglies' for *The Saint*, a popular Sunday afternoon television adventure series starring Roger Moore and adapted from the Leslie Charteris novels. The episode 'The King of Beggars' was being filmed at the old ABPC Elstree studios at Borehamwood, north of London. It was set in Rome and the studio back lot was filled with mock-ups of Italian streets and houses.

Joining Oliver for his *Saint* debut were fellow actors and future stars Ronnie Corbett and Warren Mitchell.

In one scene Oliver, playing a young villain called Joe Catelli, is gunned down and killed. As the blank cartridge was fired Oliver took the full force of the 'shot' and dramatically hurled himself backwards. The director shouted 'cut' and the stage hands moved in to set up the next scene. One by one the crew stopped working as they became aware of a strange guttural sound. A search found Oliver unconscious among the scenery.

'It was the best example of method acting I have ever seen,' recalls Johnny Goodman, the series' production manager. 'In his enthusiasm Ollie had knocked himself cold.'

To his discomfort Oliver found he was already being typecast by producers and directors, some of whom fought desperately to dissociate themselves from the finished product.

As Moise in *The Party's Over*, Oliver plays the leader of yet another vicious and hysterical teenage gang, this time a band of Chelsea beatniks. The edited film, which included scenes of necrophilia and a mock burial, was so disturbing that the Lord Chamberlain gave it an 'X' certificate – and even then only if several of the most offensive scenes were cut. In protest Anthony Perry, as producer, and the director, Guy Hamilton, removed their names from the list of credits, leaving what the British Film Institute reviewer could only describe as something 'so unrewarding the whole business seems pointless'.

Michael Winner was a director with a passion for gold jewellery and blue lamé suits and he could smell talent before it walked into his London office. He was also a man who kept his promises.

One 1962 October morning soon after Winner arrived at his Dean Street office, the telephone rang and a slow public-school voice introduced itself as Oliver Reed. Winner listened as the actor explained he had written a short screenplay and asked if the director would be interested in turning it into a film. The plot – the story of two men living in a wardrobe on the top of a hill – was too esoteric even for Winner's taste, but this was the early 60s and a low-budget cult movie certainly wouldn't do his reputation any harm. Winner arranged an interview.

Dean Street was familiar territory for Oliver. As a pre-National Service teenager in 1955, he had worked as a doorman-cum-bouncer at a St Anne's Court strip club just yards from No. 72 where Winner had his first-floor office. Winner and Oliver talked for more than an hour. Oliver came across as a 'very shy and sensitive young man' full of ideas about how he thought his film should be shot and what message it contained. Flipping through the script and reading the odd line of dialogue, Winner decided against the project: it was 'too poetic'. He did not tell Oliver. Listening to the actor talk – watching him talk – the director felt the hairs on the back of his neck rise. He had found his next leading man. All he had to do now was find the right film.

It took almost two years for the script of *West Eleven* to land on Winner's desk. Within hours he had offered lead roles to Oliver and to a young, blonde actress called Julie Christie. The auditions went well. Both Oliver and Christie were enthusiastic about Keith Waterhouse and Willis Hall's adaptation of the Laura de Rivo novel *The Furnished Room*, in which a rootless drifter is offered £10,000 to commit a murder. To his surprise Winner found his decision overridden by Danny Angel, *West Eleven*'s producer. Angel feared both Oliver and Christie were too inexperienced – 'Oliver is strictly a B-movie actor' – and ordered the director to recast the leads.

Winner was certain he had found a future star in Oliver Reed. 'There was a certain calm and quietness about the man that made me want him as an actor,' he recalls. 'Silence and quietness are important on screen, yet you always felt the human being shining through.'

By 1963 Winner approached the pair once again, this time with parts in his latest project, *The System*. Christie was too busy filming *Billy Liar*, another Waterhouse–Hall creation, and her place was taken by Julia Foster. Impressed by Winner's loyalty, Oliver agreed to head the cast of other 'looming talents' including David Hemmings, John Alderton, Derek Nimmo and Harry Andrews.

The film is set in the British resort of Roxham, and Oliver plays Tinker, a flip-talking seafront photographer who leads a group of young men in a system – the *System* of the title – to meet and share out pretty women on holiday with his mates. Accustomed to one-night sex, Tinker gets his comeuppance when he falls in love with a classy model, played by Jane Merrow, who ignites his latent ambitions of becoming a serious London photographer.

Winner felt the seafront and bed-and-breakfast side streets of Torbay had the right feel for *The System* and location shooting started in the spring of 1964. Within days he discovered two qualities his leading man possessed: one proved accurate; the other Winner used as a reminder to keep himself well away from Oliver Reeds' zealous lifestyle. 'He was very good at being still,' says Winner, 'which is the essence of stardom: not to do too much. He was incredibly handsome and had a great quality of danger. I was convinced he would be an international star.'

When he arrived on set one day, the director found Oliver being besieged by a group of young women. They were, he soon discovered, members of the Oliver Reed Fan Club. Although married with a young son, Oliver exploited his good looks and sexuality and made no excuses for his rather obvious casual affairs. At the time, Winner was still social-ising with his cast and crew, a practice, at least as far as Oliver was concerned, he never repeated. 'I was still quite young and I used to give parties and there were girls involved,' admits Winner. 'Not only was Oliver after the girls, he also started drinking quite heavily. He was never drunk on set, but he could be very difficult in the evenings.'

There was, Winner confesses, a deeper, more ominous air about Oliver. 'I could never quite put my finger on it, but you could see he was deeply troubled. He carried round postcard-sized photographs of himself and a carpet of fans, and he wanted very much to be a star. I never blamed him, but it was troubling.'

With *The System* Michael Winner laid the foundation stone to his claim to have been one of the first directors to introduce the antihero. It was a film, he later explained, that tried to peel back the onion skin of early sixties youth, outwardly searching for a good time, while beneath insecure and sensitive. A simile not lost on the film's star. 'The public image of Oliver is of a slightly dangerous roustabout,' says Winner. 'He may have grown into that, but when I first worked with him he was deeply insecure, deeply sensitive and immensely shy.'

On the first day of shooting Oliver discovered the flamboyant Winner's presence to be as intimidating as his ego. Enthused with a Cecil B De Mille megalomania, Winner insisted on issuing all his set instructions through a megaphone – no matter how close he was standing to the recipient.

Winner's whimsical sense of humour also endeared him to his latest star. Describing the first film he ever made, a short called *This is Belgium*, Winner openly admitted that much of it was shot in the London suburb of East Grinstead. 'We started in Belgium, but it rained so much we had to finish it back home.' During the making of *The System* he was asked by a newspaper to compose his own obituary. Winner replied, 'The inspiring young film director, Michael Winner, died yesterday while in his fifth year of being twenty-nine years old. He was killed on his film set by a large arc lamp dropping on him from a great height. The police investigating the accident have had confessions from all one hundred and thirty-six of the unit wishing to take credit for the event. Mr Winner leaves behind him a number of significant films all of them much enjoyed by his mother.'

Once again, a BFI critic found his star's performance lacking: 'Oliver Reed is badly cast as Tinker. In a very class-conscious film his accent places him firmly in the "U" category, while the script puts him several pegs lower: this plays havoc with the action, and we can never really believe in, let alone feel sympathy for, this rather unattractive Don Juan of the beaches.'

Edited and reissued two years later in 1966 as *The Girl Getters,* Winner's film not only established Oliver as an actor capable of representing the dreams and disillusionment of his generation, but it also fixed him as one of the last pre-pop icons.

He was a publicity man's dream: young, handsome, virile, sexual, and loving every minute of it. Few studio press releases mention his marriage or his young son, preferring to exploit his image as a new 'brooding teenage idol':

'When you get your clothes torn off your back by fans, then you know you've arrived,' says 25-year-old Oliver Reed.

He is a dark, intense young man with a peculiar brooding attraction. One of his first major roles was in *The Curse of the Werewolf*. It brought him a sackful of fan mail and more than fifty proposals of marriage from girls he had never met.

Then he played a romantic young smuggler in *Captain Clegg*. And the film company promptly received a petition signed by over 3,000 girls in a provincial town, asking for more starring roles for their hero.

In his next film, *The Pirates of Blood River*, Oliver Reed played a bloodthirsty pirate – and his fan mail increased dramatically. A group of enthusiastic fans even discovered where he lived. And early one morning they left little gifts on his doorstep. Gifts like ties, buttonholes, books, bottles of drink and gloves.

Since then he has starred in *Paranoiac*, *The Party's Over*, and a television series *Needle Match*. And an official fan club has now been formed to deal with his mail.

When success came, as Oliver's ego knew it would, he was surprisingly coy about claiming the credit. 'I look like a sixties actor, like I fell out of a garbage can. That's the look for today and that's why people like me.'

Early in November 1964 a pair of tickets arrived at Dave Mumford's mother's house in West Bromwich. The former Royal Army Medical Corps sergeant was by now married with a home of his own and established as a clubland entertainer. Accompanied by a note from Oliver Reed, the tickets invited the former Church Crookham NCO to the opening of a ten-pin-bowling alley in nearby Birmingham.

Although by now an established Hammer star, Oliver was hired to 'escort' the singer Kathy Kirby to the event. Kirby had, that week, reached number four in the hit parade with her song 'Secret Love'.

Mumford waited for a suitable opportunity before approaching the friend he had not seen for four years. 'Come and have a drink,' announced Oliver, propelling the couple towards the bar.

'I can't,' Mumford apologised. 'I'm working tonight and I never drink before a show.'

'OK,' said Oliver, handing Mumford a piece of paper. 'Well, write your new address on that.'

Mumford obliged and handed the note to Oliver. 'Now do it again on that,' said Oliver, offering a new slip of paper.

Putting one address in his top pocket, Oliver handed the second to the barman. 'My friend can't have a drink now,' he said. 'But deliver a crate of Scotch to that address tomorrow – it's on me.'

Chapter Seven

'I have made many serious statements – I just can't remember any of them. I guess they mustn't have been very important.'

'LOOK OUT, HERE COMES DRACULA.'

As he brushed past the table of jeering young men Oliver Reed bent low and whispered into the ringleader's ear. 'Watch it,' he said, forcing a smile. 'Or I'll bite your jugular vein out.'

The Crazy Elephant was a smart but dubious nightclub in Jermyn Street, around the corner from Piccadilly. It was not the kind of establishment his uncle had in mind but, with his 21st film about to be released, Oliver decided it was time to smarten himself up and get himself noticed.

The music was loud and the waitresses were tolerably attractive and Oliver and his two friends settled down for an expensive night's drinking. The trio attracted as many sideways glances for the actor's familiar face as they did for the oddity of their appearance: Oliver, well-dressed and barrel-chested; Frank, small and overly gentle, whose delicate hands were usually employed making displays from plastic flowers; and Gibby, an Australian dentist who insisted on chain-smoking cigarettes from a holder he claimed was once owned by Noël Coward.

The friends had just emptied their second bottle of champagne when they noticed someone approaching their table. 'Did you mean what you said over there?' The man nodded over his shoulder.

'Fuck off and play with yourself,' Oliver hissed.

The man grinned inanely and Oliver felt something hit his face, not hard enough to knock him over but strangely sharp like a semicircle of sharp pins grinding against his jawbone. A spatter of blood hit the man's face a millisecond before Oliver's fist.

It was too late. Surrounded by the gang, Oliver was punched and kicked to the ground. As the house lights came on he saw Frank sitting stiff-backed and still on one of the few undamaged chairs, determined to ignore the club's destruction. Oliver tried to protect his face from the storm of blows and noticed Gibby crouching cross-legged under the table, attempting to light what remained of a broken cigarette. 'He's never going to manage that,' Oliver said to himself.

Outside the club Oliver held together what remained of his face with one hand and began waving at passing taxis. He could still feel shards of broken glass in his mouth and his tongue was beginning to swell painfully.

A taxi pulled over. 'St George's Hospital,' Oliver mumbled.

The driver, whose name was Andy Cohen, eyed his fair apprehensively. 'What about my cab, mate?' he said. 'All that blood's going to fuck up my cab.'

'Fuck your cab,' snapped Oliver, falling into the back of the taxi. 'Get me to St George's quick.'

On the way Oliver fainted twice. Cohen, still concerned more about his week-old black cab than his passenger, stopped to prop Oliver upright and staunch the blood with clean handkerchiefs his wife insisted he keep in the vehicle's glove box. 'It wasn't until a couple of days later when I read about the fight in the London *Evening News* that I realised just who he was,' recalled Cohen.

By the time the cab arrived at St George's Oliver had lost several pints of blood, most of them down his jacket and trousers. The early-morning quiet was suddenly shattered as the casualty department was plunged into what could have been a scene from one of his recent Hammer horrors. Already in deep shock, Oliver was shaking violently. To stop his legs from collapsing he was forced to hold them rigid and stagger towards the first person he saw. The young nurse – confronted by a six-foot figure, dripping with blood from behind a swathe of handkerchiefs and mummy-walking towards her – first screamed, then fainted.

Back at the Homefield flat, Kate had long since retired to bed. She took one look at her lover's bandaged face and announced, 'You stupid bastard.'

Oliver, still high on the combination of alcohol and analgesic, fumbled on under the macho misconception that despite being badly beaten he needed to prove he was still capable of making love. 'You're bloody kinky,' Kate said, pushing him away.

The next morning Oliver peeled back the bandages in front of the bathroom mirror. He was appalled at what confronted him. The glass had sliced through his cheek and shredded part of his tongue. Convinced that if the stitches had saved his face they had also ruined his acting career, Oliver set off for the nearest off-licence. 'I bought a bottle of whisky and drank half of it through a straw because I could hardly move my mouth.'

Refusing his wife's advice to rest and let the wound heal, Oliver was soon touring his local pubs proudly exhibiting his disfigured face. 'Look, look what they've done to me,' he would say, peeling back the bandages and ignoring the protests of those halfway through a lunchtime hotpot or shepherd's pie.

While Winner was busy editing his latest picture, its star arrived unannounced at his Dean Street office, escorted by a silent but menacing minder. 'What's the bodyguard for, Oliver?' asked the director.

'Look what happened to me,' said Oliver, pointing to the angry red scars on his face. 'They're after me.'

Oliver was convinced that the attack was retribution for his drunken behaviour. So, too, was Winner.

'Do you think the scars will affect my career?' asked Reed.

'No, Oliver,' said Winner honestly. 'It adds a bit of interest really. You were never the conventional leading man; you were never going to play the head of a bank.'

At that moment Reed would have been happy to play any role. Apart from three television appearances and with *The System* still not released, Oliver was desperately short of money. A few weeks later Winner was approached by a fellow director who cheekily told him he had been surprised to find the minicab he'd ordered the previous night being driven by *The System*'s leading man.

By the mid-1960s Oliver was living in a world fringed by the criminal underworld and blurred by alcohol. He was fascinated by the lower-league criminals who used the Wimbledon pubs, and the first-division mobsters who frequented the West End clubs. His scars, healed but still an angry red, and his confident, punchy manner attracted their own attention – from both sides of the law.

It was not uncommon for Oliver and his circle of close friends to be offered the occasional stolen item: £500 watches for a tenner, a dozen Jermyn Street shirts for a fiver, and a regular supply of stolen or smuggled spirits. 'Ollie, like the rest of us, bought things and made a few quid,' admits restaurateur, John Hogg. 'He wasn't rich then. It was a way of getting things cheap and earning some extra money.' There was, adds Hogg, another reason. 'Ollie was from the top of Wimbledon Hill, he came from a good family and went to a public school. He even talked differently. Most of us had grown up in council houses. Somehow Ollie was trying to prove he was as good – or as bad – as us. We were the underdogs and he wanted to belong.'

One night Oliver was approached in the toilets of the Dog and Fox. The man, whom Oliver knew but had never spoken to, had a proposition: £20 for ten minutes' work. A local villain needed to be taught a lesson. Later that night Oliver dragged the miscreant into an alley and broke his nose and jaw before punching him semiconsciousness. The next morning the actor met the victim's wife on her way to visit her husband in hospital and slipped the £20 into her hand.

The attack attracted the inevitable police attention and Oliver was questioned, but never charged. The detective sergeant who interviewed Oliver was 'bewildered and shocked' by the actor's performance. 'He suddenly began to cry,' recalls the former officer. 'Here was this man, who we knew dabbled in stolen property and who was earning himself a hard reputation as a brawler, crying real tears.'

As a debt collector, Oliver delivered swift and painful justice. The nonrepayment of a loan that would forestall a friend's appearance in the South Wimbledon Club or the Green Man would be answered by a visit from the actor and a swift crack across the bridge of the nose.

If Oliver's brush with the law put the brake on his criminal exploits it did little to curb his apparently disastrous plunge towards alcoholism. Once drunk Oliver would do almost anything to increase and continue his consumption. After one party at John Hogg's Wimbledon home, the restaurateur awoke to discover his friend had swallowed the contents of every perfume and scent bottle on his wife Nita's dressing table. Out on the town, Oliver had a more devious method of securing out-of-hours liquor. Checking into Brown's Hotel near Piccadilly, he would promptly empty the minibar, before demanding a new room with a fresh stock of drinks. He was eventually banned from the hotel after changing rooms five times in one night.

Oliver loved parties, and if not parties then lock-ins at his local pub. Local licensing laws forced every pub and club in Wimbledon to close its doors at 10.30 p.m., an hour earlier than licensed premises in the surrounding boroughs. Most nights saw a mass exodus as drinkers crossed the common and the local authority boundary to indulge in an extra round of late-night drinks. At 10.30 p.m. he would slam his glass on the counter and stamp his way to the door. 'Right,' he would announce loudly and fiercely, holding the door wide open. 'Who's going and who's staying?' A few sheepish couples would tiptoe out of the bar as Oliver slipped the bolt behind them. It was a ritual strangely in tune with Oliver's self-imposed sexual and moral code.

For Oliver any alcoholic gathering was a wonderful mingling of personalities: building-site labourers, petty criminals, businessmen, would-be writers and poets, artists, the unemployed and unemployable, beautiful women and strong men, good talk against a background of laughter and lies and the latest hit record on the radio or Danset portable record player. Oliver was drinking heavily, but he had not yet become obnoxious, combative, competitive, and wanting to have sex with every woman in the room. Not yet.

For most of Oliver's circle of friends and drinking partners it was a trait apparent only with hindsight. 'Ollie was the only man in our circle who never made any kind of sexual advances or tried anything on,' recalls Nita Hogg. Drunken fumblings and dark-corner petting were a frequent ingredient in most Wimbledon parties. 'Not for Ollie,' she adds. 'Most women compare notes in the powder room, that never happened with Ollie. I can't remember him even pinching a bottom in fun.'

Nor did Oliver boast his sexual conquests. 'And there were plenty of those,' remembers John Hogg. 'Ollie never tried to hide his affairs, but he made sure they never came anywhere near Wimbledon.'

Late in 1965 Oliver made a passable thriller called *The Shuttered Room*. Set on an isolated island off the New England coast the story – adapted from the HP Lovecraft and August Derleth thriller – interweaves the village antagonism against a newly married couple and the mystery of a locked room on the top floor of a remote millhouse. Playing the double role of Susannah Kelton and her disfigured and demented sister, Sarah, was the actress Carol Lynley. Within weeks Oliver and Lynley had started a passionate affair.

To celebrate the New Year, the actor invited John and Nita Hogg out for the night. When the couple arrived in London Oliver and his latest girlfriend met them. 'It was obviously a very serious and intimate affair,' recalls Hogg. 'Anyone who did not know Ollie was already married would have assumed they were very much in love.' The evening ended with drinks and supper, cooked by Hogg, in Lynley's west London riverside flat.

During Oliver's time at Bray he died in the flames of a blazing chapel, was shot with a silver bullet, blasted by a flintlock pistol and plunged over a cliff in a stolen car. After six films with Hammer – four of them fatal to his characters – he decided it was time to move on.

If Oliver studied as a wide-eyed and ambitious freshman at the Ambassador and Odeon and Essoldo universities he was now at least a postgraduate with a degree earned at Bray. 'By the time I left Hammer I at least knew enough about maintaining a part throughout the duration of a film when it's shot out of continuity.'

In 1965 Oliver played his final death scene for Hammer, in a feeble North-West Frontier adventure called *The Brigand of Kandahar*. This time, as Eli Khan, the leader of a band of Glizhai rebel tribesmen, Oliver dies in hand-to-hand combat. It is the British Film Institute that, once again, delivers the final vitriolic comment: 'Oliver Reed sneers maniacally throughout . . . Otherwise all this tatty epic of life on the North-West Frontier has to offer is actors in streaky black-faces pottering about among cardboard rocks and bits of rural England.' There was no argument from Oliver. It was, he readily admitted, the worst film he ever made for Hammer.

Since its launch in the 1950s *Monitor* had established itself as BBC Television's most prestigious arts programme, tackling difficult and esoteric themes in an exciting and accessible way. The filmmaker Ken Russell was recruited to the 45-minute programme when he persuaded its editor Huw Wheldon, to commission a trial film about Sir John Betjeman. The documentary – *Poet's London* – was screened in March 1959 and since then Russell had made an average of five films a year for *Monitor*. The production staff had moved, mean-while, from their cramped offices in the BBC's West London Film Studios – once the home of Ealing Films – to Lime Grove.

Each weekend Ken Russell and his family watched *Juke Box Jury*, a television show in which celebrity jurors passed sentence on the latest pop releases. This Saturday Russell watched the programme with growing interest. The panel included a young actor called Oliver Reed – and Oliver bore a striking resemblance to the young Claude Debussy.

On Monday morning Russell telephoned Oliver's agent to arrange a meeting. The next day the 27-year-old actor shuffled into the office Russell shared with three other *Monitor* directors.

'I hear you're considering me for Debussy,' Oliver said confidently.

Russell nodded. 'Do you know anything about Debussy?'

'Not a thing.'

Russell related a brief account of the composer's life. Oliver seemed unimpressed.

The director waited a few seconds then said, 'Well, thanks for coming in.'

Oliver rose to leave. 'So I won't be playing the part, then?'

'What do you mean?' asked Russell.

'What about this?' Oliver stuck out his chin and moved it from side to side, as if examining himself in a shaving mirror.

'I didn't see anything,' said Russell, unconcerned about the scars. 'So do you want to do the film?'

'Yeah, sure,' said Oliver.

Before officially accepting the part Oliver telephoned Michael Winner, with whom he had made *The System*, to ask his advice. Oliver's biggest concern was the small fee on offer from the BBC, less than half he could demand for a film appearance. Winner's response was emphatic. 'I told him to go for it,' Winner says. 'Ken Russell was a director he should get close to.'

Oliver's 'attitude' was exactly what the BBC director was looking for. 'When I first saw him he looked terrific.' said Russell. 'He struck me as vivacious, cheeky and not run-of-the-mill. I remember him being very moody and glowering. I liked his spirit – everyone else I auditioned seemed to fade into insignificance.'

Shooting for *The Debussy Film* started in the spring of 1965. It would be Russell's last project for *Monitor*. The BBC had decided to axe its prestigious arts programme and replace it with a new series, *Omnibus*.

At 38 Russell had already earned himself a reputation as one of the most original and outrageous filmmakers of the sixties. This time, and using a previously rejected script co-written with a fellow *Monitor* producer, Melvyn Bragg, he intended to poke fun at traditional screen biographies, all of which 'inform and romanticise but leave the act of creation unexamined'. In Russell's unique way, his film would complete an absurd circle: with a fly-on-the-wall film crew following a television director as he struggles to complete a fly-on-the-wall film about the composer. Oliver Reed would play both Debussy and the actor who played him.

'Debussy was an ambiguous character and I always let the character of the person or his work dictate the way the film goes,' Russell explains. 'Also, one was a bit critical of artists like Debussy and I thought the time had come to ask questions, and the natural way for me to ask questions was to have a film director talking to an actor, because an actor always asks questions about the character he's playing and the director usually had to answer them, or try to, often just to keep him happy. And when I found that Debussy was friendly with an intellectual named Pierre Louys from whom he derived a lot, it seemed an analogous relationship to that of a film director and an actor. There are some points in the film, I think, where it doesn't matter if it's the director talking to the actor or Louys talking to Debussy – passages of intentional ambiguity.'

Despite its corporation kudos all the *Monitor* films were made on a shoestring budget – some considerably thinner than others.

Russell decided to shoot several scenes in Chalon-sur-Saône, the French town with close associations with the leader of the French impressionist school of music.

For some reason the French customs at Calais had impounded the unit's wardrobe and make-up. Russell decided to press on and announced they would improvise by adapting and cannibalising their own clothes. The lost make-up was replaced by scouring chemists' shops on the way to Chalon.

At the end of the week's shooting Russell was so pleased that he invited the entire nine-man crew to lunch at the town's swishest restaurant, courtesy of the BBC. Only when the wine list arrived did he realise the corporation was unlikely to sanction his wine expenses at £9 a bottle. While the rest of the crew munched on the bread and rolls, Russell and Oliver slipped across the square to a nearby wine shop. Stuffing bottles of cheap red and white wine down their trouser legs, they clanked and swayed their way stiff-legged back into the restaurant. Each time the single bottle of house wine went down it was surreptitiously topped up from the under-the-table reserve. The empties were smuggled out past the waiters to the ladies' toilet.

With his Debussy fee, Oliver redecorated and recarpeted the Homefield Road flat. After an evening in the Dog and Fox the couple invited their friends back for an impromptu party. The next morning they awoke to find their new lounge carpet so badly scuffed by the revellers that it looked as though someone had driven a tractor across it. Rightly or wrongly, Michael Monks got the blame and was instantly elevated to Oliver's gallery of nicknames as 'Tractors'.

Nicknames to Oliver were both a leveller and a ticket of admission, a label of derision and a badge of brotherhood. A

Scandinavian friend became the 'Norseman'; the dapper actor Jimmy Villiers, who claimed a distant relationship with the Queen, was 'Old Cockey Bollocks'; Ken Burgess, who had served in the navy, was promoted to 'Admiral'; Morris Maple was 'the Colonel', and John Plackett 'the Major'. The group was confronted by one Rose and Crown regular whom they had dubbed 'Eddie the Arab' because of his Middle Eastern appearance. 'My name is not Eddie, it's Edwin,' he protested.

'OK,' replied Oliver, 'We'll change it – you can be "Edwin the Bedouin".'

Within six months Oliver was earning enough to think about moving home for the third time in as many years. This time he could afford an entire house and not just a part of someone else's. From the bedroom window of his new home at No. 4 The Drive he could look across the neat back gardens to the Durrington Park Road house in which he was born. It would be the last home he would share with Kate and his young son.

At home, and on the streets of Wimbledon, Oliver remained inconspicuous. Away from the film set or the television studio, he was determined to enjoy his anonymity to the point of obsession. In 1964 John Hogg took a two-year lease on a former tobacconist's in St George's Road, just around the corner from Wimbledon Bridge and where Granny Dardin had taken her young grandsons to buy sweets. Hogg's plan was to turn the shop into the kind of themed restaurant he and his wife had seen and managed during their time in America. Keeping renovation costs down was vital. 'All my friends would come in and help,' recalls Hogg. 'When he wasn't working Ollie would turn up in his jeans and clean and scrub the brickwork. He loved it. It was something physical he did with his mates. It wasn't work, it was fun.' When the Windjammer Restaurant opened, Hogg, ever the businessman, swapped Oliver's sweat for his celebrity and invited the press along to take pictures.

Meanwhile, the promise and 'erotic delight' Ken Russell had first spotted in Oliver Reed's eyes the day they met shone through the television screen like a new and highly original light source. The camera loved him. 'Oliver was good as

Debussy,' remembers Russell. 'He captured the brooding sensuality and threatening calm that is so characteristic of the man and his music.' Unable to use Oliver's face so soon after Debussy, the director had no hesitation in capitalising on the actor's voice.

Three years earlier Russell had made a film portrait of the Yorkshire painter James Lloyd. He now hired the painter as an actor to play Henri 'Douanier' Rousseau, the customs officer and Sunday painter ridiculed by the modernist movement and yet whose pictures now sold for millions of dollars. The script for *Always on Sunday* was once again written by Ken Russell and Melvyn Bragg and Oliver Reed did the commentary.

The System was released while Oliver was in France, but *The Debussy Film* – and the weeks he spent making it – were to become the pivotal point of his career. 'It was the point at which I began to shoot upwards.'

Omnibus opened its art series with a documentary on the Victorian poet Dante Gabriel Rossetti. To Russell's amazement the glowering actor once again bore an extraordinary resemblance to his subject – 'looking like Debussy in a top hat'. Other roles were similarly cast for appearance over experience: Gala Mitchell, an amateur actress, played the part of Janey with the poet Christopher Logue as Swinburne and the artist Derek Boshier as Millais.

For those not attuned to Russell's oblique and sometimes frightening view of the world *Dante's Inferno* was equally confusing. The director was once again pursuing his Holy Grail – that 'objective truth is no guarantee of artistic reality'. In his book *An Appalling Talent* John Baxter attempts to summarise the plot:

With its grim first shot of a coffin exhumed to reveal a decomposed corpse from whose side the gravediggers plucked a mouldering book, and the following montage (fast becoming a Russell trademark), of burning academic paintings and a capering Rossetti, stresses the truth of Rossetti's life rather than the image one infers from his work. His quest for some spiritual purity to counterbalance his sensuous nature ends in the betrayal of his artistic ideals, his friends, his drug-addicted first wife – after throwing his poems into her coffin as a melodramatic gesture, he is persuaded years later to dig it up and have them published – and finally in his addiction to Chloral, premature enfeeblement and death.

It was during the filming of *Dante's Inferno* – Oliver and Russell's third BBC project together – that the director and actor began to appreciate each other's demands and delivery. Russell was beginning to distil Oliver's performances into a kind of directive shorthand, each command – 'Moody One' or 'Moody Two' or 'Moody Three' – would elicit the 'intensity of smouldering meanness required'.

Oliver soon realised that he and the other actors were, at least in Russell's scheme of things, little more than movable props directed by a man who focused as much on irony as images. 'I think there are all sorts of people who perpetrate the image of Ken as an intellect and as an intellectual director,' explained Oliver, 'when in fact he plays his players and uses his film with the panache of a great comedian, and this is his magic. Ken is very concerned about his composition and, because it's necessary for someone to speak, he allows his actors to come into this beautiful picture he has created.'

Oliver was also making less cultured television appearances. His image as a *Saint* heavy was holding good. During the 1964–65 winter he appeared in two series, both produced by Granada. The first was *Biggles,* with Neville Whiting as the airman hero and the singer-actor John Layton as his sidekick Ginger. And just after Christmas Oliver made his first of several appearances in *It's Dark Outside,* a detective drama starring William Mervyn and Keith Barron. In as many months he was acting in a third TV series, this time for the BBC. *R3* – full title *Research Centre No. 3* – was a science-cum-espionage thriller, in many ways the precursor for the highly successful cult series *Doomwatch.*

Chapter Eight

'Contrary to popular belief, I am not the greatest crumpet bumper of all time.'

ICHAEL WINNER WAS A ROUND-SHOULDERED, short-tempered, overenthusiastic film producer with the habit of puffing on large cigars while using his free hand to jingle the loose change in his pocket.

'It's a marvellous story, my dear boy,' said Winner pacing the carpet of his antique-filled London office. 'A marvellous story all about two brothers who set about stealing the Crown Jewels from the Tower of London.'

The 24-year-old actor fingered the draft script on his lap and waited for an opportunity to ask the obvious question: 'But who's going to play my brother?'

The producer stopped pacing and stabbed at the actor with his cigar. 'Oliver Reed,' announced Winner grinning triumphantly.

'Oliver Reed!' said an astonished Michael Crawford. 'You must by bloody joking.'

Crawford was an actor who owed his early successes to the Rank-owned Children's Film Foundation and his stage name (his real name is Michael Patrick Dumble-Smith) to a passing cream-cracker lorry. He was about to start rehearsals for a West End show, and, no matter how astute Winner's track record, the last thing Crawford needed now was a miscast-film disaster.

For his latest project, *The Jokers*, Winner hired Dick Clement and Ian La Frenais, whose award-winning Tyneside television comedy, *The Likely Lads*, was about to start its third and final BBC series. *The Jokers'* storyline, and the film's hook, were inspired by the director's days at Cambridge. While editing the student newspaper, *Varsity*, Winner repeatedly 'borrowed' bicycles to make the journey from his college to the newspaper's office. Despite being gated and sent down for two weeks he evaded a theft charge by invoking a legal loophole – the same loophole the jokers of the film use to escape prosecution after stealing the Crown Jewels.

Crawford loved the script, but refused to commit himself. 'There was absolutely no way I thought an audience would accept Oliver Reed and me as being remotely related,' he explains. Time was running out. Winner finally suggested the two actors should meet. Oliver arrived at the producer's office accompanied by his 'fair and skinny' younger brother Simon. 'He [Simon] could have been my double,' Crawford recalls. 'There was no more argument.'

Assessing *The Jokers* in his book *The Films of Michael Winner*, Bill Harding claims it is this physical and emotional contrast that is the movie's inherent strength. 'Oliver plays straight, allowing himself to be carried along by the plot,' says Harding. 'His assertive masculinity nicely sets off Crawford's naively introverted portrayal.'

Crawford soon discovered there was always a certain amount of physical risk working with his new co-star. On the set, Oliver took to walking with his arm around Crawford's shoulder, periodically giving the younger actor a brotherly hug – 'the kind of squeeze a fruit-extracting machine would give a ripe orange'.

In one scene, in which David Tremayne mistakenly thinks he has been betrayed, he attempts to throttle his brother. 'Ollie took my "betrayal" as something entirely real and completely personal,' says Crawford. 'His ham-like hands were fastened so tightly round my neck, I felt the end of my life was imminent. It took four people to get him off – and only two of them were scripted.'

The film was shot using some of the capital's top tourist attractions as sets – the Stock Exchange, the Tower of London and the Old Bailey. Each evening for nine weeks during the summer of 1966 Crawford left the *Jokers* set – the entire film was shot on location around London – to return to the Duke of York's Theatre in the West End, where he was starring in *The Anniversary*. Oliver took the opportunity of suggesting they try some nearby restaurants. 'Michael had very short arms and very long pockets,' recalled Oliver. 'Whenever Winner and I invited him to lunch, Michael would turn up late and leave early.'

On one rare occasion Michael Crawford invited his director and co-star for a drink at the White Elephant Club. When the bill arrived Crawford was nowhere to be seen. The pair finally caught up with Crawford in Trafalgar Square, where Oliver dangled him over one of the fountains until he promised to pay up. 'Oliver was very sensitive to injustice,' adds Winner. 'Especially in the way of paying for rounds.'

Someone with an exceptionally low alcohol threshold, Crawford insisted on drinking only half-pints of beer. What he didn't know was that on one occasion Oliver had bribed the waiter to spike each half with a double vodka. 'That gave him a very grumpy constitution after lunch and he would start shouting back at Winner,' adds Oliver.

Crawford was exceptionally dedicated and hard-working, and his style of acting was already showing glimpses of the dysfunctional and maladroit character he would unleash seven years later as Frank Spencer in *Some Mothers Do 'Ave 'Em*. 'Michael would get into a Rolls-Royce by leaping across the pavement and jumping in head first,' remembers Oliver. 'He had this wonderful knack of bringing out his natural aggression by doing his own stunts and falling off things.' Their director, however, showed a more annoying kind of enthusiasm.

Michael Winner was a brilliant and innovative director who, early in his career, had picked up the unnerving habit of issuing all his on-set instructions through a battery-powered megaphone. Oliver, who made *The System* for Winner two years earlier, was determined he wasn't going to suffer the director's 'Cecil B De Mille fixation' a second time.

First to go were Winner's designer and very expensive sunglasses, which Oliver and Crawford 'accidentally' threw under the wheels of a bus. The pair then enlisted the help of the crew to jack Winner's car clear of the ground. It was only when the pair smeared shoe polish around the mouthpiece of

Winner's megaphone, making him look as if he was wearing black lipstick, that the instrument finally disappeared.

When it was released a year later *The Jokers* found almost universal praise. Even the traditional sceptics at the British Film Institute conceded, 'Oliver Reed has found a useful comic line by imposing a Bogarde-ish smoothness on to his characteristically tough exterior'. The London *Evening Standard* went still further: 'The lean-line droopiness of Michael Crawford and Oliver Reed's big-drum bravado make them the best double act since Laurel and Hardy.'

While taking minor pot shots at the film – 'the colour is on the crude side' – a few critics managed to appreciate Winner's subplot. Almost three decades later, in his 1991 biography of Michael Crawford, Anthony Hayward successfully explains: '*The Jokers* said much about Sixties London, still swinging but not at the pace depicted by the media. Winner's aim was to reveal the truth of a society becoming richer but less happy. The brothers intend to show that they will not conform to the practices and hypocrisies of high society. David [Reed] is a failed architect and Michael [Crawford] has been thrown out of Sandhurst where he was training for the Army. Their planting of small bombs, so that they can monitor security procedures, is followed by police and Army blundering, which was intended by Winner as a dig at Services mentality.'

Peter Draper was getting fed up with the telephone calls. The scriptwriter was committed to his television work and was working to a very tight deadline. Creating *The System* for Winner the writer accepted the idea it was to be the first in a trilogy of films. He was now finding it hard to commit himself to the second script.

The director-cum-producer had already announced his intention to rehire Oliver Reed to allow Tinker, the character Draper created in *The System*, to be developed still further as Andrew Quint, a disillusioned London advertising executive. Explaining the continuation, Draper has since said, 'Assuming Tinker had gone to London . . . and you leapt five or six years. But the looks and age of the character didn't change. This is why it was good that Oliver was playing both parts. He was a kind of *doppelgänger* of Tinker. So if you see the two characters working at the same time both films hang together.'

Michael Winner recruited Orson Welles to play Jonathan Lute, Quint's ruthless boss. It was, the American later admitted, his best part since his legendary Harry Lime in *The Third Man,* coincidentally directed by Carol Reed, his co-star's uncle. Sparked by the director's relentless pestering, Draper based Jonathan Lute squarely on Michael Winner. 'I made the Orson Welles character a symbol of Michael's persistence, of never letting you leave,' says Draper. 'The advertising background was a symbol of commercial filmmaking. Michael is a combination of a successful commercial filmmaker and someone who wants to make serious movies. I wanted a symbol of commerce which would give the opportunity to use *art,* for want of a better word.'

The film's title - *I'll Never Forget What's 'isname* - was meant to symbolise the trendy and quick-silver mentality of the sixties' advertising industry. The plot, suitably splashed with sex and violence in a variety of stylish settings, tells the story of Andrew Quint (Reed), a commercial director, separated from his wife and daughter and bored by a succession of wealthy mistresses. After destroying his desk with an axe – providing Oliver with one of his most memorable entrances – Quint rejoins the literary magazine on which his career started. There he falls in love with a sexually innocent woman, played by Carol White, whose death in a car crash forces him to make sense of the life he has abandoned and come to terms with his own flaws and frustrations.

Oliver Reed and Orson Welles met a few days before filming started. Their friendship would last until Welles's Hollywood death in October 1985. 'Orson was a paradoxical creature, a poetic visionary and a mendacious con-man magician,' recalled the comic actor Kenneth Williams, whom Welles had earlier befriended. 'His mercurial nature oscillating between rancorous rudeness and humorous charm.'

Whatever his reputation, Welles's larger-than-life persona was perfectly in tune with Oliver's already rumbustious lifestyle. Working with him, declared Oliver, was an 'honour'. One day over lunch the American offered his British co-star a singular piece of advice. 'If in doubt,' Welles told him, 'do nothing.' Eight years later, while filming the rock musical *Tommy*, Oliver proffered the same advice to his friend and acting protégé, Keith Moon. 'I learned so much technique from Ollie,' admitted the Who drummer. 'More than I can ever repay.'

The third and final 'Tinker' film was never made. Winner and Peter Draper discussed a setting but not a plot. 'It was going to take place out of season in a seaside town,' explains the writer. 'The kind of people who inhabited Andrew Quint's urban world down there and a kind of amalgam of Quint and Tinker was living in the resort.'

By the end of shooting Oliver developed another, more physical, relationship with a co-star he first flirted with while filming *Beat Girl* and whom many now regarded as his female rival for media icon of the sixties.

Carole White was born in 1941, the daughter of a prosperous London scrap-metal dealer. Following a brief film appearance at the age of eleven she dropped the 'e' from her first name and started a promising film career with a part as a wayward schoolgirl in *The Belles of St Trinian's*. By 1959 she had appeared in thirteen films, including *Carry on Teacher, Around the World in 80 Days* and two of the highly successful *Doctor* series. Her first marriage, at the age of eighteen, produced two sons and put a temporary hold on her acting career.

In November 1966, BBC Television broadcast *Cathy Come Home*, by Nell Dunn, a documentary-style play which aroused a nationwide response to the problem of homelessness and rekindled Carol White's career. White – herself a wispy five-foot-two-inch, strong-boned woman who radiated a down-to-earth sex appeal – played the rootless young mother of the title. From pushing a pram down Hammersmith High Street she found herself being offered Hollywood contracts and instant celebrity.

The following year White starred in another Nell Dunn film. *Poor Cow* depicted the life of a young London mother who lives in squalor with her criminal husband. This led to her being named the most promising new female star by American cinema owners.

By the time she appeared in *I'll Never Forget What's 'isname*, White's career was once again on the slow slide to disaster. From specialising in playing women with problems, she progressed to becoming one herself. Her affair with Oliver Reed was brief and passionate and went a long way towards destroying her first marriage. In 1972 White moved to Hollywood. It was a disaster. When the film offers dried up she earned a dubious living by selling her sexual confessions to newspapers and television. Along with Oliver she claimed a series of affairs with, among others, Frank Sinatra, Warren Beatty, Richard Todd, Adam Faith and Peter Sellers.

In 1982 and after descending into a lifestyle of debt and shoplifting and suicide attempts, the actress would be sacked from a successful run of Nell Dunn's *Steaming* for missing fifteen West End performances – absences she blamed on her drug binges. It was in White's company that Oliver Reed experienced his first encounter with drugs.

'At first Ollie wasn't that keen,' she admitted to an American journalist shortly before her death. 'Ollie was much too interested in booze and the effect that had on his brain than he ever was about drugs. One night I got him to smoke his first joint, he was so drunk I don't think he even noticed it.'

For several weeks Oliver refused to progress to harder drugs. 'In the end I had to spike his drink with LSD,' admitted White. 'The effect was awesome. You could see the trip bubbling behind Ollie's eyes, but nothing surfaced. He was floating; dancing; flying; all in his head, externally he was the same drunken Ollie. No change. Talking. Inside he was having the time of his life.'

The sensation left Oliver with a psychedelic hangover and an angry determination never to repeat the experience. Carol White died of liver failure in Miami on 16 September 1991. She was 48.

Sometimes it was not necessary for Oliver to progress to physical seduction: he needed a wife at home and a mistress to cheat with and an endless supply of women with whom he could flirt. From his first sexual encounter to the day he died, Oliver needed the presence of more than one woman within range of his magnetism.

As witnesses would later testify, arguments between Oliver and his wife would follow an established set of rules and, until his affairs became the battleground, invariably centred on his upper-class background and her working-class roots. Oliver would spark the dispute; Kate would retaliate; Oliver would reluctantly apologise; Kate would threaten to walk out; Oliver begged her to stay; Kate would maintain her undying love. It was a strategy heavy on manipulation and with each player employing temper tantrums, public embarrassment, vulgar insults, ridicule, sarcasm and bitter irony. 'When Ollie and Kate erupted, the safest thing was to duck,' recalls a friend.

Coping with the press was still fun, especially if the examiner was a woman. Oliver had not yet developed a private life worth sniping at – interviews were angled almost exclusively on his career. When the questions became too personal – or the questioner too boorish – Oliver invariably sought his own debunking revenge. He told one charming but probing Japanese journalist he would be interviewed only on Wimbledon Common and only if the young woman accepted a local 'tradition' that she drink at least four pints of lager before twelve noon. Another woman writer reluctantly agreed to interview Oliver in the Dog and Fox. Sensing she was becoming increasingly uncomfortable, Oliver asked, 'Do you like French food?' The journalist nodded. 'Right, we'll go to Jacques,' he announced in a thick French accent. Five minutes later the woman found herself at the bottom of Wimbledon Hill holding out her plate as the Cockney-born Jack Messenger dispensed a Telfords pie and two spoons of beans from his roadside stall.

It was not until June 1967 that Oliver's presence attracted the attention of his local newspaper. Wedged between a Budget Rent-a-Car advertisement for '25/- a day and 4d a mile' Vauxhall Vivas and an Eastern Carpet Store offer of free underlay, his interview is wrapped around a picture of a scowling Oliver clutching the inevitable glass of beer. The *News* piece reads more like a curriculum vitae than a profile of the actor and, despite the predictable errors, tells us more about the son than the father:

He has lived in Wimbledon all his life. He was born in Pepys Road and now lives with his wife Kate and young son Mark in a flat in Arterberry Road.

'I can't see my ever leaving here – it's the perfect place to live. Who wants to live in some grotty flat in town when you can wake up to the sound of birds singing on the Common? It's much better for a hangover,' he said, half in jest.

Son Mark has inherited much of his father's personality. He is also something of a firebug, having once set fire to his bed and basement flat in Homefield Road. And he is generous to the extreme – the other day he was caught handing out junior aspirins to his classmates at The Squirrels . . .

The piece ends with Oliver's Eireann dream:

One day I should like to live in Ireland. I love the Irish, the more I see of other races the more I believe the Irish are the only real people left – and apart from that they've got space and clear air in which to wander and think and to feel free.

What he hadn't told the reporter was that his dream had already come true. Oliver Reed had an Irish wife and a half-Irish son. Long ago his relatives – on his mother's side – had emigrated from Ireland and settled in Scotland. It was, although this time through a stranger, the same route that led Oliver back to his first home in 'the land of fairy-tale people'.

Pat Clancy was an Irish-born ex-soldier who spoke with the rough, throaty accent of a Glasgow Scot. Pensioned out of the army after 25 years' active service in World War Two, Korea and Malaya, the veteran first met Oliver in 1960 while attempting to liquefy the last few pounds of his severance pay in a Wimbledon pub. He had just returned to England after disposing of most of it on a nine-month tour of Dublin's bars and brothels. 'That was fairly spectacular,' said an impressed Oliver. 'What would you have done with the money if you hadn't blown it?'

Clancy's voice softened: 'I wanted to buy myself a little cottage and keep chickens and maybe a few ducks.'

'Tell you what,' said Oliver, 'when I become a rich and famous movie star, I'll buy you that cottage and let you live in it for as long as you like.'

Six years later, just before Christmas 1966, Oliver met the former soldier a second time. He was sitting in the same corner of the same Wimbledon pub. 'Do you remember what I promised you?' asked Oliver.

'Och, aye,' said Clancy.

'Then when do you want to start looking for that cottage?'

By the end of January Clancy had driven across most of Scotland, in a car paid for by Oliver and with the actor settling the trail of hotel and bar bills, without success. The search switched to southern Ireland. In February an excited Clancy telephoned his benefactor to report he had at last found a cottage in a 'magical place inhabited by amazing characters, where the locals poach salmon and throw them up on the bank for bottles of beer'.

The cottage was called The Ferry and was situated in County Clare on Ireland's west coast, between Kilkee and Kilrush and where the River Shannon washes into Colley Bay. It was surrounded by acres of peat-fed turf and its nearest neighbour was Molly Turbetty, whose farmstead was fenced by hundreds of upended sleepers stolen from the abandoned Clare Railway. Oliver flew out to inspect his latest investment and was captivated.

Years later, and long after he had given The Ferry away to a homeless couple and their two children, Oliver remembered his escapes with a childlike whimsy. 'When I stayed at The Ferry I would go fishing in the currachs with the boys or duck shooting with Barry Howard, the village chemist, though I always made sure I miss because I hate killing any kind of creature. It's exhilarating and exciting and deeply satisfying and an entirely different world from any film studio or location.'

One of the stage hits of the early sixties was a Lionel Bart musical called *Oliver!*. For the film director Carol Reed it held a special fascination. An adaptation of Dickens's *Oliver Twist* was one of his father's, Herbert Beerbohm Tree's, greatest hits.

The film would be produced by John Woolf. Already pricing the project out of existence, Woolf was determined to make what he rightly feared would be the last great film spectacular and wanted to lose none of the all-singing, all-dancing action that made the West End show a sell-out success. As with the costumes and sets, nothing was skimped on the cast, which included Ron Moody as Fagin and Harry Secombe as Bumble the Beadle and Shani Wallis, Leonard Rossiter, Hylda Baker, Peggy Mount and Meg Jenkins. The part of the Artful Dodger went to Jack Wild.

Auditioning for the title role of Oliver Twist took more than two months. Young boys from stage schools across the country travelled to London hoping to launch their careers with one of the biggest parts of the year. A short list of twelve was eventually whittled down to three. After a final round of auditions the part was eventually given to a seven-year-old Londoner. Mark Lester's mother was telephoned by the director Carol Reed and told her son was needed on the Pinewood set at eight the following morning.

A decision on one of the film's other starring roles caused Carol Reed still more problems, but for quite different reasons. Among the actors auditioning for the broody, brutal villain Bill Sykes was the director's 28-year-old nephew Oliver Reed. This time it was the older Reed who was anxious about claims of nepotism. With the cast list complete he continued to procrastinate until John Woolf telephoned him at home and ordered him to hire his relative. 'Oliver was quite clearly the best actor for the part,' the producer later admitted, 'so I took the decision and the responsibility.'

Meeting Oliver Reed for the first time, after several weeks of 'happy and very enjoyable' filming, was a frightening experience for the young Mark Lester. The day's shooting would be in Fagin's rooftop lair and include a violent disagreement in which Bill Sykes grabs the Jew by the throat. 'Oliver arrived on the set fully made up and mentally into his part,' recalls Lester. 'He terrified the living daylights out of me. I think we were all frightened of him. I remember looking into Ron Moody's eyes during the fight and, even at my age, seeing real fear.'

Lester noticed that his co-star never lingered on the film set; it was part disdain and part aloofness, even though

Oliver's conceit was a kind of bluster covering up the rueful knowledge that he was no more than a big fish in a tiny and socially rather murky pond.

Oliver's sullen, scowling demeanour was equal to that of Robert Newton in David Lean's 1948 *Oliver Twist*. There was also a prophetic irony in Oliver's accepting – and surpassing – Newton's legacy. Not only did both men win immediate and lasting acclaim for their portrayal of the Victorian thief and murderer, but both died in surprisingly similar circumstances. Newton, like Oliver, was a heavy drinker. He died of an alcohol-provoked heart attack in 1956, only days after completing the major photography for *Around the World in 80 Days*, the biggest and most expensive movie in which he would ever appear. Newton managed to keep his promise to stay sober during the principal filming, but collapsed during a public drinking binge.

Oliver!'s apparent commercialism did not sit well beside Dickens's message about the iniquities of child labour, pimping, abduction, prostitution and murder. A concern shared by critic Jan Dawson:

> There is a heightened discrepancy between the romping jollity with which everyone goes about his business and the actual business being gone about . . . such narrative elements as the exploitation of child labour, pimping, abduction, prostitution and murder combine to make Oliver! the most non-U subject ever to receive a U certificate.

For many years Oliver would tell a story, quite possibly apocryphal, of how he provided an additional line for the Vernon Harris-written script. Oliver claims he was strolling along one of London's busy shopping streets when he spotted a young woman with her nose pressed against the window of a shop. She was coyly trying to persuade her boyfriend to buy her a pair of shoes. When the man said he couldn't afford them his girlfriend fluttered her eyelids and asked if he really loved her. 'Loves you,' said the man. 'Of course I loves you, I fuck you don't I?'

The next time he met his uncle, Oliver urged the director to use the response in a scene where Nancy asks Bill Sykes the same question. The suitably modified line eventually appeared in the musical as 'Love you? Course I love you. I live with you, don't I?'

For six days a week Oliver drove his new Jaguar E-Type sports car across London to Shepperton Studios. On Sundays he pottered in the garden or sauntered down to the pub. One weekend he arrived in the Dog and Fox to discover a besuited Michael Monks about to leave for a 21st-birthday party with his girlfriend. 'I'll come,' pleaded Oliver. 'Please let me come.'

'It's invitation only,' said Monks. 'I'll have to call and make sure it's all right.'

The trio arrived at the Esham address to find it was a magnificent house besieged by equally impressive and expensive cars. The only person who failed to recognise Oliver, still wearing his gardening jeans and a grubby shirt, was the birthday girl's mother. As the guests found their seats and began filling the tables for the celebration supper she appeared with a small mat and placed it on the floor beside Monks's table. 'It's perfectly clean,' she reassured him. 'The dog uses it.'

Gasps of horror swept the room as each table in turn spotted Oliver, cross-legged and balancing his plate on his knees, eating his meal apparently unconcerned and unoffended. The women made a second appearance. 'I'm terribly sorry,' she said, looking down. 'My daughter tells me you're somebody on television.'

Attempting to save his wife from digging an even deeper hole for herself, the owner of the house arrived and invited Oliver and Monks into his library for brandy and cigars. By ten o'clock the decanter was almost empty. 'Wonderful party,' commented Oliver, puffing on his Havana. 'How good of you to put it on for your daughter. Do you have any other children?'

'Yes,' said the man, 'I had a twenty-eight-year-old son, but he hung himself three days ago.'

'Well, I think you're a very brave man,' offered Oliver. 'And you have my deepest sympathy.'

For Monks it remains a defining moment of his friend's compassion and confidence. 'Bang. I thought, my God, how are we going to get out of this. I just froze. I couldn't taste the brandy and I couldn't work the cigar any more. And Ollie never even changed gear, he knew the right thing to say at just the right moment.'

The musical won six Oscars and, overnight, transformed Oliver Reed into an international star. It also confirmed him as one of Britain's highest-paid film actors, a price tag he was never truly comfortable with. For the first time in his life he insisted on picking up everyone else's tab: for drinks, for meals, for days out, for holidays, for anyone he knew or wanted to know. 'Don't argue, just let me get on with it. Indulge me.'

While tipping his bank balance into the millionaire bracket the film would also bankrupt his marriage.

One of the dancers hired for *Oliver!* was classically trained Jacquie Daryl. Within days Oliver had invited the South African-born dancer to dinner. By the end of the film they were lovers.

One afternoon not long after the *Oliver!* release, Oliver was dining in the revolving caravanserai-style restaurant on top of London's Post Office tower. Someone at the table complained that 'nuggets' of English heritage were being swept away and destroyed by property developers. Oliver demanded an example and, as the glass observation windows turned, was shown the roof of 35 Maple Street. Before returning to Wimbledon the actor had called at the house and introduced himself to 75-year-old Harry Jonas.

The elderly artist, restorer and erstwhile juvenile lead in numerous black-and-white films led Oliver to his first-floor studio littered thigh-deep with canvases, busts, paints and Bohemian bric-a-brac. The house, he explained, was a famous centre for Bloomsbury artists: at one time or another Sir William Orpen, Augustus John, Charles Conder, Ambrose McEvoy and Sir William Rothenstein. It was even possible Thackeray used it as the model for the studio in *The Newcomers*.

Three weeks earlier Jonas – whose picture of a Balinese dancer with water lilies and few clothes is still being reproduced and sold by the thousand – had received notice to quit his studio. A property company had purchased the entire block and obtained planning permission to demolish most of Maple Street and replace it with shops and flats.

Sitting quietly amid the debris of the studio, Oliver appeared 'concerned and deeply moved'. He drank tea from a stained and mismatched cup and promised to do all he could to save the building. 'I really didn't expect to see him again,' recalled Jonas. 'I suppose I thought it was just a bit of company, someone to share my worries with.' Captivated by the 'graceful and talented' artist, Oliver set about launching a fighting fund. Within a week he had raised £5,000 – much of it his own money – to repair and restore the house and return it to a sanitary condition. It would not be the last property Oliver snatched from destruction.

It was while Reed was shooting *Oliver!* that several offers arrived. The most prestigious and certainly the biggest film he never made came once again from Michael Winner.

Late in 1967 Lew Wasserman, the president of Universal Pictures, sanctioned an ambitious multimillion-dollar project called *William the Conqueror*. The studio was determined to break away from its low-budget image and felt a *Spartacus*-style epic the perfect vehicle. A script was commissioned from Howard Clewes – although later rewritten by Michael Hastings – and Michael Winner was asked to direct. Shooting, Winner was informed, was already scheduled for early the following May.

Wasserman and his Universal board eagerly accepted Winner's suggestion that, at thirty, Oliver Reed was the ideal choice to play Duke William II of Normandy. They were less pliable when it came to money. Winner claimed the ear-marked budget of $6 million was far too low and that he felt 'nervous' about attempting the epic on anything less than $8 million. 'Anyone else would have demanded $12 million,' the director later said. To his amazement Wasserman agreed – and cancelled the project.

Winner, who in the meantime had turned down *The Prime of Miss Jean Brodie*, was surprised to find himself temporarily out of work. Not for long. Ever prepared, the director was already successfully pitching his next project to United Artists. It was the true-life story of a prisoner of war and would earn a special place in Oliver Reed's heart.

In the late sixties Tom Wright was a Norfolk house painter who, more than twenty years earlier, was captured in France after taking part in the D-Day landings. He was sent to Mustag camp, near Munich, and ordered to clear debris caused by Allied bombing. Late in 1944 he volunteered for special duties at Munich Zoo, where he looked after and formed a special attachment to an Indian elephant called Stasi. Nine months later Wright was liberated by the Americans but returned each day to work at the zoo until he was ordered home.

Throughout his captivity Wright kept a diary. After the war he used it as the basis for *Hannibal Brooks*, an unpublished novel which describes what might have happened if he and Stasi had escaped across the Alps to Switzerland.

With Oliver Reed already contracted to make his fourth film for Winner the director faced two major casting problems – one a good deal bigger than the other. To attract cinema audiences across the Atlantic the film needed an American star. Winner settled on the diminutive Michael J Pollard – who shot to fame as Faye Dunaway and Warren Beatty's silent sidekick in *Bonnie and Clyde* – to play the trigger-happy GI escapee, Packy. Auditioning the film's third star produced some cinema firsts of its own.

Winner was searching for a very special elephant. Not only would it have to be trained to obey simple commands but would need to be consummately calm surrounded by the cast and equipment and unfazed by some precarious mountain scenery. Photographs poured in from every circus in Europe and the world's first elephant screen test was organised three miles outside Munich.

'It was an absolute disaster,' recalls Winner. 'Firstly, most were extremely small. The trainers had sent photographs of the elephants with people in the picture to show their enormous size. In order to deceive us the elephants were photographed with people little more than midgets. The result was twenty-two elephants accompanied by twenty-two very small people.' Most of the animals were also too nervous to work with anyone but their trainers.

Eventually Winner came across an Indian elephant called Aida. The fifteen-year-old animal, owned by a Dutch zoo, had already appeared in several films and was being temporarily housed in a Rome slaughterhouse. 'Not only was she incredibly intelligent,' says Winner, 'she enjoyed working and learning new tricks.'

Oliver flew to Austria and was introduced to his five-ton co-star, renamed Lucy for the adventure-comedy. It was, recalls Aida's handler Stefan Heckle, a deep and trusting love at first sight. In the actor's presence, Aida would become docile and listen intently as he talked and shared whispered secrets. Because she was afraid of the dark and susceptible to mountain chills, a member of the crew was on duty throughout the night to keep a light burning and ensure the elephant was wrapped in a special coat. Heckle looked in early one morning to find Oliver curled up and fast asleep between his co-star's front legs.

The bond forged during pre-filming training sessions produced a unique and impudent trust between man and elephant. Long and intricate takes were frequently ruined when Aida, who had behaved impeccably, took a cheeky sideswipe at Oliver with her ears. To show off, the elephant would suck up a handful of pebbles in her trunk and blast Oliver with them. If they were anywhere near water, Oliver would get a soaking. 'They were like two naughty children bursting with energy,' says Heckle.

The script called for Lucy to hide under a waterfall. Winner decided to extend an existing waterfall with a sixty-foot overhang and with a special path to stop the animal getting her feet wet. He was then informed elephants are afraid of the sound of running water and it was unlikely Aida would perform. Without flinching she allowed Oliver to lead her through the scene.

The mountain stream was not the only thing altered by Winner's unstoppable energy: four thousand television aerials were removed from houses in the picturesque villages around Lutasch, and the privately owned Montafon Railway was hired and taken over during a peak tourist week. In contrast with the situation in Britain, 26 landowners and 17 local authorities readily gave assistance to the filmmakers.

On 6 June 1968, Michael Winner awoke to find the clouds so low on the mountains surrounding Lutasch that he felt it would be impossible to shoot any of the day's sequences. By the time he reached the hotel's restaurant, he discovered an even darker mood had descended on the unit: Robert

Kennedy, brother of assassinated American president John F. Kennedy, had been gunned down the previous night while addressing a rally in a Californian hotel. The cast and crew were listening to US news reports of the senator's worsening condition. Shot twice in the head, Kennedy died that afternoon, never having regained consciousness. Winner decided to abandon the day's filming.

Just after lunch Oliver Reed was informed that Ken Russell, dressed in a purple velvet coat, had arrived, with his producer Marty Rosen, to see Oliver. The pair had flown out from England to persuade Reed to star in a film adaptation of the DH Lawrence novel, *Women in Love*.

That evening Oliver took Winner aside. 'Russell wants me to do a film with him,' confided the actor. 'But he's a television director. I'm in movies now, I don't want to go back to television.'

'I think Ken Russell is very talented,' admitted Winner. 'My advice would be to do it.'

'It's a very arty script,' said Oliver. 'I'm trying to be a commercial actor.'

'Do it, Oliver,' said Winner. 'It will do your career good.'

Although impeccably behaved on set, Oliver, who had shipped his wife and seven-year-old son out to Austria, had the unnerving habit of instigating flour-bomb fights between the cast and crew. But with his family safely asleep one night, his rabid patriotism triggered another kind of skirmish. After a heavy drinking session, he tore down the Austrian flag from outside the Lutasch hotel and urinated on it. Winner had to apologise for his wayward star before he could restore goodwill between the locals and the film crew – and avert a diplomatic incident.

Reed's co-star, Michael Pollard, had a different problem. 'You know you really must stop taking these drugs,' Winner warned him. 'You are a young man and you are going to ruin your career if you take all this junk. I beg you not to take them,' pleaded the director. 'Why do you take them, Michael?'

Pollard's usually impish face turned serious. 'Have you ever been in a hotel with Oliver Reed?'

'Michael, you have won the argument,' conceded Winner. 'Take the drugs.'

Chapter Nine

'Being nice doesn't particularly interest me and I only do things if they interest me.'

'I KNOW YOU'RE IN THERE, Jesus. I saw your poofy candles through your poofy lace curtains.'

The voice was familiar. Ken Russell cast a despondent look at his wife Shirley across the kitchen table. Only one person claimed the director's sandals and shoulder-length hair made him look like the Messiah.

'Sit tight,' said Russell. 'I smell trouble.'

The flap of the letterbox rattled open. 'If you don't open up I'll kick your poofy purple front door down.'

Oliver Reed was wearing a dinner jacket and black bow tie. He was followed into the kitchen of the Russells' South Norwood home by a beautiful young woman he introduced as Jacquie Daryl.

'She says the wrestling scene is different in the book, Jesus,' said Oliver. 'In the script you've got the two naked men wrestling in the poofy moonlight on a river bank.'

'Then they fall in the water and continue wrestling in the water,' continued Russell.

'All in slow motion,' said Oliver. 'Like a poofy commercial.'

In *Women in Love* the fight scene between Rupert Birkin and Gerald Crich takes place in the aristocrat's stately home. Russell attempted to explain he wanted a more natural setting for his adaptation of the DH Lawrence novel.

Oliver looked at his girlfriend for support. 'But that's how it is in the book.'

Russell, irritated by the interruption, kept his voice level. 'It's one thing to get away with it in a book and quite another to bring it off on the screen.'

'You mean it's more of a challenge?' countered Oliver.

'It's bloody impossible.'

'Is it?' Oliver looked around the kitchen, eyeing the shelves of Shirley Russell's china collection before focusing on the hearth and the imitation-log gas fire. 'And she tells me they're both in evening clothes enjoying a drink by the fire . . . Make mine a brandy.'

Oliver took his drink and dragged two easy chairs to the fireplace. He motioned the director to join him.

'Sometimes I have an overwhelming desire to hit something,' said Oliver. It was a quote from the script he had been studying for the past two weeks.

Russell followed his lead. 'Meaning me?'

'Not necessarily.' Oliver sipped his brandy. 'Have you ever tried jujitsu?'

The director exchanged a nervous glance with his wife. They had both read the original book and the Larry Kramer script and knew where Oliver was heading. 'No, and I have no desire to,' said Russell.

Oliver got up, crossed the kitchen and turned and removed the key from the door. 'Oh, you'll like it,' he said. 'I'm sure you'd like it. Once you enter into the spirit of things.'

The pair tiptoed around the script and each other. 'I'm not interested,' said Russell, attempting to retrieve the key from the actor's outstretched hand. 'The servants . . .'

The producer heard his wife gasp as he flew through the air, landing on his back on the far side of the room.

'You see how easy it is,' said Oliver, distracted by a tap at the door. Russell's cook wanted to clear away the dinner things.

'Will you unlock the door or shall I?' said Russell once again reaching for the key.

This time he landed near the fireplace. A stab of pain shot through his shoulder. 'I see what you mean,' Russell said from the floor. The game was over. 'I think this has the making of a very good scene.'

Shirley Russell took the key and unlocked the door. 'You'll live to thank me for this, Jesus,' said Oliver, helping her husband to his feet.

Work on the *Women in Love* project had started two-and-a-half years earlier in 1966 when Larry Kramer, a former story editor with Columbia, was asked to write the screenplay. Kramer read all of Lawrence's published novels and short stories and wrote four different versions of the screenplay.

Casting *Women in Love* was just as problematic and remained fluid almost to the moment shooting started in Derbyshire in June 1968. Part of the dilemma was a near-crippling shortage of money.

For Russell the solution was easy: he would persuade his two leading actors to exchange part of their traditional fee for a share of future profits. It was a practical solution never before tried on a British film.

Russell's next recruit was Alan Bates, an actor whose theatrical training and social life were vastly different from those of his co-star. The oldest son of a 'middle-middle-class' insurance broker, Bates was born in Derbyshire four years to the week before his fellow actor. After studying the classics at RADA he returned from two years National Service in the Royal Air Force to make his 1955 stage debut with the Midland Theatre Company. A year later he was starring in both the West End and Broadway productions of John Osborne's *Look Back in Anger*. Bates was also an accomplished and experienced film actor whose credits included *The Entertainer*, *Whistle Down the Wind* and *Far from the Madding Crowd*.

'I like physical things about a part,' Bates once admitted. 'I like to let the part creep through me, become part of me. I can start walking with a stoop without being aware that I'm doing it.' Informed of his fellow actor's successful attempt to bring the wrestling scene closer to that of the novel, and aware of Oliver's energetic enthusiasm, Bates started a course of judo lessons.

When he read the first draft of the screenplay, Ken Russell's imagination had cast Oliver in the role of Rupert Birkin, a self-portrait of Lawrence, and Bates as Gerald Crich, the son of a local colliery owner. Weeks later, after Russell had finally settled on his two leading ladies, it was decided that Oliver and Bates should swap roles.

Jennie Linden, whom Russell wanted to play Ursula, had vowed not to work for at least four months after the birth of her son Rupert. The actress, who had fled to a cottage in Wales, changed her mind only after being confronted by an executive deputation late one Sunday night.

To fill the part of Gudrun Brangwen, the autocratic and arrogant sculptress, it was Russell who needed persuading.

'At the moment, what I want more than anything in the world is to go into films,' Glenda Jackson admitted in the London *Evening Standard* in March, 1968. The film the 31-year-old actress had set her heart on was *Women in Love.* Throughout the winter Jackson's agent, Peter Crouch, pestered Russell for an audition. With time running out Russell finally agreed that Jackson could try for the part. Her performance was 'impressive' but there were several problems with her appearance. 'Part of the problem,' she later admitted, 'was my inability to see myself as I really am – very "ish". Shortish, thinnish, plainish, palish.' Russell, however, was far more concerned about the ugly varicose veins disfiguring her legs. When he complained about them Jackson instantly booked herself into hospital to have them removed.

In late May, and with less than two weeks before shooting was due to start, Oliver, Bates, Linden and Jackson met for the first time. An invitation to Ken Russell's home was combined with a script read-through. Glenda Jackson was the last to arrive. Russell turned to Oliver and informed him, 'You're going to work with an actress from the Royal Shakespeare Company.'

'Oh, jolly good.' responded Oliver in a quack-quack voice.

Women in Love chronicles not only the battle of the sexes but the daily skirmishes between the British Midlands' elite of the 1920s. Jackson, who was quite happy to accept the part of the emasculating and eccentric sculptress Gudrun Brangwen, openly detested the sexual politics of Lawrence's novel. She had also read Russell's script with increasing alarm, not so much for the nude scenes she would be expected to perform – 'where nudity is essential to the role it would be fraudulent to shrink from it' – but more as a reaction to the director's view of women in general and female actors in particular. 'Glenda was acutely perceptive about portrayals of women that she thought were simply inaccurate or improbable,' says Chris Bryant in his biography of Jackson. 'She tried to make the women Lawrence and Russell wrote about more realistic.'

Disagreements between Russell and Oliver and Glenda Jackson were numerous and heated – and always centred on sex.

Oliver had never met a woman quite like Glenda Jackson. When charm failed he turned to macho logic: 'How could a beautiful, feminine girl like you emasculate a tough, rugged character like me?' And, when that failed to spark a response, he turned uncharacteristically to sarcasm: 'I'm articulate on the subjects of horses, dogs, cats, actors, pissoirs – but not Glenda.'

More confusing to Oliver was Jackson's refusal to accept his male-dominated view of life and sex and, therefore, his interpretation of how his on-screen character should behave. 'I swear to God, I admired her for what she was,' admitted Oliver. 'But I wouldn't budge one inch when it came to putting my masculinity on the line.' A strange comment from an actor being asked to portray the decadent homosexual son of a wealthy colliery owner.

A rumour broke the surface after the film's release claiming Oliver had, not long after the first read-through at Russell's house, demanded the director replace Jackson because Oliver could not imagine himself making love to her. 'Whether or not it was true it was obvious to the crew that the mutual respect between Glenda and Oliver was so powerful that, paradoxically, it sometimes bordered on manic antipathy,' says Ian Woodward in his biography of Jackson, *A Study in Fire and Ice*. 'Each recognised the other's strengths and weaknesses, and they manoeuvred around each other like two powerful motorboats forced to compete in a narrow dangerous waterway.'

A potentially volatile moment came when Russell and Oliver were attempting to explain to Jackson how they wanted her to play one of the film's more violent sex scenes.

Once again the actress refused to play the submissive female they were both demanding.

'Russell and I were trying to convince her that I should rape her and be the dominant factor in that particular love scene,' Oliver Reed recalled some years later. 'She was so aggressive about it, saying no, *she* should dominate *me*. In the end we had to call in the producers, because this unknown girl was being so headstrong ... She thought she had to rape me, had to completely dominate me, had to climb on top and be the aggressor. But she wasn't experienced enough to know that to be on top is not the be-all and end-all of the conquest. I don't think she would ever have compromised had she not believed that there was still enough superstition left in male vanity to warrant the leading man, and the director, to think that she should be underneath getting fucked for the things that she had said.'

A far more dangerous situation, for both Jackson and the film, involved the actress's decision not to inform Russell she was pregnant until shooting was well under way. Alarmed at the way the director had fired one actor on the first day of rehearsal, Jackson attempted to disguise her swelling waistline. With her first nude scenes looming she finally confessed collectively to Russell, Larry Kramer and the producer Marty Rosen. Predictably Kramer and Rosen were 'incandescent with rage'. Russell, however, had just sat through the first rushes and was delighted with his leading lady's performance. Ever the opportunist, he suggested they reschedule the nude shots for when Jackson's breasts were even larger.

The script included an adaptation from the 'Gladiatorial' chapter of the book in which Rupert Birkin – a self-portrait of Lawrence – and Gerald Crich, the son of a local colliery owner, exhaust themselves with a bout of 'Japanese wrestling' in the library of Gerald's home.

So they wrestled swiftly, rapturously, intent and mindless at last, two essential white figures working into a tighter closer oneness of struggle, with a strange octopus-like knotting and flashing of limbs in the subdued light of the room ... Often, in the white interlaced knot of violent living being that swayed silently, there was no head to be seen, only the swift, tight limbs, the solid white backs, the physical junction of two bodies clinched into oneness.

It was a powerful and essential scene. Through Russell's eyes – *with* Russell's eyes – it took on almost mystical symbolism. Oliver was naturally nervous about the wrestling scene: not only was it the first time he had been asked to act without clothes but he was about to become the first actor to appear fully naked in a mainstream film. The wrestling scene was shunted further and further down the shooting list. As the day loomed Oliver conveniently started to limp and Bates began to sniffle. More worrying for the director was the fact that both men developed a previously unfound friendship.

Despite medical certificates confirming Oliver's damaged ankle[1] and Bates's worsening influenza, Russell 'went on directing as if both actors were fighting fit, because I noticed that during "takes" Oliver managed not to limp at all and Alan managed not to sniff, though they more than made up for it when I shouted "cut".'

Russell was getting jittery. So, too, were his producers. The marketing potential of two of Britain's biggest stars romping naked for the first time in a general release picture was enormous. If both actors refused to perform it would cost time and money. The night before the scene was due to be shot the director and the film executives met to draw up an emergency schedule. The call sheet, kept secret from the crew and other cast members, would be used only if Oliver and Bates failed to show next morning for the 8.30 call.

Russell was tired and apprehensive. More than anything he needed a drink. The director called at a nearby public house and ordered a glass of wine and a plate of whelks. 'I'm sorry, sir,' said the landlord, tipping his head to the far end of the bar, 'we've just sold the last whelks to Mr Reed.'

As the actor raised his glass Russell turned and headed for the door and back to his car. He slipped the Toyota Estate into gear and looked up – just in time to see Oliver hurl himself on the bonnet.

---

[1] In his autobiography Oliver claims it was his elbow and not his foot he injured.

Russell wanted to get to bed and he wasn't going to let a stupid actor stop him. Into second. The car bumped and bounced out of the car park and on to the road with Oliver Reed spread-eagled on the bonnet, his feet braced on the wing mirrors and his hands clamped on the windscreen wipers. Into third. Oliver's ear and cheek and nose flattened on the glass screen. Into fourth. The speedometer was nudging 70 m.p.h.

'Since when do you refuse to take a drink with me?' Oliver bellowed over the slipstream.

'Since you ate all the whelks,' Russell shouted back.

'You want whelks,' Oliver shouted back. 'I'll give you whelks. Turn back.'

A mile down the road Russell swung the car around a roundabout and headed back to the pub. In the car park he slammed on the brakes and watched as Oliver shot off the bonnet, flew through the air and landed, still spread-eagled, on the gravel.

Oliver dusted himself down. 'You want whelks,' he said, marching across the car park and down the adjoining estuary foreshore. Fully clothed and, Russell noticed, without the slightest hint of a limp, his leading man waded into the sea until only his head and shoulders were above the water. A second later he was gone.

Fearing he may have witnessed the death of one of his stars, Russell got out of his car and began scouring the water. Suddenly two fists, each holding a string of seaweed, appeared above the water. Slowly and deliberately, his eyes fixed on the director, Oliver walked out of the water like some weed-festooned monster from one of his early Hammer movies. At the car he opened his fists and two mud-coated shellfish landed on the white bonnet.

'Thank you,' Russell said, examining the dubious offering and noting they weren't whelks.

'What'll you have?' asked Oliver.

'Half a shandy.'

Inside the bar Russell borrowed a knife and prized open the shellfish. 'It was worse than swallowing two globs of phlegm soaked in sump oil.'

Early the next morning Oliver was back at the pub and hammering on the front door. It may have been before six in the morning but the publican was not about to offend one of his best, if temporary, customers. He sold Oliver two bottles of vodka and a bottle of lime cordial and went back to bed.

Alan Bates had been awake most of the night. When his co-star entered his caravan on the film set he was deathly pale and shivering nervously.

'How do you feel?' asked Oliver.

'Bloody terrified,' admitted Bates.

'Then drink some of this.' Two hours later the vodka bottles were empty and Oliver and Bates, each wearing only a dressing gown, marched giggling on to the set.

Russell was an uncompromising director who thought nothing of demanding 25 or 30 takes on a single scene. He also believed creating 'atmosphere' on the set was vital to releasing an instinctive performance. It was a potent chemistry of tension and frustration experienced the following year by Richard Chamberlain on the set of *The Music Lovers*. 'We would all be there with our preconceived ideas of how the scene was going to go,' recalled the American actor. 'We'd run through the scene just prior to shooting but, instead of commenting on the interpretation Russell would say "That chair is *ridiculous!*" The emphasis would suddenly be on an inanimate object that couldn't act, couldn't do anything. Seventy people would be running around in a blind panic because the chair wasn't right. And then, in the confusion, he would suddenly yell, "Right. Turn over camera. Action." '

Russell used the same technique for the nude scene in *Women in Love*, only this time the 'inanimate object' was a piece of foam rubber placed under the carpet to cushion Oliver's fall. The initial takes were abandoned, and the foam was hurriedly removed, when Russell claimed the public would know the actors were falling on something soft.

'Suddenly the object, whatever it is, is more important than they are,' admits Russell, 'and while they're still off-balance I start shooting, so they have to go to their natural reactions. Since they know the story well enough I get something extra out of them I wouldn't have got if I hadn't made a fuss.'

The vodka may have anaesthetised the pain of repeatedly being thrown on to the thinly protected floor, but it had little effect on Oliver's masculinity.

Between takes he would pretend to rub himself down with a towel while frantically massaging life – and length – back into his penis. No one noticed except the continuity girl. 'She was watching me with growing interest and got very embarrassed when she glanced higher and saw me looking at her looking at me,' Oliver later boasted. 'Then she went bright red when I told her to fetch a ruler and measure it, just for continuity of course.'

The expected clash with the censors, at least in Britain, failed to materialise. Far from condemning *Women in Love*, the chief film censor John Trevelyan thought it a 'fine film' instinctively in tune with the rapidly changing public acceptance of screen sex. 'Although there were strong and explicit sex-scenes, we passed it without cuts,' Trevelyan admits in his memoir, *What the Censor Saw.* 'We had little criticism, possibly because of the film's undoubted brilliance.'

Even the 'remarkably brilliant' nude wrestling scene was left unscathed. 'In a sense this was a milestone in censorship since male frontal nudity was still a rarity,' added Trevelyan. Unlike the censor and the general public, the critics were unimpressed. One reviewer advised, 'They should take all the pretentious dialogue out of the soundtrack and call it *Women in Heat.*' Michael Billington, writing in the *Illustrated London News*, was more generous. His verdict: 'Two-thirds success, one-third failure.'

In Britain the film broke all box-office records. International reaction was mixed. The *New York Daily News* pronounced it a 'visual stunner and very likely the most sensuous film ever made'. It was a view shared by the US film industry, which, the following year, awarded Glenda Jackson a Best Actress Oscar.

In most Catholic countries the response was swift and uncompromising. Curious South American audiences packed the cinemas for weeks after the censors inadvertently gave the Birkin–Crich relationship a homosexual twist. The 'great buggering scene' – which nobody actually saw – was generating more interest than the film itself.

Italian censors were taking no chances and banned the entire film. French critics, as ever, treated it as cinematic art. The off-screen antics of its star were far more entertaining.

The production executives and stars gathered in Paris for the premier of *Women in Love*. Most were booked into a small exclusive hotel whose sole claim to fame was that Oscar Wilde had died in one of its rooms 68 years earlier.

The day before the screening Oliver arrived at the hotel carrying two bottles of champagne and a huge bouquet of flowers. One gift was destined for Ken Russell the other for his wife, Shirley. Oliver asked for his room key only to be informed he was not staying in the hotel proper, but at the annexe a few doors away.

'Oh no, I'm not,' announced the disgruntled actor. 'I'm staying here.'

The receptionist attempted to explain all the rooms had been allocated. Oliver was having none of it and strutted to the middle of the foyer where he lay full-length on the floor, using the bunch of flowers as a pillow. The reception area began to fill with other arriving guests. Still Oliver refused to move and popped the cork on a bottle of the bubbly.

The black-suited manager pushed his way through the crowd. 'Will you please desist from bedding down here for the night?' he pleaded.

'If this hotel was good enough for Oscar Wilde to die in,' answered Oliver from the floor, 'then it's certainly good enough for me to sleep in. Would you like a drink?'

The manager declined and a few minutes later offered Oliver the hotel's Scarlet Room.

Later that evening Oliver, who had spent several hours in the hotel's bar, began prowling for company. As he was crossing the lobby he spotted the film's associate producer, Roy Baird, climbing the stairs. Bounding after the executive, Oliver ripped off the man's braces and pulled down his trousers. As the man lost his footing and tumbled backwards down the stairs Oliver once again bounded after him, hauled him to his feet and planted two very wet kisses on each cheek.

Startled and dazed the man began shouting something in French, a language the actor had never attempted to master. Oliver had picked on the wrong man and frantically began to apologise. For the second time that day Oliver had brought the foyer to a standstill.

From the corner of his eye Oliver caught sight of the real Roy Baird entering the hotel and dragged the two lookalikes together. The Frenchman, still with his trousers round his ankles, accepted Oliver's hand-signal apology and a bottle of champagne.

Another drunken spree ended less amicably. 'After the showing we had a reception and I got stoned,' Oliver recalled. 'Alan Bates and his fiancée, Victoria Ward, gave me a lift back to the hotel. I started to sing some bawdy rugby songs, but Alan was most offended about me singing in front of his girl so I jumped out of the car and sang to a crate of horses' heads in a French market.'

Chapter Ten

'I may look like a Bedford truck but somehow I unconsciously give the promise of having a V8 engine – uncomfortable perhaps – but fast.'

ON 13 FEBRUARY 1969 OLIVER REED turned 31 and, while he was too old for a Prince Charming, the public was already accepting him as working-class royalty.

It was a perception focused even sharper by revelations of his private life and public antics, which, in the late sixties, offended no one except the conservative upper classes and powerful movie moguls. By day he was photographed in the company of famous golfers or pop stars or arriving to open fêtes in the back of a builder's lorry and, by night, pouched-eyed and slightly tight in various London pubs or clubs. And it was this popularity – this overfamiliarity – that would lose Oliver perhaps the most prestigious and lucrative role of his career.

After a worldwide search for a new James Bond, Cubby Broccoli and Harry Saltzman had finally drawn up a short list of actors to replace Sean Connery. 'Oliver Reed was very near the top of that list,' Broccoli admitted in a rare interview shortly before his death.

There was certainly no doubt of Oliver's acting ability. In *Women in Love* he displayed a technical grasp of his craft and the ability to sustain the harsh psychological scrutiny of the tight close-up that equalled, and frequently surpassed, Brando in *Julius Caesar* or Olivier in *Spartacus*. For their latest Bond adventure the producers had chosen *On Her Majesty's Secret Service*, a fatalistic love story adapted almost word for word from Ian Fleming's original.

With hindsight Broccoli admitted it was a lost opportunity. An oversight shared by the critic and writer Andrew Rissik. 'Oliver would have brought a glowering menace to the mayhem, while he might have been able, in the romantic scenes, to do what Connery had never attempted: to bring to the comic-strip fantasy of the films the emotionally obsessive, Byronic loner of the later books,' says Rissik. 'He would also have spared us George Lazenby . . . and perhaps Roger Moore as well.'

For Broccoli the decision to discard Oliver in favour of Lazenby was far more a question of image than imagination. 'Lazenby was an unknown,' he admitted. 'We could mould Lazenby into the public perception of James Bond, into the kind of Bond we knew the fans wanted. With Oliver Reed we would have had a far greater problem. Oliver already had a public image; he was well known and working hard at making himself even better known. We would have had to destroy that image and rebuild Oliver Reed as James Bond – and we just didn't have the time or the money.'

Another factor – although both producers have since pleaded ignorance – was the rumours of Oliver's disintegrating marriage and his increasingly public affair with Jacquie Daryl. While Oliver was apparently unaware of this lost professional opportunity, there was another victim of his crumbling relationship. Undeterred by what the frequent fights and bitter skirmishes might be doing to his nine-year-old son, Oliver refused to save his marriage which, by now, had degenerated into a grotesque parody of his parents' own stormy relationship.

Equally destructive was Oliver's drinking. When he was in a bad mood, which usually coincided with his proximity to Kate, the booze would make him vicious. The pettiest thing – her hair, her cooking, her shoes – would become the target for his verbal gnawing until Kate left the room in tears. Unable and unwilling to deal with his drinking, Oliver refused to accept the shift even the smallest alcoholic intake had on him, changing a fairly reasonable, charming man into a sadistic bully. His anger, he claimed, was coming from some other place.

When Oliver was drinking there was a lack of joy and spontaneity and a kind of grimness took hold of everything he did and said. His eyes developed a mean squint, the corner of his mouth would turn down in a hateful sneer, and he would speak in a mid-Atlantic drawl. When he was drunk, it was worse still: he looked like an angry dog, straining at his chain, dying to get at whoever he imagined had offended him. John Plackett, a friend and later the gardener at Broome Hall had his own method of gauging Oliver's aggression. 'Mr Nasty' was a twitch in Oliver's cheek which became active only as he began to lose control. 'I would announce, "Oh, Mr Nasty's arrived," and everyone knew what that meant and left before Ollie blew up.'

The end came when Kate was informed by one of their friends – Oliver always claimed it was a tip-off from a newspaper reporter he had offended – that her husband's lover was pregnant. While Kate's solicitors were drawing up and filing the divorce papers, Jacquie was giving birth to a daughter. None of this did Oliver any harm with the general masses, although the screen old guard were already hissing they had inherited a 'cad' as one of the film industry's up-and-coming princes.

Everyone agreed Jacquie was the perfect fit for Oliver. She was the devoted mother of his second child; she loved gardening; and, above all, she shared his love of animals. For his part Oliver was grateful she had given up her dancing career and looked set to be the wife he considered Kate had never been.

Kate, however, refused to let go of the man she considered had deserted her after years of shared poverty, only to be exchanged for a 'younger and prettier' model once the years of loyal support and encouragement were beginning to pay off. In a flurry of legal letters she demanded support for herself and their son. Oliver protested, but was advised to come to some sort of financial agreement. His anger boiled over. Responding to Kate's claim on 50 per cent of his estate her ex-husband began sawing tables and chairs in half. 'His hatred of her was a terrible thing to see,' says one Wimbledon associate.

For Kate, who took custody of their son, it was the inevitable end to a frustrating and agonising relationship. For Oliver it was a chance to defend his concept of marriage. A woman's place, he suggested, was in the home: 'Because you sign a piece of paper and say "for better or worse" and you stand up in front of God and vow that you will remain faithful to the exclusion of every other woman for the rest of your life doesn't mean you can do it. I can't believe that it's possible to be sure that you'll live up to that vow,' he confessed. 'I might get drunk one day and fall in love or fall over a hooker outside, and I would have consummated a relationship that I couldn't necessarily believe in.' It was a monolithic working-class attitude remarkably at odds with the social flow and progression of the late 1960s.

Once again Oliver decided to move back to Wimbledon – this time to a £20,000-plus house in the exclusive Copse Hill area south of the common and overlooking Wimbledon Common Golf Course. Parked in the drive of his Ellerton Road house was a Rolls-Royce Silver Cloud.

Temporarily freed from the responsibilities of marriage – if not fatherhood – the 31-year-old actor teamed up with his younger brother, Simon, to form the Portley Club. The all-male membership was subjected to a series of initiation rites, one of which included drinking from the Penicillin Glass, a goblet that had never been washed and was left to grow its own particular strain of green mould.

The club had just two rules. The first was that either of the brothers could order, day or night, a 'gargantuan feast'. The second was that, whatever the hour, all members must immediately attend and stay for as long as at least one Reed remained conscious.

For years his neighbours were puzzled when, each spring, the name 'Portley' was spelled out by the emerging daffodils on the front lawn.

'Actors and actresses are strolling players,' Samantha Eggar once informed a *Times* feature writer, 'wandering where ever life takes them.' In 1969 the London-born actress who, five years earlier had set up home in America, was back in Britain and eager to work with 'one of the sexiest men I know'.

It was the first time the green-eyed, flame-haired actress had met Oliver Reed, who, ten years later, would mysteriously describe Eggar as his 'first love and oldest friend'.

The daughter of an army officer and a Dutch-Portuguese mother, Victoria Eggar was a late theatrical starter, abandoning her convent education and adopting the stage name Samantha Eggar to make her acting debut alongside Donald Wolfit and Mona Washbourne in a Cecil Beaton play at the Dublin theatre festival. Seasons at the Oxford Playhouse and the Royal Court were quickly followed by offers of film work and in 1965 Eggar was named as best actress at the Cannes Film Festival for her part in *The Collector*.

The Lady in the Car with Glasses and a Gun – originally released in French with the title *La Dame Dans L'Auto Avec Des Lunettes Et Un Fusil* – is a clumsily titled suspense thriller shot at Pinewood and on location in the South of France. It follows the journey of an English secretary working in Paris who decides to drive to the coast and arrives, after various adventures, convinced she is either mad or amnesic. The director, Anatole Litvak, decided Eggar was perfect to portray the confused secretary opposite Oliver as Michael Caldwell.

Oliver had completed his first full decade as an actor and just finished his 35th film. His next contract would pass another milestone in his career: he was about to make his first western.

The Hunting Party was being filmed in Spain. Oliver would play the tough but moving role of Frank Calder, a surly and illiterate gang leader who realises there must be more to life than riding around the American southwest of the 1890s. Calder kidnaps a schoolteacher – or a woman he thinks is a schoolteacher – and orders her to teach him to read. But Calder has made a tragic mistake and his victim, played by Candice Bergen, is the wife of a millionaire cattle baron, Brandt Ruger. Armed with .54-calibre Remington rifles Gene Hackman's Ruger forms the eponymous hunting party and sets off in pursuit.

Oliver's contract stipulated a preshooting period in Madrid, where he would be taught to ride and handle a gun like a cowboy. When he wasn't loading and drawing and finger-spinning his Colt revolver, he was being schooled by the Master of Horses at the Medina stables just outside the Spanish capital. Oliver's mount for the film was a horse called Archibald. The pair became so attached to each other that the horse, like Oliver's *Hannibal Brooks* 'co-star', began to play tricks on his rider, nibbling his ear or nudging him when he felt he was being ignored. When Oliver's offer to buy the horse and have him shipped back to England was rejected he resolved 'to get myself a horse just like him'.

Released in 1971, the film failed to impress the critics. One described it as 'the epitome of permissiveness, replete with gore, rape and sadism'. Oliver defended the screen violence with a strangely philosophical statement: 'In this picture, men are the victims. It's violence that's the enemy.'

While not working Oliver began haunting the sales and show-jumping events in his search for a replacement Archibald. He was finally introduced to Johnny and Jane Kidd, the grandson and granddaughter of Lord Beaverbrook. The pair invited him to inspect their Ewhurst stables, south of Dorking, and it was there that Oliver was introduced to an enormous hunter called Dougal. The next morning he strolled into London's most exclusive riding outfitters and announced he had just bought 'the most magnificent horse in England' and wanted him kitted out.

Ten years after his return to Wimbledon, Oliver convinced himself it was time to establish his own set of roots – and find a permanent home for Dougal. The plot of land he settled on was a 63-room former monastery on the top of a rolling Surrey hill south of Dorking.

'I fell in love with Broome Hall the moment I saw it,' admitted Oliver. Set amid 65 acres of fields and paddock and overlooking its own lake, parts of the main house dated back to 1740. A hundred and forty years later the estate was bought by an extended family as a monument to their shipbuilding empire. Among the guests who took tea on the manicured lawns or strolled majestically through the grounds were Queen Victoria and, only months before his death, her Conservative prime minister Benjamin Disraeli.

During the Great War the family offered most of the house for use as a military hospital. In 1940 it was handed over again to the army, this time as barracks and a training establishment for Canadian special forces. While the Canadians learned the art of espionage in the makeshift classrooms and sabotage and demolition in the grounds a company of Sherwood Foresters, stationed nearby, took pot shots at Broome Hall's chimneys just visible over Leith Hill.

When the war ended Broome Hall was bought and occupied by more than a hundred members of the White Fathers, an African missionary order. Its maintenance and upkeep, as all its owners soon find out, was crippling. The monks were replaced in the 1950s by Sir William Pigott-Brown, the millionaire racehorse breeder and jockey. By the time Oliver saw the mansion for the first time in the spring of 1971 Broome Hall was a near-derelict wreck and had been empty for years.

Peter Reed was horrified by his son's determination to buy an £85,000 'heap of rubble in the country'. To mollify his father – a motive he did not admit at the time – Oliver bought Peter and Kay a new home of their own. After 35 years of marriage the couple moved out of their Merton Mansions flat and into 326 Fir Tree Road on Epsom Downs.

The house and its history fascinated Oliver who, unlike his family and friends, could focus on the long picture. With the walls bare and mouldy, the window frames rotten and the floorboards and plumbing dangerously in need of attention, he and Jacquie and their one-year-old daughter established a bedroom in the hall's old chapel. Ignoring the dereliction, Oliver admitted to a friend, 'I like living in a Victorian house surrounded by Victorian furniture and Victorian wallpaper.' Publicly his ownership of Broome Hall needed no justification: every brick and room and acre trumpeted Oliver Reed's arrival.

To Simon Reed his brother's sense of history and continuity came a far second to his ego. 'He liked people to know how well he had done and how much he had achieved, and Broome Hall was a good way of showing it – he had a peacock about him.'

Local reservations about Oliver Reed's tenure at Broome Hall, no matter what the misgivings during his first few months, dissolved once they saw the childish charm of his escapades rather than any malicious intent. One neighbour, paraphrasing a television advert of the time, says they soon realised that Oliver was 'naughty, but nice. You had a sneaking admiration for his adventures. They were the kind of thing you wanted to get up to, but never had the nerve.'

An early Oliver discovery – and victim – was the Cricketers at nearby Leith Hill. The management were attempting to maximise the premises' potential by opening it as a country pub for lunches and, with a deft change of menu and tablecloths, transform it to an old-world restaurant for the evening trade. As one midday session was coming to an end Oliver invited his cronies, and anyone else within earshot, back to Broome Hall for more drinks. First they had to find him. While no one was looking the actor had climbed up the inside of the restaurant's massive stone fireplace, stretched out on a chimney ledge and promptly fallen asleep. Down below his guests had abandoned the hunt and gone home and the pub staff locked up for the afternoon. Six hours later Oliver awoke to the smell of food and the faint chink of crockery. Clambering back down the chimney a dirty and dishevelled Oliver bowed majestically to the silence-struck diners before planting a sooty kiss on the barmaid and walking out.

While Broome Hall provided Oliver with a sense of arrival, it also left him feeling strangely isolated, even vulnerable. A friend explains: 'For the first time Ollie could not walk down the road to one of his favourite pubs or haunts. He loved being the new lord of the manor. He would have loved it even more if the manor was slap-bang in the middle of London.' For Oliver the solution was simple. One by one he surrounded himself with the Wimbledon friends he trusted most and needed to impress the least.

Simon, in his early twenties and already an experienced journalist, was recruited as his half-brother's press agent. David was already working as his business manager, reading scripts and fielding approaches from producers and directors and, vitally, attempting to keep track on income and expenditure. 'You know,' said Oliver throwing his arms around his siblings, 'one day we're going to be bigger than Warner Brothers.'

To manage the garden and oversee the day-to-day work on the house Oliver hired Bill Dobson. His wife, Jenny, became the Broome Hall housekeeper. 'Dobbo' was first introduced to his future employer in the sixties while working in a hospital boiler room and bringing home more each week than the actor earned for most of his early film appearances.

Anyone who drank with Oliver was considered an equal. When he invited his friend to a celebrity London dinner Dobson was predictably hesitant. 'What can I say to them?' he protested. 'I feel as if I've got nothing to talk to them about.'

'Don't think of it like that,' reassured Oliver. 'You're as good as any of them. Just have a drink and enjoy yourself.'

Courting stardom and hating celebrity, Oliver would shun any kind of deferential treatment. 'That is why he went around with people he knew well and was sure they would not change towards him,' says Simon Reed. 'As soon as there was anything artificial about a person or the way they treated him, Oliver would run a mile.'

Persuading journalists to write about his brother was, Simon quickly discovered, a task made even harder when the subject treated the entire exercise as little more than entertainment. 'Ollie's main problem was that he got bored,' admits Simon. 'And when he got bored he would create a threatening drama, nudging things along fairly sharply until the drama really got intense.'

Sometimes Oliver would tip his brother a warning wink. Most times he kept Simon in the dark, watching his reaction like a sideshow to the main event. Arriving with a reporter for an eleven o'clock interview Simon would ask, 'Where's Ollie?'

'He is upset with something he read,' Jacquie would attempt to explain. 'He doesn't want to talk to any journalist today.'

While Simon attempted to placate the guest Oliver would observe his quarry through the crack of a door or from behind a curtain. Returning to Jacquie, Simon pleaded: 'I've got one of the country's best film writers in the front room, he can't do this to me.'

'Well, he has.'

'Can't you do something? Make him see sense.'

'No.'

Just as Simon's despair was plunging in direct proportion to the journalist's rising blood pressure, Oliver would sweep into the room scattering apologies and charm. 'Ollie's antennae were infallible,' claims Simon. 'He knew exactly how much he could get away with and how much a person would put up with. His sensitivity to someone's character was extraordinary.'

After a few minutes Oliver would invariably suggest they adjourn and continue the interview at a local hostelry. By closing time both would be legless and Simon would first have to drive his brother to Broome Hall before delivering his second charge back to Fleet Street. The journey was not without its own dramas. Twice in a single week Simon stopped on the same stretch of the A24 to allow his passengers to urinate behind a hedge only to have to rescue them when they fell head first into a ditch.

Reading what his guests had written was never a priority with Oliver. David Orde met the actor several times during the late 1960s and 70s. 'As a hunting pack of reporters we quite liked Ollie,' he admits. 'He could be a right shit one minute and then Prince Charming the next, but you knew he was always being honest. Whatever attitude you were getting was because you deserved it.' For those who took it personally and took it out on Oliver – 'Fuck 'em. They've lost the plot.'

When the press discovered he had deliberately sidestepped the stage – and after a brief flirtation the television studio – in favour of a 'hands-on' apprenticeship in films it mischievously demanded an explanation. He told *The Times*:

On television you just speak like an ordinary person. In cinema you mustn't overlap and you've got to allow false pauses and you cheat your looks, but I don't speak like that [projecting very loudly]. Simon where are we going tonight? Let's go down and have some fish and chips. Immediately the veins begin to stick up here and I'm not behaving normally. I'm pantomiming life. I believe the essence of cinema as a creative and interpretative art form belongs to the fact that the camera can embrace you. The theatre audience is always a voyeur.

I don't act to a cinema audience. I make love to the camera. Literally in *Women in Love*. The camera makes love to me. It's a mechanical, rather ugly old maid and it's always black. I have no prejudice. And if I want to so involve myself with the masturbatory experience of having people applauding everything I do, then I suppose I should get on the stage. I've only been to a theatre about three times in my life but I remember on those three occasions I wasn't too distressed I'd missed the first act. But I'm constantly distressed if I've missed the first minute of a film.

In interviews Oliver had already taken to calling himself 'Mr England'. To one journalist he made the boastful claim: 'I'm the biggest star this country has got, destroy me and you destroy the whole British film industry.' His resolution to defend his status as one of Britain's top actors – while still living in Britain – would lose him some of the choicest film roles of the decade and millions in lost earnings.

David Reed, watching one golden opportunity after another slip through his brother's fingers, could stand it no longer. 'You have got to go to America,' said David one afternoon at Broome Hall. 'Sean Connery has gone. And so has Michael Caine. You've got to spend some time in America.'

It was an argument Oliver did not want to hear. 'What about this place?' he said. 'There's too much to do.'

'We'll put the whole of Broome Hall in mothballs,' countered David. 'We'll keep a team going and when you come back it will all be here waiting for you. I promise you will not lose it.'

'I'm not going,' Oliver told his brother. 'I'm a Brit and I'm staying here.'

Within months Oliver was offered two leading roles – in *Jaws* and *The Sting* – by the Hollywood producer Richard Zanuck. He turned down both and both parts went to another British actor, Robert Shaw. Patriotism and pride, which Oliver possessed in bucket loads, had ended the 'Warner Brothers' dream. 'At that stage I think he had done it all,' reflects Simon Reed. 'He was the biggest star in Europe and he needed another step up to be among the top five actors in the world. In Oliver's eyes, moving to Hollywood would have been like tarting himself around and he wasn't prepared to do that. It may not have had a lot of logic for most people, but it had raw logic for him.'

Twenty years later Oliver admitted it was the biggest mistake of his career. 'I turned down an approach from a very powerful American agent,' he explained. 'He wanted me to move to the West Coast, but I had just bought a big house, a lot of horses, was going through a messy divorce and my girlfriend had just had a baby.' At the time there was still a powerful British film industry, 'so it seemed probable that I could make Europe my stomping ground. Ultimately I ended up making obscure European films that paid well, but did nothing to further my reputation.'

Unknown to Oliver, his public bad behaviour did more to slam the Hollywood door than his misguided patriotism. 'There isn't an actor or actress in history who hasn't – eventually – been bought by the West Coast studios,' admits one 1970s Hollywood executive. 'Reed didn't turn us down. We turned him down. We like our stars to have respect – Oliver Reed didn't respect anyone and he showed it.'

The final disenchantment came when Steve McQueen flew to England to meet Oliver and discuss a possible film collaboration. 'Reed showed me his country mansion and we got on well,' recalled McQueen. 'He then suggested he take me to his favourite London nightclub.'

The drinking, which started at Broome Hall, continued into the night until Oliver could hardly stand. Suddenly, and with no apparent warning, he vomited over McQueen's shirt and trousers. 'The staff rushed around and found me some new clothes, but they couldn't get me any shoes,' said McQueen. 'I had to spend the rest of the night smelling of Oliver Reed's sick.'

Chapter Eleven

'Mine is simply an animal way of translating a script into a film the best way I know how.'

'THERE IS NO WAY SHE CAN SAY "cunt".'

John Trevelyan fiddled with his screening notes before looking back across his desk at the long-haired director-cum-writer. 'It has taken me ten years of struggling just to get "fuck" accepted,' he said. 'Believe me the British public aren't ready for "cunt".'

Ken Russell left Trevelyan's Soho Square office and began fumbling with a tin of Dr Rumney's No. 1 Snuff. The nails of his fingers were bitten so low he could only just manage to prise open the lid. After months of writing, shooting and editing Russell was prepared to fight for every inch of his latest project – 'it was meant to be a disturbing film.'

John Trevelyan's tenure as chief films censor overlaid almost exactly Russell's career as Britain's most innovative and adventurous filmmaker. The chain-smoking Trevelyan had taken over as secretary of the British Board of Film Censors in the late 1950s, after seven years as an examiner. His signature on thousands of certificates flashed on screens before the opening credits was familiar to thousands of cinemagoers. Guiding the film industry through a period of enormous public liberalisation and change, he earned himself a reputation as an enlightened censor who deeply cared about films and freedom of expression.

Set up on the initiative of the rapidly expanding film industry in 1912, the British Board of Film Censors was an independent nonstatutory body that undertook the censorship of all films, except newsreels. With no written rules or standards its examiners viewed each film and rely on 'personal judgement and experience' to determine whether cuts are required. Throughout its sixty-year history the board attempted to reflect what it believed was the opinion of most 'reasonable and intelligent' people.

In 1969 Ken Russell had sent Trevelyan a script of *The Devils* and asked him to let him know anything in it that might produce censorship problems. Trevelyan read the screenplay with admiration and growing concern. 'After studying the script I sent him a detailed letter containing numerous items I felt would almost certainly need to be censored,' explained Trevelyan. Two years on and about to retire, he found himself in the difficult position of having to demand cuts to *The Devils* fully aware that any public backlash would land on the desk of his successor, Stephen Murray.

Several cuts were demanded, both by Trevelyan and the film's distributor, Warner Brothers. One scene, in which the actor Murray Melvin climbs on to the roof of a church and 'masturbates', was lost completely. Another controversial sequence was the erotic exploits of a group of nuns and a huge figure of Christ naked on the cross. The film was eventually released – with an 'X' certificate – twelve minutes shorter than Russell envisaged. Its making was equally fraught with problems.

Russell adapted *The Devils* from Aldous Huxley's book, *The Devils of Loudun*. The story had also been turned into a stage play by John Whiting. It is an intricate and complicated story best told through the Warner Brothers campaign book issued to cinema managers prior to release.

Seventeenth Century France is a country torn by religious wars and political intrigue. Louis XIII (Graham Armitage) sits on the throne but the policy of France is directed by Cardinal Richelieu (Christopher Logue), the King's chief Protestants and the Nobles of France.

The Huguenots are crushed by force and the feudal nobility lose their independence by an edict calling for the destruction of castles not needed for defence against invasion.

Richelieu persuades the King that self-government of the small provincial towns of France must cease.

It is to the walled town of Loudun that Laubardemont (Dudley Sutton), an agent of Richelieu, arrives to demolish the fortified walls. There he is stopped by Father Grandier (Oliver Reed).

Urbain Grandier is a strikingly handsome priest of 35, a sensualist, an intellectual, a man born to be a leader were it not for a streak of cynicism which lurks forever behind his large, dreamy blue eyes. Above all, Grandier is a realist. His vows of celibacy have not prevented him from bedding most of the pretty girls of Loudun. He fathers a bastard child with Phillipe (Georgina Hale), the young daughter of Trincant (John Woodvine), the town magistrate, and performs an illicit marriage ceremony between himself and Madeleine (Gemma Jones), with whom he falls in love.

Within the walls of Loudun is the Convent of the Ursulines where a group of nuns are ruled strictly by their Mother Superior, Sister Jeanne of the Angels (Vanessa Redgrave). She is in her mid-twenties, has a slightly humped back, but a truly angelic face. Sister Jeanne is sexually obsessed with Grandier, although they have never met. She often has visions of a sensual nature, which always involve the young priest.

When Jeanne hears of Grandier's illicit marriage to Madeleine she is furious and falsely accuses the priest of lewdness and sorcery.

Grandier's enemies – including Laubardemont, Trincant, Father Mignon (Murray Melvin), and the two medi-aeval 'witch-doctors', Adam (Brian Murphy) and Ibert (Max Adrian) – recognise in the accusation the means with which to bring about Grandier's downfall. They send for Father Barre (Michael Gothard), a professional exorcist.

And so begins a series of exorcisms, the like of which has never been seen before in France. The methods that Father Barre and his helpers employ to extract the devils that are reputedly within the bodies of the nuns are the most base and erotic ever used.

Sister Jeanne, the chief accuser, is the first to undergo treatment in the convent chapel. Her continual screams rapidly affect the assembled nuns. Sister Agnes (Judith Paris) is the first to go. She shrieks, shrieks again – goes into screaming convulsions. The hysteria spreads – soon all the nuns are at it – pandemonium.

A few voices in the congregation are raised in objection to the spectacle. Rangier (Andrew Faulds) and LeGrand (Ken Colley) cry out that the good Sisters are innocent – they have been deliberately provoked by the priests. It is the priests that are depraved. The two dissenters do not go unnoticed by Laubardemont who later orders their arrest as accomplices of Grandier and the Devil.

The nuns revel in their notoriety and as they become more hysterical, their fantasies become more unreal and debauched.

The arrest of Grandier and Madeleine comes as no surprise. Laubardemont and Father Barre have done their work well. The lies of the nuns are believed by many and those who are skeptical are forced to keep quiet or face arrest.

Grandier is tried and found guilty. He is imprisoned and viciously tortured as his tormentors vainly try to extract a confession of his guilt.

So the downfall of Urbain Grandier is complete. Both Richelieu and Laubardemont are well aware of the young priest's innocence but their vile and corrupt use of Sister Jeanne and the Ursuline nuns as weapons for Grandier's destruction has proved successful.

The public square in Loudun is packed as Grandier burns at the stake. The shouting hysterical crowd rejoices at the public execution, oblivious to Laubardemont's demolition of the city walls behind him.

By the late sixties Ken Russell had assumed an almost mystical presence in British society. An *Observer* survey rated him England's seventeenth most influential person – above Malcolm Muggeridge and Harold Wilson – and claimed his television films were both 'trendy and good'.

Throughout the summer of 1970 one of the largest sound stages at Pinewood, a Rank-owned studio in the Buckinghamshire countryside not far from Iver, was transformed into a sixteenth-century replica of Loudun, a walled city in provincial France. By the time Oliver and the other members of the cast arrived it had taken on an enchanting, almost magical feel. 'One can't help but be very conscious that one was walking into something extremely beautiful,' said Oliver. 'It was very impressive and immensely moving; marvellous cathedrals and houses and people, all hand-picked by Ken Russell for their fantastic character faces.'

Before filming started Russell called all the extras together to inform them what they could expect: most would have to play at least one scene naked, some would be 'flagellated' and those playing nuns would have to have their head and pubic hair shaved, for which they would be paid extra.

Oliver, as Father Grandier, was also told to have every hair removed from his head and legs, an order he accepted 'without a murmur'. When Russell demanded the eyebrows also go, the actor decided to make a stand.

'God!' shouted Russell, waving his arms in the air and walking around in ever-decreasing circles. 'We might as well not make the film at all.'

'Don't be bloody silly,' Oliver countered. 'It can't make all that much difference.'

'Of course it's important,' said Russell. 'They shaved off all of Grandier's bodily hair and then stuck red hot pokers up his arse.'

The actor pondered the image for a minute and decided to trade his eyebrows for the pokers. 'All right,' said Oliver, 'but I want them insured for half a million pounds in case they don't grow back properly.'

Russell reluctantly agreed and sent the production manager off to track down a Lloyd's underwriter willing to risk an insurance claim against the chances of Oliver's eyebrows failing to regrow properly.

The next day Oliver called the film's associate producer Roy Baird to his caravan and announced he was quitting the film. This time it wasn't the make-up but the Latin in the script that was giving Oliver the jitters.

Russell hired a friend and classical scholar as a consultant to translate parts of the screenplay into sixteenth-century Latin. The script was changing almost daily during filming and Oliver found it difficult to read, let alone pronounce, most of his speeches.

'I'm not a scholar,' he informed the producer. 'If I wanted to be a scholar I would have gone to Cambridge. The only reason I didn't go to university was because I can't spell, I can't add up and I can't sodding well stand Latin. Now I want off this film because I didn't sign up to read a script that was full of Latin. So tell Ken Russell to piss off.'

Nothing was said for the rest of the day and the shooting continued as normal. The next morning Russell tapped politely on his star's trailer door. He was wearing a Donald Duck cap over his shoulder-length hair and looked like an errant schoolboy about to apologise for breaking a window. 'I've been thinking about all this Latin,' said Russell, avoiding eye contact. 'And I don't think it all that necessary.'

'That's good, Ken,' said Oliver. 'Because I was getting a bit worried about it.'

'I thought you were. Well, Latin's out, except for a few small lines.'

Unknown to the director Oliver had already come up with a plan to cope with the 'few small lines'.

In one scene Oliver had to dip an object in holy water and anoint the bodies of his congregation while chanting a Latin Mass. He got through the take by writing his lines on tiny scraps of paper and surreptitiously floating them on the water and out of sight of the camera.

In another profile shot, Oliver, as Father Grandier, had to kneel and break bread while continually intoning a Latin prayer – *'Non intres in judicium cum servo tuo Domine'*. Russell was speechless and the set remained silent in amazement.

'That was bloody marvellous,' Russell eventually conceded. 'You told me you couldn't learn all that Latin.'

Oliver smiled innocently and prepared himself for a second take. This time the director noticed that the actor's eye further from the camera, which should have been closed, was slightly open. Russell crept up on Oliver without stopping the take – and discovered that the Latin lines had been pasted to the middle of the bread.

'We can't have that,' exploded Russell, before sending Oliver off to his caravan to learn every word by heart.

A week later it was Oliver's insistence on absolute authenticity that nearly cost him his life. In the closing minutes of the film Father Grandier is burned at the stake. Russell found himself having to choose between the safety of his leading man and his belief in 'accurate and honest' cinema. The answer, claimed Oliver, was simple. He could act out the execution scene standing on a hidden trap door; when the flames got too close for comfort Oliver could release the flap and drop to safety.

The set was rigged and the pyre torched. As the flames rose the director and crew watched as Oliver acted out Grandier's death scene. Still he refused to quit. With the flames at waist height and a 'very strange smell' coming from his legs, Oliver pressed the hidden release mechanism. Nothing happened. The heat from the fire had swollen the wood and jammed the trap door. Only the rapid intervention of the studio firemen saved Oliver from serious injury.

It was during the filming of *The Devils* that Equity issued a document called *Our Profession in Peril*. The circular was in response to the government's Industrial Relations Bill, which would, effectively, end the actors' union's long-standing right to a closed shop. At the same time an organisation called the Liaison Committee for the Defence of Trade Unions launched a campaign for a one-day strike against the Conservatives' anti-union legislation. Vanessa Redgrave, with her actor brother Corin, promptly proposed an Equity resolution that actors and actresses should support the strike and walk off every set and studio in Britain.

Redgrave was not the director's first choice to play the hunchbacked, sex-crazed nun. Russell sent an outline of the story to Glenda Jackson, who declared it 'interesting'. She eventually declined after reading the completed script, informing Russell: 'I don't want to do another sexually neurotic lady.'

Redgrave was heavily pregnant with her third child, a fact that, unlike Glenda Jackson's pregnancy during *Women in Love*, she had not kept secret from Ken Russell. When Redgrave attempted to secure Oliver's support for the industrial action the actor tried to explain that what he considered a 'futile strike' would only worsen the already ailing British film industry. As ever with a Russell film, Oliver was on a share of the profits, and any delays and extra costs could eventually mean less money in his pocket.

'That's typical,' exploded Redgrave. 'You're so selfish.' A large proportion of her own salary from the film had already been donated to the Vanessa Redgrave Nursery School.

'Don't be so bloody silly,' responded Oliver. 'And stop involving politics in your profession.'

For ten minutes the argument rattled back and forth until Redgrave finally broke down in tears. Oliver cuddled his fellow star but refused to support the strike.

The next Sunday, the cast and crew's only day off, Redgrave was alone in her St Peter's Square flat and feeling 'terribly tired and in pain'. When she realised she was having a miscarriage she telephoned the baby's father, the Italian actor Franco Nero, in Rome and they both cried. Long after midnight and still alone she buried the tiny baby in the garden of their West London home. She spent the next five days in the Samaritan Hospital for Women.

The Devils was being premiered at the 1971 Venice Film Festival. In a clever publicity stunt the Italian distributors invited a cross-section of society – taxi drivers, teenagers, right- and left-wing extremists, prostitutes, politicians and church leaders – to sit through the first screening. Only the theologians objected. When the Doge of Venice called for yet another embargo on a Russell film his effigy was burned in a street protest and the ban on *Women in Love* was finally lifted. The festival judges were also unanimous in presenting Oliver with a Silver Mask Award for his performance.

At home the film received its first British showing in a Leicester Square cinema; fans queued around the block and every seat was sold. Far more important would be the verdict of the professional critics. They were not good.

Alexander Walker thought it a 'garish glossary of sado-masochism . . . a taste for visual sensation that makes scene after scene look like the masturbatory fantasies of a Roman Catholic'. While Stanley Kauffman thought, 'Russell's swirling multi-coloured puddle . . . made me glad that both Huxley and Whiting are dead, so that they are spared this farrago of witless exhibitionism.'

The first threat to a general release came a few days later when the new chairman of the Greater London Council's film viewing committee, Dr Mark Patterson, called a special viewing at County Hall. Any local authority had the right to reverse or modify the Board of Censors' decision and a GLC ban would almost certainly have triggered a chain reaction by councils nationwide. The committee agreed by just three votes to allow *The Devils* to be shown in cinemas across London.

Waiting in the wings was the Festival of Light, an organisation that claimed to be the 'authentic voice of the British backlash'. It contacted churches outside London, encouraging ministers and congregations to pressure local authorities to ban Russell's film. Few councils agreed.

In America critics capitalised on the resultant hype by claiming hundreds of cinemagoers were walking out and some were even vomiting in the aisles. One New York writer, Judith Crist, was so vociferous in condemning what she branded pornography that Oliver repeatedly challenged her to a head-to-head television confrontation. Crist never responded.

For Russell *The Devils* remains a film worth making. 'It was a political statement,' says the director. 'Although the events took place over four hundred years ago, corruption and mass brainwashing by Church and State and commerce is still with us, as is the insatiable craving for sex and violence by the general public.'

Oliver, like the rest of the cast, loyally supported the film. There were, he admitted, 'some ridiculous' scenes in *The Devils,* but it wasn't outrageous or horrific or blasphemous. Oliver also empathised with Russell's attempt to subdue his audience with moments of accuracy and total belief only to make them gasp with lightning jolts of insane stupidity – much the same as Oliver lived his own life.

Oliver and Russell were undeniably disturbed by the experience of making *The Devils.* They could no longer hold a conversation or look each other in the eye. Sometimes they could not bear to be in the same room. There was an emptiness in the relationship which needed to 'lie fallow' until it recharged.

'When I worked with Ken on *Women in Love* he was starting to go crazy,' said Oliver. 'But in the days when he made television movies about composers and writers, he was a sane, likable director. By the late sixties he was an insane, likable, film director.'

Oliver also suspected the director-writer's motives for making the film. For ten years Russell's Catholicism had supported and sustained him. When it could no longer deliver, when he found it lacking, he chose to destroy and attack it rather than search for a deeper purpose. Russell turned himself into his own demigod. 'Count how many times his name appears in the titles,' asked Oliver. 'I suspect him a bit.'

No matter what else happened in his life – sick children, angry wives and petulant lovers, hangovers, bad weather, demanding friends – the one thing that Oliver never stinted on was his work. If he was less than an attentive father, a faithful or unfaithful husband, an unpredictable and disloyal friend, the single standard of self-measure that remained constant was the energy and quality of his acting.

There were, for Oliver, no such things as rehearsals: every time – on and off the set – was a first take and needed to be right. For the first reading of a new film script he would frequently arrive without his script; while the other cast members read their parts Oliver would perform word-perfect.

'I never am at all conscious of the fact that I'm playing a different character from one film to the next,' he said. 'For instance I've just finished playing an American cowboy [in *The Hunting Party*], now I'm playing a priest. There's a big difference – I'm told by friends – in my attitudes, in the way that a film part affects me. I'm not conscious of the change myself.'

For Oliver Reed, one of the tragedies of his career was that he never played Shakespeare or the classics on stage, early on turning down an offer to play Falstaff. There were one or two whimsical thoughts of stage productions, but never anything serious.

'Oliver Reed was up there with Peter O'Toole, John Hurt and Anthony Hopkins,' claims Derek Malcolm, film critic with the *Guardian*. 'The fact that people never treated him as seriously as they treated other English actors was his real tragedy. It may have been a self-created tragedy, but personally if I had put those four actors into a room I would have been very surprised if Oliver Reed would have seemed a lesser actor.'

A superbly rich instrument, Oliver's voice often sounded like someone trying to speak after downing a tumbler of rye whiskey and shaved ice. For someone suffering from dyslexia – or maybe because of it – his line delivery was extraordinarily good, articulating sexual despair or high physical excitement with equal dexterity. He was equally at ease with dialects. Each of his films offered a new challenge – from the Cockney Bill Sykes in *Oliver!* to the educated casino boss in *The Big Sleep* and encompassing just about every regional accent in between.

One trick Oliver learned early was the technique of punctuating dialogue. The preparatory half of a statement would be delivered in a high-pitched, bellicose roar. While the audience waited for the inevitable blast, Oliver shifted down a gear to sell the line as a whispered threat. The effect, framed in a tight close-up, was insolent and dangerous and pure Oliver.

Graham Cottle had bought the film rights to *The Triple Echo*. While the screenwriter Robin Chapman adapted the HE Bates novel, the producer began his search for a director.

'The producers wanted someone rather more substantial to make the film,' admitted the television director Michael Apted. 'In the end it was a question of making do with whoever was available. Me.'

Two of the film's three stars were already under contract. It would be the first time Oliver Reed and Glenda Jackson had worked together since *Women in Love*, a film that won Jackson an Academy Award and Oliver an international reputation. The pair would soon be joined by a newcomer, Brian Deacon. Aware of Apted's relative inexperience as a big-screen director – as with Deacon, it would be his first film – Cottle took the unusual step of allowing the actors power of veto over his choice of director.

Jackson welcomed the chance to work with a 'new and fresh director'. Oliver, once again offered a 'short fee' and a percentage of the profits, flexed his box-office muscles by threatening to decline the film unless the script was changed.

'In the script it said I had to kiss the soldier while feeling his bollocks – I said no,' explained Oliver. 'So they said Glenda Jackson was in the film, and I still refused to do it. I said, "Do I have a love affair with Glenda?" and they said, "No, she has a love affair with another fellow, but the fellow is dressed up as a girl."' In the end Oliver capitulated. 'As long as I didn't have to kiss the fellow.' The £200,000 film was shot entirely on location in Dorset and Wiltshire and took just six weeks to complete. Filming began early in April 1972, and Oliver was informed he would be needed for a week at most.

For Oliver the plot generated one or two echoes of its own. A young soldier (Deacon) is out walking in the summer of 1942 when he comes across a remote English farm, owned and run by a lone woman (Jackson) whose husband is a prisoner of war. When the soldier announces he has deserted, the woman takes him in and the pair begin a passionate affair. To protect her lover the woman dresses him in her sister's clothes. The claustrophobic relationship is put under still more pressure when a bombastic and lecherous sergeant (Oliver) arrives and attempts to flirt with both 'sisters'. The deserter, still dressed as a woman, agrees to attend a Christmas ball where the sergeant discovers the truth while attempting to rape him. In the final scene the woman raises a shotgun to both men, eventually shooting her lover dead.

To the former members of 18th Field Ambulance, most of whom had not seen their former NCO for almost fifteen years, Oliver's portrayal of a tyrannical parade-ground bully was frighteningly nostalgic. 'The only difference was that the soldier Oliver played on screen had another stripe,' recalls one Sek-Kong veteran. Another remembers watching *Triple Echo* in a local cinema and thinking, Jesus Christ, Ollie's caught in a time warp. His voice and manner were exactly the same; he was even making the same guttural sounds he used when marching us around the drill square.

Friends who got to know Oliver after his National Service recognised a deeper, more chilling, depth to his latest character's attitude. 'Ollie hated any kind of cowardice, and particularly anyone who refused to fight for their country,' says a Wimbledon associate. 'So tracking down a deserter, even on screen, had a special meaning for him. Not that Ollie would have quite seen it like that, but anyone who heard him talk about his father [who had registered as a conscientious objector] knew exactly where his motivation for the character came from.'

On the location set, a near-derelict farm cottage near Salisbury, Glenda Jackson did her best to cope with her director's nervous inexperience and Oliver's 'overbearing presence'.

The first scene on the shooting script involved Jackson milking a cow. The clapperboard snapped shut. Nobody moved. As the seconds ticked by the actress and the crew froze in silence. Eventually Simon Ralph, the film's first assistant director, leaned forward and whispered something in his boss's ear. 'Action,' shouted Michael Apted.

Fearing that another personality clash with Oliver might well unnerve the director, Jackson left her co-star free to dominate the set during his week in attendance. 'Visitors to the set noticed that Glenda, with a scarf over her 1940s wig and gum boots on her feet, invariably sat alone on a rickety canvas chair between takes, almost cold-shouldered by the other actors and totally ignored by Reed,' recorded Ian Woodward, one of Jackson's biographers.

The future Labour minister's latest biographer, Chris Bryant, gives a different impression: 'There were rumours that Glenda was behaving badly on the set, and a BBC documentary on the filming seems to show a different Glenda at work, but Apted (who says "I am pretty thin-skinned about actors shouting at me, so I would have remembered it") does not remember anything of the kind.'

Whatever the truth of the situation Oliver remained the gentleman and publicly branded their feud a 'myth'. In a less guarded moment he returned to his *Women in Love* metaphor: 'Working with Glenda is rather like being run over by a Bedford truck.'

Oliver and Jackson viewed each other from distant and separate summits. Although Oliver disliked Jackson as a woman – almost from their first meeting – he admired her

Above Oliver Reed was born on 13 February 1938 at No. 9, Durrington Park Road, Wimbledon, the house just passed by the milkman. (© Merton Library Service)

Below Oliver Reed as a young man: Oliver's uncle, the director Carol Reed, advised his nephew to study at RADA or join a repertory company. He also told him to spend as much time in the cinema as possible, studying films. (© Fiona Adams)

Below With his first wife, Kate, at the opening of friend John Hogg's restaurant, The Windjammer. After nine years of marriage, Oliver's very public affairs finally destroyed the relationship and resulted in divorce in 1969. (© John Hogg)

From sketch to screen: Leon – the man and the werewolf. Oliver spent nearly two hours in make-up every day for filming of *The Curse of the Werewolf* (1961).

(Tomahawk Press)

(Tony Hillman Collection)

Above As Bill Sykes in *Oliver!* (1967), Reed hit the big time. During rehearsals for this scene, with Shani Wallis as Nancy, Oliver met his long-time lover, Jacquie Daryl. (Tony Hillman Collection)

Below In *The Jokers*, directed by Michael Winner, Oliver and Michael Crawford acted as two brothers who decide to steal the crown jewels from the Tower of London. Crawford initially refused to take the part on the basis that he looked nothing like Oliver . . . until he met Reed's younger half-brother Simon, who could have been Crawford's double. (© Michael Winner)

Top left With Michael Winner, on location in the Austrian Tyrol for the filming of *Hannibal Brooks* in 1969. It was during filming here that Ken Russell arrived to ask Oliver to star in *Women in Love*.
(© Michael Winner)

Middle left Women in Love (1969) was classic cinema, and Oliver's performance as Gerald Crich (alongside Alan Bates and Glenda Jackson) was one of the strongest performances of his career. He also made cinema history by appearing 'stark bollock naked'.
(Tony Hillman Collection)

Below Oliver Reed made three films with Glenda Jackson, the third of which was the 1979 *The Class of Miss McMichael*. Oliver based his part – of a bombastic headmaster, Terence Sutton – on some of his own teachers. (Tony Hillman Collection)

Right And still the parts came. As Gerald Kingsway in *Castaway* (1987), Oliver, his co-star Amanda Donohoe and the other cast and crew were shipped to the Seychelles for filming. The relationship between the two stars was strained and there were even allegations in the press that Oliver had exposed himself to his co-star. (Tony Hillman Collection)

Below Oliver was also in demand abroad. Reed and Albert Moses (pictured) were the only two British actors in *The Great Quest*, which was never shown in the West. (Albert Moses)

Above Once he'd moved to Guernsey, Oliver's time was more his own. He loved gardening and was a member of the Guernsey Gardener's Club . . .
(Richard and Ivy Hall)

Left . . . and he was an enthusiastic sportsman. It was on the golf course or the cricket pitch that Oliver's patriotism really shone through.

Above In 1979 Oliver Reed published his autobiography, *Reed All About Me*; his friend, Stephen Ford, is pictured at the launch party. Also shown behind Reed are his Broome Hall housekeeper and gardener, Jenny and Bill Dobson. Asked by one interviewer to sum up his book, Reed replied, 'It's a load of old bollocks really.' (Stephen Ford)

Right In 1985, at the age of twenty-one, Josephine Burge married a man twenty-six years her senior. The second Mrs Reed learned to deal with her husband's excesses and enjoyed their quiet times at Petit Houmet in Guernsey. (Richard and Ivy Hall)

Above Oliver Reed in 1993 at Petit Houmet: one of Josephine's favourite pictures of her husband. (© Fiona Adams)

Left Always living life to the full: Oliver Reed poses with Joseph Borg, the concierge of his Floriana hotel in Malta, where Reed was based during filming for his last film *Gladiator*. Four hours later, on 2 May 1999, he was dead.
(© Joseph Borg)

talent as an actress, and was never afraid to say so: 'When all the great ladies of the theatre are dancing round the maypole upstairs with their petticoats showing, Glenda will be resoundingly applauded by the great pundits of the theatre.'

Shooting was completed before the end of May. By the time *Triple Echo* was released that autumn Oliver Reed was involved in his third film of the year. *Triple Echo* soon turned a profit in Britain and Europe, especially in France, but its American release was delayed because of a bankruptcy wrangle. Renamed *Soldier in Skirts* it suffered a bungled release the following year, when, for some inexplicable reason, it was hyped as a 'sexploitation' movie.

No matter how conscientious, Simon could never maintain a 24-hour guard on his half-brother's exhibitionism. Oliver maintained the first time he produced his penis – 'My snake of desire, my wand of lust, my mighty mallet' – in public was at a crowded 1972 press conference. An event uncorroborated by Simon.

The questions turned from his recent performance in *Triple Echo* to Burt Reynolds, who had just appeared as a *Playgirl* centrefold. Oliver admitted declining a similar offer, joking that his penis was too big to fit on the page.

'Prove it,' demanded an elderly woman reporter in the front row.

Oliver, never one to refuse a challenge, promptly downed his trousers and flashed the end of his member. 'Is that it?' the woman demanded. 'Why have you stopped?'

'Madam,' said Oliver, readjusting his dress. 'If I'd pulled it out in its entirety, I'd have knocked your hat off.'

In years to come Oliver would take little persuading to produce his penis – in bars, hotels, private parties, on planes, on film sets and still more press conferences. 'I don't display it as often as it is reported,' he said once by way of defence. 'I certainly don't do it at the drop of a hat. I don't mind taking it out occasionally. A winkle's a winkle and I'll happily pull it out to get a reaction. If people are hurt or outraged by what I do, then they're missing the point. The point being that life shouldn't be about sitting around staring at frosted glass. Life should be lived and that's all there is to it.'

Chapter Twelve

'I assumed from the outset I'd be successful.'

OLIVER REED'S CAREER APPEARED FATALLY out of sync. 'I knew the way to the bar, but not to the bizarre,' he admitted with eerie foresight. 'I was taking my life and my work a little bit too seriously.'

By 1973 only one director still believed in the 36-year-old actor. Unlike the rest of the British film industry – which, by now, was almost universally blind to the creative possibilities underpinning Oliver's proven commercial pulling power – Richard Lester was the only mainstream filmmaker who appreciated what Oliver was capable of.

There was no shortage of work. But Oliver seemed either to receive starring roles in less-than-great pictures or supporting roles in greater pictures. It took Richard Lester, with whom Oliver had never yet worked, to recognise the truth: that Oliver Reed was unquestionably at his best stealing scenes in vast adventure stories and oozing his unique air of tightly reined menace. A year later, as the first sword is drawn in the latest remake of Alexandre Dumas's classic swashbuckler *The Three Musketeers*, it is Oliver's name that appears on the screen.

Forty years earlier John Wayne had starred in the first *Three Musketeers*, a black-and-white, twelve-episode adventure in which three Foreign Legionnaires defy the Devil of the Desert. Two years later a more traditional version directed by Rowland V Lee sank without trace. The first memorable *Musketeers* came in 1939. Released as *The Singing Musketeer* for British audiences, it was a burlesque of the familiar story and starred Don Ameche. A high-spirited postwar remake, the first film in colour, featured a host of stars including Gene Kelly, Lana Turner, June Allyson, Angela Lansbury and Vincent Price.

The latest *Three Musketeers* – not yet subtitled *The Queen's Diamonds* – would be a three-and-a-half-hour blockbuster, shot almost entirely in Spain and costing more than its four predecessors combined.

To ensure its American success Lester sprinkled the cast with international stars. Michael York would play D'Artagnan, with Richard Chamberlain as Aramis, Simon Ward as the Duke of Buckingham, Racquel Welch as Madame Bonancieux, Geraldine Chaplin as Anna of Austria, Faye Dunaway as Milady de Winter and Charlton Heston as Cardinal Richelieu, along with Christopher Lee. For Lester there was only one part big enough for Oliver Reed: he would play the smouldering and world-weary swordsman Athos, at all times honourable and relentlessly fearless, but barely in control of his temper. Oliver need do little more than change his clothes.

William Hobbs, a 33-year-old fight arranger, was chosen as the film's swordmaster. He quickly persuaded Lester to abandon the traditional Hollywood-style stage swords and arm the actors with heavier, longer and more authentic rapiers and daggers. As a trade-off every fight scene, from a clash of swords to a full-blown battle, needed to be blocked and rehearsed in detail. Hobbs had yet to convince Oliver Reed.

With less than two weeks before the cast and crew departed for Spain Hobbs called the first fight rehearsal. Before choreographing the stunts Hobbs needed to see how agile the actors were and how quickly they could absorb the complicated directions. Michael York and Richard Chamberlain obediently arrived for the rehearsal in the gymnasium of a Swiss Cottage school. Oliver refused to attend.

A rehearsal session was arranged with Oliver at Broome Hall. Hobbs arrived and was shown into a huge baronial hall. The sparsely decorated room appeared deserted except for a high-backed leather chair facing the window. Minutes passed. Suddenly Oliver's head appeared around the side of the chair. 'Right,' he announced leaping up. 'Let's get on with it.'

On the flagstoned patio Hobbs showed his pupil the assorted armoury he would be using and the pair exchanged a few trial thrusts and parries. After fifteen minutes Oliver hobbled to a halt, claiming he had developed a cramp in his leg. It was a common excuse: whenever boredom overtook a conversation or meeting Oliver would shuffle off rubbing his 'painful' leg.

To Hobbs, who faced nineteen weeks of the star's lack of interest in any kind of rehearsal, the cause was obvious. 'Oliver was never a trained theatre actor,' says Hobbs. 'He had no notion of rehearsing a fight over and over again to perfect it. He was very good and very quick at picking up a routine, but tough shit on the poor guy who had to face him on set after a single run-through.'

In Spain shooting for *The Three Musketeers* was delayed while Racquel Welch and the producers wrangled over her costumes. Welch insisted she should be allowed to wear dresses designed by her boyfriend. The producers refused and the dispute rumbled on for days until a compromise was reached.

The rest of the cast filled their time by organising and hosting evening parties. Welch's hairdresser arrived at Oliver's party to confess that her employer was upset because she had not received a formal invitation. Oliver explained that his drinking sessions were always an open house and added loudly that 'while she [Welch] was keeping the whole unit waiting, I was spending my time drinking, not writing out fancy invitations'. It was the first shot in a series of transatlantic tabloid skirmishes.

Welch considered she had been badly and publicly snubbed. The only words she would exchange with Oliver were those in the script.

A few days later Oliver was cornered by a London journalist. 'Tell me, Ollie,' asked Don Short. 'How are you getting on with Racquel?'

'I'm not,' said Oliver. 'She's jealous because I fancied her hairdresser instead of her.'

When the story hit the streets Short had put enough top spin on the reply to make it sound as though the American actress was dismayed because Oliver was having an affair with a hairdresser instead of an international sex symbol. The crack widened still further. 'Racquel Welch is someone I can live without,' Oliver confessed to another reporter. 'She loathes me and I can't say she is one of my favourite people.'

According to Oliver, and his press agent brother Simon, it was more a question of reputations: Welch was one of the most attractive women in the world, whom every red-blooded heterosexual man wanted to bed; and Oliver was one of the most charismatic actors in the world, who, it was claimed, wanted to make love to every woman in the world. 'It was a very difficult situation and I remember it terribly well,' explains Simon Reed. 'Racquel was ringing, making loads of calls, and only because Ollie just wasn't interested.

'My brother was with Jacquie at the time and I think he was trying to behave himself. Which didn't help Racquel's cause. He was probably the only man on the *Musketeer* set who wasn't interested in climbing into Racquel's knickers.'

Filming eventually started in Toledo, the ancient Spanish city itself famous as a medieval sword-making centre. The equipment was set up on the shore of the River Tagus for a fight involving all the musketeers. As the cameras rolled for the first seconds of the 210-minute adventure Oliver slammed his rapier across the head of the chief stuntman, Jaquin Parrae. It was the disaster William Hobbs had been expecting. Parrae vomited his breakfast on to the shingle but was not seriously hurt.

'It was pure macho,' reflects Hobbs. 'All four actors were performing for the first time together – and in a fight scene – and Ollie was not going to be outshone physically by anyone. He was going to show his metal and did so in the only way he knew how.' Oliver's reputation was so well established that all forty Spanish stuntmen insisted on drawing lots to decide who would fight the British actor.

Hobbs's concern grew as the shooting progressed. Within days he outlined his fears in an undelivered letter of resignation. And of the two injuries suffered during the filming of *The Three Musketeers*, Oliver was responsible for both – one to himself.

Unlike his fellow stars, Oliver insisted on doing all his own stunts. As ever, he skimped on rehearsals for a one-to-one sword fight. The Spanish extra confused the sequence of moves and lunged at Oliver, stabbing him in the forearm. After an overnight stay in hospital Oliver was ready to reshoot the next day.

For Hobbs, as fight arranger, there were definite benefits from Oliver's zealous machismo. On the *Oliver!* set Ron Moody had found Oliver's spitting anger terrifying. With a sword in his hand Oliver could be truly petrifying. 'The wonderful thing about Ollie was that he put everything into a fight scene,' adds Hobbs. 'You only have to look at the aggression to see that he was doing it for real, life-and-death stuff; he was really going for people and that was what was so frightening.

'There were some wonderful actors in the *Musketeers,* but the tone was set by Ollie in that first sequence. From that moment everyone else performed with that little extra panache. He lifted everyone and we had some rather special action scenes thanks to Ollie.'

Off duty, Oliver's behaviour was just as erratic and presented Richard Lester with a clutch of not unforeseen problems.

At weekends and during breaks in the shooting schedule the cast and crew retreated to the five-star Hilton Hotel in Madrid. Early one morning Richard Lester was woken by the night manager and informed that the police were in the lobby and about to arrest one of his stars.

Oliver had spent the night drinking. Arriving back at the hotel he shed his clothes and clambered into the hotel's giant goldfish tank, where he made an elaborate display of swallowing the wriggling fish whole. More and more police officers arrived until the aquarium was surrounded. Naked and dripping he bowed to his 'audience' before splashing off to his room.

The story made headlines around the world. It was rumoured – incorrectly – that he was threatened with the sack. Animal protection groups issued a stream of angry and disapproving noises. 'They've all missed the point,' mumbled Oliver cryptically. His 'point' was that he spent most of the previous afternoon whittling 'goldfish' from carrots. It was all an intricate hoax 'to tease the press and relieve the boredom'.

Two months later Oliver once again clashed with the hotel management. This time it landed him in court and on the streets.

On 18 July 1973 Oliver and a party of friends stopped off at the Hilton's coffee bar after a night out in Madrid. What started as a round of drunken banter quickly degenerated into the inevitable tests of strength. Short of arm-wrestling opponents, Oliver challenged the other occupants of the restaurant, shouting, 'I am the greatest. I'm British True Blue. I'll take on anyone.'

Gerald Edwards, a 27-year-old Concorde flight engineer, was enjoying a late-evening coffee. 'It was a disgusting display of drunkenness,' said Edwards, in Madrid to complete the supersonic airliner's hot-weather trials. 'Reed overturned tables and smashed glasses and ashtrays. People rushed out not wanting to get hurt or involved.'

It took five policemen to subdue the actor and drag him into a police van. 'Leave me alone,' protested Oliver. 'I am Athos, of *The Three Musketeers*. You can't touch me.'

At Madrid's police headquarters the 35-year-old actor was placed in a cell to cool off. The next morning he appeared before an examining magistrate and was offered an ultimatum: find a new hotel or face charges of being drunk and disorderly. Oliver opted for a lift back to the Hilton and the ignominy of walking the streets of the Spanish capital looking for another hotel.

Back on the *Musketeers* set, Oliver attempted to defuse the incident. 'It was just a skirmish with the police,' he said. 'I was having a laugh with a mate and we turned over a couple of tables. When two giants start wrestling things are bound to get broken.'

Violence was not the only thing the drink produced. Sometimes it turned to neat vitriol. Even his brother Simon has admitted, 'He could be malicious, very rarely, but he could be.'

One evening William Hobbs was having dinner with Roy Kinnear, a mild-mannered, roly-poly English comedy actor hired to play Planchet. Oliver staggered over and scooped up Kinnear's dinner plate. Clicking his fingers at a passing waiter Oliver announced, 'This meal is not good enough for my friend, take it away and bring him a new one.'

When Kinnear attempted to retrieve his plate, apologising to the waiter, Oliver's face tightened. 'Who do you think you are you lousy little actor?' he stormed. 'You wouldn't know good food from bad, you little shit.'

Sometime between filming and editing the producers decided their three-and-a-half-hour epic was too unwieldy and certainly too long for most cinema audiences. The film would be cut almost exactly in half and issued as two separate features: *The Three Musketeers: The Queen's Diamonds* in 1973 and *The Four Musketeers: The Revenge of Milady* a year later. Double the profits at half the cost.

Within weeks the majority of the stars, including Oliver, had threatened a joint legal action. The cast successfully claimed that a second release constituted a second film and, therefore, a second pay cheque. 'It was reasonable to do this, rather than waste the richness of the material, but there were actors and agents engaged who thought that modern skulduggery had intruded on Dumas's plot,' commented Christopher Lee.

At Broome Hall Oliver led the baronial life: the wealthy master of a 47-bedroom mansion with its own swimming pool, a fifty-acre country estate including a seven-acre lake and a coach house and stables. As a sporting patron he was sponsoring the middleweight boxer, Mick O'Neill, and financing a cousin to compete on the show-jumping circuit.

The warm Gulf Stream air blowing in from the Atlantic had soon revived and invigorated Oliver. He had returned to Broome Hall 'ticking' with an idea for a film. For weeks he closeted himself in his Surrey home and worked on a film script he called *The King's Man*. Its climax was the 1170 slaying of Thomas à Becket in Canterbury Cathedral. When it was finished Oliver telephoned Ken Russell and invited him over to discuss the script's potential.

The director arrived at Oliver's country house and rang the doorbell. As the huge studded front door was flung open the actor leaped into view wearing his Athos costume from the *Musketeers*, swept his plumed hat low and announced, 'Welcome, Your Eminence.'

The hair on the back of Russell's neck began to bristle – 'I knew I was going to be put to the test again.'

Inside the great hall a log fire was blazing. With a glass of brandy in one hand Oliver began cutting and thrusting with his rapier. 'Shouldn't we talk about *The King's Man?*' said Russell, attempting to distract his energetic host.

'I'd clean forgotten about that,' said Oliver, throwing his rapier aside and lifting down a giant broadsword from the chimney breast. 'The man in the shop swore it was a thousand years old. I'm sure it's authentic.'

Russell examined the blade. 'It's certainly very rusty.'

'Blood. Dried blood. A sword like that killed Becket.' The sword was in the air and Russell fumbled a catch. 'Priest or no priest, Becket was quite a swordsman. He must have put up a hell of a fight before they killed him.'

Flashes of the pre-filming wrestling match filled the director's mind.

'Imagine you are standing on the altar steps, Jesus, and I'm coming at you, coming to spill your guts and rub your sanctimonious nose in them. It's you or me, trying to split each other in two.'

'Where's yours?' Russell took a gulp of brandy.

'My what? My sword? You don't imagine I've got two of those big bastards, do you? I use the rapier.'

'I rather see Becket defending himself with a crozier,' said Russell. 'I don't suppose you –'

'Bullshit, Jesus!' Oliver swished his rapier at a wooden chest in the corner of the room. 'Now get up on the altar steps.' Russell obeyed. 'Prepare to meet thy maker, heretic.' Oliver charged and Russell used both hands to raise the broadsword above his head. The blade sliced down and the actor dropped his rapier in horror. As the colour drained from his face a dribble of blood began to ooze from a long thin gash in his chest. 'Christ!' mumbled Oliver. 'Now we're blood brothers.'

Not surprisingly, Oliver remembers the incident differently. It started, according to his autobiography, as a 'friendly' sword fight and developed into a revenge attack by the director. 'I soon realised I was fighting for my life. I was dripping blood all over the floor from where he had caught me in the chest and had to run for my life, screaming for him to stop.'

For Russell the 'fight' was not so much serious as yet another example of Oliver's life-at-full-tilt philosophy: play to win or don't bother playing at all. 'Everything was a game to Oliver and must be played by two simple rules,' explains Russell in *A British Picture*. 'The game must be played in deadly earnest and it must be played through to the end, whatever the outcome. Any infringement of the rules incurs not only Oliver's displeasure but, what is worse, his contempt.'

Chapter Thirteen

'Darling! Remind me! Did I really wave my chopper around in the casino last night?'

KEITH MOON WAS OLIVER'S SELF-APPOINTED guide down the road to insanity. It would prove a boozy, blustering, bumpy journey, frequently dangerous and all too often illegal.

'He was the path I was looking for,' confessed Oliver. 'Keith Moon was the fellow who convinced me that there is a sense of the bizarre in life, that life should and cannot and *will* not be taken seriously. It can be taken seriously in as much as there is pain and there is laughter and there is sweetness, but in between those olfactory senses, and the senses of smell and hearing, there is a sense of the bizarre.'

Keith Moon discovered at a very early age what Oliver, in his middle thirties, was only just coming to accept: that life is there to be lived shambolically, bottle by bottle, confronting disapproval and humiliation with nostrils flared. Catching the coat-tails of the pop age, Oliver willingly embraced its three basic and enduring icons: sex, booze and the ability to monumentally piss about.

Keith John Moon was born in Willesden, West London, on 23 August 1946. By the age of eighteen he was a bona fide pop star as the drummer and youngest member of the Who. At 21 he was touring America making music and mayhem. By his 25th birthday he had entered the hierarchy of British pop.

Much like his future friend, Moon soon realised it was easier to bend – to manufacture – the truth than it was to tell it. In his biography *Dear Boy: The Life of Keith Moon*, Tony

Fletcher says, 'Falsities and fibs fell from his mouth with ever-increasing regularity. Keith was not so much a compulsive liar, however, as a compelling liar, one whom people wanted to believe.' It was a description equally applicable to Oliver Reed.

The drummer's unannounced and noisy arrival at Broome Hall is a prime example of how both men preferred their own version of history.

According to Oliver he was soaking in his bath on a Sunday morning when he heard the roar of a landing helicopter. 'I rushed to the window,' he continues, 'exposing my full frontal, and there was this strange, frail-looking punk-type creature staring at me through his binoculars and nudging a dishy girl who sat alongside him.' More enraged by the fright the noise had given his horses than the damage the helicopter had done to the lawn, Oliver grabbed his antique broadsword from the hall and charged on to the terrace. 'Without turning a matted hair, he introduced the girl as a "Swedish model" and himself as Keith Moon of the Who.'

In reality there was no 'Swedish model'. Moon had flown across Surrey with Dougal Butler, a one-time mod who first gained employment as a Who roadie before rising through the ranks of the band's entourage.

Oliver, barely a fan of pop music and never of rock, had only just become aware of the Who. A month earlier he had never even heard of Keith Moon.

Pete Townshend, the creative force within the Who, had written his rock opera *Tommy* in 1969. Its theme, inspired by Townshend's own adolescent years among the debris of his parents' ruptured marriage, deals with the alienation of the postwar child. 'I was trying to show that although we hadn't been in the war we suffered its echo,' explained the musician a generation later.

First issued on record and later adapted for the stage, *Tommy* had won five Tonys, a Grammy and an Olivier. Robert Stigwood decided to make a screen version. By 1973 negotiations were complete and the producer began by signing Ken Russell as director. Stigwood had also managed to secure cameo appearances from Tina Turner and Jack Nicholson and persuaded the American actress-singer Ann-

Margret to take on the role of Tommy's mother, Nora. Two members of the Who also exercised their long-standing right to film parts: Roger Daltrey, who had sung the part of Tommy on stage for years, and Keith Moon as Uncle Ernie.

As director, Ken Russell made only one demand: that the part of Tommy's Uncle Frank should go to Oliver Reed. A surprising decision considering every word of the 108-minute film – about the cure of a deaf, dumb and blind boy and his subsequent rise to rock celebrity – was to be sung.

Russell promptly arranged an 'audition' for Oliver at the Who's Ramport recording studio in Battersea. Trudging through the first January snow of 1974 the pair arrived to find Pete Townshend agitatedly pacing up and down in the tropically heated studio. He was dressed in a luminous-blue ankle-length coat, swigging neat brandy from a half-pint beer mug and munching crisps. Townshend later admitted his driver brought him five bottles of Remy Martin a day for a year. 'I must have spilt most of it, but I remember sometimes drinking three.'

Russell made straight for the control room. 'OK, Ollie,' the director informed Oliver through the loudspeakers. 'Grab a mike and start singing.'

'I don't know any songs,' pleaded the actor. 'Listen, Peter,' Oliver said to Townshend, 'all I can give you is "The Wild Colonial Boy".'

Townshend shrugged and rammed another handful of crisps into his mouth. Still crunching, he turned to Russell behind the glass screen and said, 'Why don't we just listen to Ollie's range with this song of his?'

'That's no good,' said Russell. 'I want him to sing the songs from the film.'

Townshend gave a second, resigned shrug and handed Oliver a page of sheet music before sitting down at the piano. Oliver croaked like a 'rugby forward' and attempted to sing a few unco-ordinated and out-of-tune lines.

Townshend abandoned his piano accompaniment and downed the entire contents of his beer glass. 'Are you fucking joking?' he said, glaring at Oliver.

As with most musicals the songs would be prerecorded and dubbed on to the soundtrack when filming and editing was complete – a practice that, as far as Oliver was concerned, presented Ken Russell with a unique double problem. Not only was the actor an incompetent singer, but it was also obvious he would be incapable of miming to the play-back on set.

The session was abandoned and Oliver was sent home clutching a tape of his songs and ordered to listen until he could sing along by heart. Badly in need of advice and encouragement, Oliver drove back to Broome Hall and ran himself a bath. Through the mist of his imagination he explained his dilemma to Grandfather Tree. He was, Oliver admitted, no singer: his attempts at pop singles had disappeared without trace and Bill Sykes's only song from the original stage version of *Oliver!* was dropped from the film largely because of his inability to carry a tune. As ever, his ancestor's counsel was honest and accurate. 'He warned me against trying to play it for real with professional pop singers.'

Two weeks later, in early February, Oliver joined Ann-Margret and Elton John and members of the Who at Ramport to record the film's musical tracks. The American actress, who, like her co-star, had never heard of *Tommy* or the Who, had learned all eleven songs during her transatlantic flight. For Oliver it was hard disheartening work. One of Oliver's songs took two studio days to perfect and, once shooting had started, fifteen takes before he could get his lips in sync with his own words.

Having secured, and successfully defended, his hiring of Oliver Reed, the director was intent on capitalising on Oliver's star name. Rewriting Kit Lambert's original script, Russell effectively swapped Oliver's and Moon's on-screen roles. 'Everything you see Oliver Reed doing in the film Keith was supposed to do,' said Townshend.

The filmwriter John Fletcher describes the change in greater detail: 'Ken Russell shifted almost all the focus from Moon's Uncle Ernie to Oliver's Uncle Frank. He managed this by switching the events of the key song "1921", which was revamped as "1951" to modernise the film's era. In Russell's movie, the lover (Uncle Frank) kills the father (Captain Walker) after being discovered in bed with the mother (Nora), rather than, as Townshend's initial composition had vaguely insinuated, the other way round. Uncle Frank then becomes

Tommy's legal guardian and Uncle Ernie becomes little more than Frank's stooge.'

There was another, more personal, reason for Russell's script changes. 'If Ken had had his way,' remembers Oliver, 'Keith wouldn't have been involved in the film at all.' As far as the director was concerned Moon was unpredictable and unreliable. The first time Russell met the group Moon breezed in six hours late, a sackable misdemeanour for any other actor. And the thought of Moon and Oliver, whose temperament Russell had only just controlled on *The Devils*, skylarking on camera together would prove 'too explosive and unmanageable'.

Shooting started in April. 'I spent the first few days of production trailing Pete [Townshend], asking him questions about my character,' Ann-Margret admits in her autobiography, *My Story*. 'Since I'd never done a film remotely like *Tommy*, which was as wild and exaggerated as an hallucination, I wrote reams of notes and studied them before each scene.' Ken Russell – whom she found 'wild, indulgent, kind and funny' – was soon landed with his first casualty when the actress gashed her hand while smashing a television set with a champagne bottle. The wound needed 27 stitches and the next day's scenes were shot with Ann-Margret's bandaged hand hidden under a table.

As ever, Oliver proved himself the consummate professional. Off camera he found it hard to keep pace with Moon's anarchy. The sixteen-week schedule ranged from the Lake District to the south coast of England, taking in London and Middlesex on the way. When the crew moved to the locations at Weymouth in Dorset, Stigwood and Russell decided the two troublesome members of the cast should be booked into different hotels and as far apart as possible. 'Within days Keith had moved into my hotel and Russell had moved out,' recalls Oliver. 'I was there with my stand-in and bodyguard [Reg Prince], and Moonie was there with Dougal and lots of crumpet . . . the place was heaving with crumpet.'

The first weekend Oliver drove the hundred miles back to Broome Hall to be confronted by the news that a film magazine had voted him Britain's sexiest actor. The change in the off-duty Oliver was immediate. He couldn't wait to get back to Weymouth and the rock-and-roll lifestyle and flaunt his 'official sexiness'.

One member of the Who coterie remembers Oliver's overnight conversion. 'Ollie always had a reputation as a womaniser, but never on the scale of Moonie and other pop stars. He came back rampant and eager to fuck anything in a skirt that moved. Someone, somewhere, had told him he was sexy and Ollie took this as an official command.'

Moon, sniffing mischief, promptly announced he had organised a party in Oliver's honour and invited a cache of Bunny Girls from the Playboy clubs in London and Portsmouth. On the night of the party Oliver suddenly found himself alone and besieged in his bedroom. 'The room had a fire escape with a glass door,' he recalled. 'I'll never forget there were six girls pressed up against the window, waving dildos at me, and banging on the glass trying to get in.'

Another of Moon's victims was an elderly and well-known comedian who booked into the same hotel. After plying him with enough drink to knock him out, Moon got two of his girlfriends to strip the man naked, cover every inch of his body in lipstick kisses and, after spraying the room with perfume, leave a smouldering love note and various sex toys.

Tommy was not the only film Oliver made in the early summer of 1974. His contract with Russell allowed him two weeks to fly to Germany to play the bombastic Count Otto von Bismarck in George Macdonald Fraser's adaptation of his own book, *Royal Flash*. While he was away Oliver agreed to let Keith Moon take over his hotel room.

Shooting for *Royal Flash* finished early. After a night at Broome Hall, Oliver returned to the *Tommy* location set and his bedroom. The television was blaring. Moon, apparently naked, was attempting to concentrate on the programme while three attractive and exceptionally well-endowed young women were each performing an inventive – and possibly illegal – sex act on a different part of his body. 'Oh, hello, Ollie,' said Moon, emptying his mouth. 'Come on in and get your clothes off.'

Another absentee from the *Tommy* set was Roger Daltrey. The Who's lead singer occupied the hotel bedroom next to Oliver. For some reason Moon had left his favourite jacket in Daltrey's room and no one could find a pass key. That afternoon Oliver returned to his room to find that Moon had borrowed an electric drill from the film crew and was in the process of hammer-drilling his way through the adjoining wall.

On numerous occasions Oliver and his friends could only watch open-mouthed as 'Moon the Loon' pressed the destruct button. 'We would be sitting in a pub and Keith would whisper, "I'm going to chuck that table through the window",' recalls Mick Monks, a friend of the actor since Wimbledon. 'Ollie and I would look at each other and before we could say anything Keith had hoisted a table on to his shoulders and demolished the window.'

A few days later Moon called Oliver to his hotel bedroom to help him fix a 'broken' television. Unaware of his friend's motives, Oliver helped Moon to drag the set towards the balcony window. Before Oliver could stop him Moon had upended the television and sent it plummeting into the car park below. A few seconds later a porter charged into the room. 'Good, there you are,' said Moon off-handedly. 'Next time, answer the phone when I call.'

During filming Keith Moon fell hopelessly in love with Ann-Margret – 'a lovely girl with huge tits' – who plays Tommy's mother, Nora. When she innocently admired a diamond ring on the drummer's finger he slipped it off and gave it to her as a present. To Oliver the Swedish-born singer-actress, who had appeared in *Viva Las Vegas* with Elvis Presley, was 'one of the most charming and personable' women he had met. There was no question of refusing to attend her birthday celebration at a London riverside pub.

Oliver arrived to discover the guests outnumbered by the press. Sold to the *Tommy* cast as a small private celebration, the event had been stage-managed by the actress's husband Roger into a media feeding frenzy. Oliver had been used and resented it.

After a perfunctory photo session with the actress Oliver was cornered by her husband. 'I thought you were a professional,' he said snottily. 'And professionals don't behave like that.'

'Listen, cocksucker,' snapped Oliver. 'This is London, not New York, and that's the Thames through that window, not the Hudson River. This is an English pub and they are English press. That's Ann-Margret over there and she's my co-star and you are not. So fuck off!'

By June the *Tommy* crew transferred to a base on Hayling Island, a holiday resort near Portsmouth and Southsea. Shooting for the day had finished and Oliver persuaded Moon and Dougal Butler to cross the Solent and visit a friend working as a Greencoat at an Isle of Wight holiday camp. By the time the drunken trio returned to Ryde the last Portsmouth ferry had long departed.

'Christ,' said Oliver. 'I've got to be back for the dawn call.'

'Easy,' replied Moon, looking into the gathering gloom of a storm. 'We'll hire a fishing boat.'

Four hours later they eventually bribed a girl and her father to ferry them across to the mainland in an outsized rowing boat. 'It was like Flora MacDonald,' said Oliver. 'The father rowed us with his daughter steering. And Keith stood on the prow with all the waves coming over, shrieking and shouting at the sea.'

By the time the boat was approaching Hayling Island the storm was blowing offshore, making it impossible to approach the shingle beach. Moon, followed by a nervous Butler and an even more apprehensive Oliver, dived into the breakers and swam ashore.

The film crew and technicians had already started breakfast when Moon and Oliver entered the dining room. They were wet and shivering and totally naked. 'Two brandies, love,' ordered Oliver. 'We haven't got time for a breakfast.'

It was while the *Tommy* crew were filming in Portsmouth that Simon Reed was first introduced to his brother's new friend. 'Ollie kept telling me "You've got to come down and meet this amazing person called Keith Moon," ' Simon recalls, aware of Moon's reputation as a hell-raising rock star and never quite sure what to expect. Simon waited for a break in shooting before being introduced.

Moon, dressed as Queen Victoria, was perched on a stool behind his drum kit. Every few minutes he would dive down to suck brandy through a straw. 'Keith, this is Simon Reed,' said a member of the crew. 'Oliver's brother.'

A flash of mischief burst behind the drummer's eyes and he collapsed in a fit of giggles. A few seconds later Moon straightened his back and lowered his voice and announced: 'We are not amused.' It never got any better: however hard Simon worked at a conversation he always got the same response. 'We are not amused.'

With a break in filming, Oliver retreated to Jacquie at Broome Hall and Moon returned to his girlfriend Joy Bang and the Kensington flat he was sharing with the *Tommy* writer Kit Lambert. Arriving unannounced at the Surrey estate was becoming a weekend habit. This time Moon brought down a newly acquired American video camera.

The next day, and at his house guest's insistence, Oliver turned the hall's terrace into an improvised set and, with Moon directing from behind the camera, Oliver and Joy Bang and Dougal Butler attempted to perform *A Midsummer Night's Dream* – 'All I could hear from Moon was not so much directing as highly coloured cursing as he kept tripping over the edge of the lawn and falling into the rose bushes.'

Oliver spent all the next day, a Monday, on location. When he returned home it was late and he was tired and he went straight to bed. Within minutes Moon was tapping excitedly on Oliver's bedroom door. 'Come and see the film I've made,' begged Moon. 'You must come and see my film.'

Oliver takes up the story: 'I went to his room and there was Joy Bang in bed with nothing on, and Moonie turned on the video and I recognised my garden. And all of a sudden I recognised one of Jacquie's tops, except it was being worn by Joy Bang. She came down the steps, Moonie went staggering back. Then Joy took off her clothes, lay on the back of the old Victorian pool and opened her legs . . . There is Jacquie and me expecting to see some great art thing, and the only thing my girlfriend could say was, "Why is she wearing my clothes?" '

Other surreal ideas took shape in Oliver's and Moon's brains. Some lasted no more than a weekend – like the time Oliver dressed as a clown and Moon a court jester and the pair invited the press to watch and photograph them romp around the grounds of Broome Hall. Others – like *The Dinner Party* – took on a shape and form and reality of their own.

The pair would spend days talking over the production, making notes and plans, and even discussing finance. Not that a shortage of money was ever a problem.

The Dinner Party was to have been a bizarre live production which, considering the reputation of its creators, would almost certainly have been a sell-out. 'We were going to have a dinner table on stage and then invite a restaurant around to serve dinner,' explained Oliver. 'Keith would invite his friends and I would invite my friends. There would be telephones on the tables, and upstairs, in the shape of an Easter egg, would be a snooker table. And we'd have Alex Higgins and people like that playing snooker, and us eating, and people coming on and off, and waiters serving. Five people from the audience would be invited up to join us every night. Everybody in the audience would have a little pair of opera glasses. That would be it. The poster would read: "Have you been to *The Dinner Party?*" '

On the second Sunday of July 1974 Moon arrived at Broome Hall, as usual unannounced, but strangely subdued. Never the healthiest-looking individual, to Oliver and Jacquie the musician appeared 'very pale and depressively washed out'.

Moon's wrist was bandaged and it was obviously causing him considerable pain. 'He told me he had had a fight in a bar and cut his wrist,' recalled Oliver. It was a deliberate lie. The previous Monday, and only hours after driving back to London from the actor's home, Moon had attempted to commit suicide by slashing his wrist with a broken bottle. He refused to have the wound treated and it slowly turned septic.

There were other things Keith Moon did not tell his host. One was that he had found a new girlfriend – a nineteen-year-old Swedish woman called Annette Walter-Lax. Another was his decision, glimpsed through the endless fog of alcohol and drugs, to book himself into a Hampstead rehabilitation clinic.

Moon and the Who were due to fly to America in two weeks to join Eric Clapton – another *Tommy* star – on tour. Oliver would not see his friend for almost a year. Before he left the drummer had one more surprise for his newfound friend.

One morning in late July 1974 Oliver and Jacquie were still in bed at Broome Hall when they heard the sound of a lorry crunching its way up the gravel drive. By the time Oliver reached the pantechnicon the delivery men had started unloading. First out was a huge tiger rug. Then a chess set. The foreman handed Oliver a note. It was written in Keith Moon's spasmodic hand asking him to look after a few things while he was away. There was a postscript: 'The rhino's name is Hornby and the dog's is Beanbag.'

'What bloody rhino?' Oliver demanded.

'This one,' said the foreman helping to drag a full-size replica of a charging rhinoceros from the van.

Beanbag didn't wait to be introduced. The Harlequin Great Dane bounced down the ramp and into Oliver's arms.

'Sign 'ere,' said the foreman.

Beanbag, which Moon frequently described as his 'best friend', had inherited several bad habits from its original owner, including head-butting glass doors and panels in an attempt to reach its food. The dog remained with Oliver until its death.

The fibreglass mammal was placed in the rhododendrons at the top of the drive to dissuade the uninvited visitor. It, too, moved house several times with Oliver.

Still basking in the critical acclaim he earned as Tommy's Uncle Frank, Oliver was at least thankful that his second film in less than a year for Ken Russell remained uncredited.

Lisztomania was Russell's preposterous attempt to retell the life of the Hungarian composer through the expectations and perceptions of a 1960s pop star. Russell had, on the strength of *Tommy,* persuaded Roger Daltrey to head a cast which included Sara Kestelman, Paul Nicholas and Ringo Starr. Oliver, as a servant, would be seen for just a few seconds and escaped the lunacy of a script that included lines such as 'Piss off, Brahms.' It was, for one critic, Russell's 'first completely unmitigated catastrophe', while Patrick Snyder saw *Lisztomania* as the climax of the writer-director's long campaign to 'bludgeon into pulp some of the finest music civilisation has produced'.

A year on and Keith Moon was back in town, this time ensconced in the lavishly decorated and astronomically priced George V suite at London's Inn on the Park. Although he had not yet admitted it publicly, nor to many of his closest friends, Moon had effectively settled in America. That May, on his way back to California from the Cannes Film Festival, where *Tommy* was being exhibited, the expatriate drummer decided to stop off in London.

Accepting Oliver's invitation, Moon and Annette Walter-Lax arrived at Broome Hall for dinner. This time the pupil outclassed his tutor. 'Ollie had a stone fireplace in the dining room and he just smashed the wine bottles open against it,' remembers Walter-Lax. 'His wife had cooked this meal and she came in with a great pot of gravy and Ollie put his shoe in it and made shoe marks all around the wall. He couldn't reach up to the ceiling so he went out and got a broom, put the shoe with gravy on it and put foot marks on the ceiling that way.'

For various reasons – most financial – Oliver's contract for his latest film started and ended in Los Angeles and spanned the weeks either side of Christmas 1975. David Reed arranged for his brother to make several films in quick succession before returning to England and Oliver flew out of London in late November accompanied by nine pieces of luggage. Arriving at the Beverly Wiltshire Hotel dressed in a pinstriped suit and followed by a chain of porters, Oliver asked if his co-star had checked in.

'No, sir,' said the receptionist. 'Mr Marvin is outside waiting for his wife.'

A bellboy was sent to find the American actor and Oliver watched as he approached a scruffy, white-stubbled 'tramp' stretched out on a bench and using a stained old satchel as a pillow. Lee Marvin, still half asleep and obviously annoyed at being woken, shuffled into the lobby.

Pointed towards Oliver, the American held out his hand. 'How do you do?' said Marvin in a twee Oxbridge accent. 'Pleased to meet you, I'm sure.'

It was not a good start. Marvin, whom Oliver regarded as the 'roughest, toughest movie star in the business', looked old and frail. His hands were trembling and every few seconds he would shake his head, as if he were trying to empty his ears of water. However decrepit his body, Marvin's sarcasm was still intact. 'I was told I was going to work with Britain's biggest hellraiser,' he later admitted. 'And all I see is this tailor's dummy dressed like a fucking banker.'

Things did not improve. 'Lee Marvin detested Oliver Reed from the moment he first saw him,' claims one of the American star's closest friends, 'and it only got worse the more they worked with each other. Lee tried to explain it, but he couldn't. It was not a professional thing – he honestly thought Oliver was a natural and gifted actor. It was simply personal chemistry.'

A few days later Oliver was sitting in the dining room of the Beverley Wiltshire when the production co-ordinator for *The Great Scout and Cathouse Thursday* arrived to collect him. 'Sit down and have a drink,' Oliver said to the attractive and very nervous young woman.

The pair chatted and drank their way through a bottle of white wine chilling in an ice bucket. It was obvious he had downed several more over lunch. Suddenly, and for no obvious reason, Oliver leaped to his feet and announced, 'Well, this isn't much of a party.' Hurling the empty bottle aside, he balanced the still-full ice bucket on his head before 'dancing' through the crowded restaurant, showering diners with ice cubes and freezing water.

The city of Durango de Victoria has an old Spanish atmosphere and a dry pleasant climate ideally suited to filmmaking. Situated on the Sierra Madre Occidental it can be reached from Mexico City by a 26-hour train ride or a bumpier, but surprisingly quicker, seventeen-hour bus journey. The *Great Scout* producers decided to ship the cast, crew and equipment into Durango's single-shack airport in a relay of daily flights.

The best accommodation in Durango was a complex called Campo Mexico Courts. 'It was a dive, but the best dive in town,' recalls the film's accountant, David Ball. The motel offered only the basic cuisine, served in a huge tiled dining room. Because of its size the cast and crew soon adopted it as an out-of-hours lounge.

Each evening after dinner Oliver Reed would hold court, never allowing anyone to pay for a round of drinks and always ordering six bottle of Mexican white wine at a time.

'The entourage would get bigger and bigger,' recalls Ball, 'and we would tell jokes and funny stories and it was a marvellous way to relax.'

The accountant was the only member of the crew who had invited his female partner on location. The pair were in the restaurant one night when Oliver said, 'Good night, Dave.'

'Are you going to bed, Ollie?' asked Ball.

'No, you are,' Oliver informed him.

Ball assumed he had somehow offended the star. 'Ollie, please forgive me if I have said anything that upsets you,' he stammered. 'I am most terribly sorry. You obviously want me to leave the table.'

Oliver leaned forward and said in a loud whisper, 'Dear boy, dear boy, nothing of the sort. Only I am going to smash this fucking place up in ten minutes and I wouldn't want your lady to get hurt.'

As they crossed the motel courtyard Ball and his partner heard the sound of two wooden dining tables being hurled through a floor-to-ceiling picture window.

The next evening Oliver arrived to find the window replaced and the furniture repaired. As he entered the dining room he was stopped by an irate manager. 'Buenas noches, Señor Reed,' said the man. 'This is the bill for the damage.'

'Let's have a look, then,' said Oliver taking the piece of paper and pulling a wodge of dollar bills from his pocket. After paying the $300 repair bill and slipping the manager a $50 tip Oliver announced, 'OK, now that's settled, let's have six bottles of wine.'

Always an extravagant tipper, Oliver did not restrict his generosity to hotel and bar staff. Two or three weeks into the twelve-week shoot he opened a book on the outcome of a world title fight between John H Stracey and a Mexican contender. All eight Mexican members of the crew backed their countryman and Ball, as an accountant, found himself holding thousands of pesos and hundreds of dollars in stake money. To inflate the rivalry Oliver took to wearing Union Jack underpants.

On the night of the contest every single member of the cast and crew squeezed into the motel dining room to watch the televised fight. Stracey won by a knockout. As the

Mexicans shuffled despondently away Oliver leaped on to a table and chanted, 'En-ger-land! En-ger-land!'

Once the excitement was over Oliver waved over his bagman. 'Have you still got the money, Dave?' Ball produced the banknote roll. 'Right,' said the actor, producing an even bigger clip of dollars. 'Add this and treat the crew to a party.'

The producers had every right to fear the consequences of a clash – friendly or otherwise – between Oliver and Marvin. Both were dominant males with a championship history of drinking and fighting. Locking horns and destroying some dusty bandit-filled bar was good press but bad public relations.

Oliver had flown south to Mexico under strict orders from the film's executives not to drink with his co-star. Marvin, who was on the same flight, was by now an ailing alcoholic and under the loving but tyrannic care of his wife Pamela. 'Lee was at the stage in his illness when just unscrewing the top of a whisky bottle and sticking his nose in made him fall over,' said one the film's senior executives.

Los Angeles and then American and then British newspapers began to arrive at the location splashing stories of rowdy nights out and near disastrous clashes with disgruntled Mexican ranch hands. 'They just never happened,' says David Ball. Frustrated by the lack of material coming out of Durango, the film's Hollywood publicity machine began manufacturing its own fiction. To protect its source – and the myth, which by now was earning the project millions of dollars in advance publicity – all press visits were gently but strategically refused. Oliver and Marvin are tricky enough to handle, one agency reporter was told, without giving them an audience to play up to.

Not once did the *Great Scout* accountant see the actors sharing a drink. 'Lee and Pam would come in and she would let him have a single beer or something very light,' recalls Ball. 'And he would chat to Ollie, but Ollie never offered or slipped him a stiffer drink. He respected the man's problem.'

By the time he arrived in Mexico Oliver Reed's entourage consisted of barflies, freeloaders, a few convincingly genuine friends – and Reg Prince.

In 1962, when the pair first met on a film set, Prince was a 26-year-old extra and Oliver a star in the making. The day's shooting had not gone well. Putting his arm around the actor, Prince said, 'Come on, son, let me buy you a light ale.' Within a few years Prince was working as Oliver's stand-in double and stuntman, an unconvincing illusion considering the difference in height and build. Mostly they drank. 'If he had a heavy day's filming the next day, he wouldn't drink much,' admits Prince. 'But, if it was what we called a winger, he would drink heavily.'

Prince was a hard, uncompromising character who had the unnerving habit of sidestepping any question about his upbringing or career. He was a man cloaked in rumours who enjoyed the power it gave him: he had served in an elite army regiment; he had worked for British intelligence in the Far East; he was an underworld hit man; he was a reformed criminal with heavyweight connections. None of these claims were proved, but all made him eminently qualified to become Oliver's confidant and unofficial bodyguard.

One member of the *Great Scout* crew commented on a gold ring Prince was wearing. 'But they're not your initials, are they Reg?' he asked.

'No, they're my brother's,' said Prince tersely. 'He fell foul of some people and they topped him.'

'Good God, Reg. I'm sorry.'

'It's all right,' Prince mumbled, turning away. 'I'll sort it when I get back to London.'

There were less mysterious – and highly profitable – demonstrations of Prince's talents. The pair arrived at the Campo dining room one evening carrying an eight-by-four-inch rounded pebble, weighing at least six pounds. When David Ball asked Prince what he was going to do with the stone, Oliver replied, 'He's going to break it with one chop of his hand – and I'm going to open the book.'

Ball once again found himself holding the stake money, with most of the bets firmly against Prince's alleged karate skills. 'Is he really going to do this?' asked Ball.

'Oh, yeah, he'll do it,' said Oliver.

A few minutes later Prince placed the pebble on the floor and held it at a 45 degree angle with his left hand. Raising his free hand he let out a deep guttural sound before chopping the stone neatly and cleanly in two. 'It was,' recalls Ball, 'one of the most awesome things I have ever seen and proved to everyone in that room that Prince was not to be messed with – he was a killing machine.'

The Great Scout and Cathouse Thursday was an oddball western which, despite its star pairing and the publicity they generated, fatally failed to live up to its all-star hype. 'It sounds like the latest in the cute twosome series launched by *Butch Cassidy and the Sundance Kid*,' wrote *Newsweek*'s Janet Maslin. 'In fact it features not two but seven wacky westerners who all seem addicted to stealing, hee-hawing, falling into puddles and punching each other in the privates.' It was so bad that even a renaming and reissue as *Wildcat* failed to show a profit.

Oliver's second film of the year was an irrelevantly titled 1976 mystery in which an evil house restores itself by feeding on its tenants. The project bore some uncanny *Great Scout* echoes: for the second time in six months Oliver found himself playing opposite one of America's legendary stars, and one who, once again, took an immediate and antagonistic dislike to the British actor. *Burnt Offerings* was yet another US-financed picture which badly misjudged its audience.

Bette Davis took her first look at Oliver Reed and sniffed the air as if he had arrived with something very nasty stuck on his shoes. From then on the veteran actress referred to him as 'that man' and spoke directly to her co-star only when the script or the director demanded. 'He is possibly one of the most loathsome human beings I have ever had the misfortune of meeting,' she told one interviewer. By some miracle of management Davis and Oliver were spirited through the studio and allowed to meet only on the set. When the filming was over the feud rumbled on, with each protagonist using television chat shows and magazine interviews to take pot shots at the other. 'She said I went out every night and turned up on the set at six every morning with a terrible hangover,' Oliver admitted to one television audience. 'When she spoke to me on the set it was all smiles and sweetness. Obviously, it's a different story when my back is turned.'

It was time, Keith Moon decided, for him to introduce his friend to one of Los Angeles's most exclusive 'clubs'. Oliver, who was about to attend a premiere, describes his inauguration: 'They were trying to groom me to behave like an Englishman should in America – like an American. You've got to wear a dinner jacket; and there was Moon in his red crocodile boots and shammy leather parrot gear. I introduced him to the girls I had to escort to the premiere. He was very quiet for Moon. We both went out through the swing doors. There was lots of cameras so I had a lady on each arm and then . . . Blatt! A lemon-curd pie full in the face.'

As Oliver wiped the remains of the pie from his eyes and face someone stuffed an envelope into his hand. On the front was printed, 'Pie In The Face International: You have been selected by Keith Moon to become a member. Here is your certificate.'

Hiding in his Knobhill Drive home, Keith Moon was a man alone – shut out of and shutting out the glitzy world he so desperately needed to be part of. One of his few visitors was Oliver Reed. 'That was when I probably saw him as flat as at any time. Flat as opposed to effervescent,' said Oliver. 'I suppose it was wrong of me, because I was never flat when I was with him.' Sitting together on a huge white sofa the pair took turns to choose and play records, listening to each record in silence. 'It was very flat. He was very flat.'

Tony Fletcher, in his biography *Dear Boy: The Life of Keith Moon*, adds, 'Confused, insecure, insomniac, struggling with alcoholism, impatient for the next Who tour, dreaming of an acting career while doing nothing of note to pursue it . . . he felt compelled to make up for it on public display.'

In the next four weeks Moon, aided to a greater or lesser extent by Oliver Reed, crept closer and closer to the edge. And always in public.

David Puttnam was leaving the Beverly Wiltshire after a business lunch when he heard a rumpus behind him. 'It was Oliver Reed and Keith Moon. I was picked up and bundled into this white Rolls-Royce,' remembers the British film director. 'They drove me out to the Pacific Coast Highway. It was mad. I had a meeting to go to. They were laughing and it was stupid and edgy. I knew I could handle Keith, but the two of them together I certainly couldn't handle.'

The Wiltshire was traditionally a meeting place for Hollywood executives, most of them Jewish. A few days after the Puttnam kidnap Oliver and Moon were drinking in the hotel.

'You're Jewish, Moonie, I know you are,' goaded Oliver.

Moon denied his ancestry and Oliver repeated the claim, this time loud enough for everyone in the lounge to hear. 'Of course you're Jewish, Moonie. You look Jewish.'

The argument climaxed when Moon stepped on to a table, lowered his trousers and pants and waved his uncircumcised penis at the astonished circle of suits. 'Look at that, you can see I'm not fucking Jewish.'

The 'explosive and exhaustive' end came a few days later, once again at the Beverly Wiltshire, when Oliver arranged a surprise fortieth-birthday party for his older brother and business manager David.

'I invited some people that I knew,' says Oliver. 'And Keith asked if he could invite Ringo [Starr] and people like that. I'd always heard about these girls jumping out of the cakes, but I'd never seen one. So I got this girl who volunteered to jump out of the cake and introduced her to my brother beforehand at the cocktail party, and there was Keith rolling his eyes, he couldn't wait.

'We sat the girl next to David, everything went fine, and I got a sign from the man and went into the kitchen, and Moon was up like a rat out of a drainpipe, and the girl undressed and went into the cake. And the chefs helped ice her in. We went back and sat down. This huge great cake with forty candles on it was dragged down, and then boom! Up came the girl out of the cake, with her boobies hanging out of the top tier: "Surprise surprise!" And with that Keith picked up a bun or a bread roll and threw it at the girl.

'Moonie then got up and started grabbing tablecloths – the pink ones that I'd ordered to go with the pink crockery – and dragged them off the tables. All the crockery went up in the air. He then went and jumped on the table and got these pink chairs and started smashing the chandeliers, and I just dived at him and dragged him into the kitchens . . . He had gone completely berserk.'

Moon had cut his hand. 'People were screaming and running out because Moon was spouting blood everywhere and the whole thing was in chaos. The waiters were going crazy, and bodyguards were punching people out . . . And Ringo was sitting at the table, just shaking his head like he'd seen it all before.'

The new carpet in the first-floor function room was ruined. So, too, was the chandelier and thousands of dollars' worth of crockery and tableware. Oliver was handed the bill, which he later claimed came to more than £8,000, and informed he would not be allowed to enter the hotel again – with or without Keith Moon.

Chapter Fourteen

*'The tragedy of my life is that women always leave me in the end –
and usually before they get to know me properly.'*

OLIVER REED SAW THE YOUNG MAN marching towards him
across the floor of the London restaurant. 'Like to
make a swap?' The man was American. 'Your leather
jacket for my shirt?'

'You must be joking,' said Oliver, brushing the offer away
with his hand.

Undaunted, the man began unbuttoning his white shirt.
This time Oliver waved away the manager intent on sal-
vaging the reputation of his establishment. 'Look.' The
stranger held the tail of the shirt under the actor's nose.
Stitched to a seam was a laundry label and beneath a
Hollywood studio number the name 'Errol Flynn'.

'It's a deal,' said Oliver, removing his expensive jacket.

Back at his Surrey home Oliver tried on his hero's shirt. To
his surprise it hung on his 42-inch chest 'like a marquee'. For
two days he rarely took it off, posing in front of each mirror
he paried or slashed his way through the house with one of
his collection of swords.

Oliver was still wearing the shirt two days later when the
telephone rang. It was a director offering him a part in the
remake of *The Prince & the Pauper*. The director, Richard
Fleischer, wanted Oliver for the role of Miles Hendon – the
part originally played forty years earlier by Errol Flynn.

Adapted from a novel by Mark Twain, the story is set in
Tudor London and follows the adventures of the young
Edward VI, who changes places with a street urchin and

exposes a traitor. Despite its lavish sets and star-studded cast the 1937 version attracted little critical acclaim and was saved from box-office oblivion only by Flynn's appearance. The seventies remake would include some of the biggest names in British–American cinema, including Rex Harrison, George C Scott, Ernest Borgnine, Racquel Welch and Charlton Heston as Henry VIII. The title roles of 'the prince and the pauper' would both be played by the teenage Mark Lester, who had made his film debut opposite Reed in *Oliver!*

Location shooting would start in Budapest in mid-May 1976, and Alexander and Michael Salkind were taking no chances. The producers of the two *Musketeer* films had experienced Oliver Reed's drunken mayhem first hand. This time they insisted that a river and several kilometres separate Oliver from the rest of the cast.

The Hungarian capital straddles the River Danube with the Buda half of the city on the right bank and Pest on the left. When Oliver arrived he discovered that all the other members of the cast were booked into the impressive Hotel Gellert, overlooking the Szabadsag Bridge, while he and his minder and drinking partner Reg Prince had been given a suite in a Buda hotel across the river. It was a futile gesture.

The next day the cast assembled in the Gellert's Art Nouveau lounge only to discover that the pair had already arrived. 'They downed a bottle of vodka between them,' recalls Mark Lester. 'It was the first time I had seen anyone pick up a bottle of spirits by the neck and empty it straight down. In the films, yes, but never in real life.'

As ever, Oliver behaved impeccably on set. His only disruptive influence came from his 'lazy eye'. A legacy of the measles he contracted at Hoe Bridge School, his eye would twitch and wander uncontrollably during takes, distracting his fellow actors, who invariably collapsed in a fit of giggles. Oliver found the affliction, for which he wore prescription glasses, acutely embarrassing. Unlike his off-duty antics.

One evening while *The Prince & The Pauper* cast were relaxing over dinner Racquel Welch was chatting to her screen servant, Michael Ripper. The actor looked up to see Oliver, with whom he had worked on three Hammer films, staggering towards them. From somewhere in Oliver's imagination had come the idea of staging a lavish West End production and he began enthusiastically describing his fantasy cast. 'You'll come, won't you, Michael?' Oliver asked.

Ripper mumbled under his breath and Welch, catching the tone of her companion's remark, began to giggle. Oliver's face turned to stone. Grabbing the glass from Ripper's hand he splashed the drink in the actor's face before stomping out of the dining room.

'I remember the incident clearly,' recalls Ripper. 'I don't normally drink and it was the first gin and tonic I had ordered for some considerable time. Half an hour later he was back and did the most bizarre thing.'

This time Oliver was standing in front of them with a huge gateau in his hands. Without saying a word he smashed the entire cake into his own face. 'You see, Michael,' said Oliver, grinning through the mask of chocolate and cream. 'In this business you have got to be able to laugh at yourself.'

The way the shooting schedule had been arranged Oliver found himself with two or three days off each week. These he and Prince reserved for drunken binges and nightly romps through Budapest's roughest bars, most ending in a scuffle or mild fracas. When one disgruntled local came back the next night intent on revenge Oliver 'slapped' the man, knocking over a table. Prince intervened, but before the pair could escape the police arrived and the two men spent the rest of the night in a police cell before being bailed by one of the film's executives – a favour Oliver repaid by staggering into a cast party one evening and threatening to 'knock the lights out' of one of the associate producers.

By early July the filming was almost over and the crew had moved to northern Hungary to shoot a few country sequences. As a seventeen-year-old, Mark Lester was legally still a minor and had been chaperoned during the three-month trip by his mother. To celebrate his eighteenth birthday – on 11 July – the producers and director organised a special dinner.

Oliver failed to turn up for the dinner and the dozen or so guests, including all of Lester's co-stars, started the meal without him. As the sweet was being served the doors of the banqueting room were kicked open and a dishevelled and drunken Oliver staggered in. 'This,' announced Oliver, leaping on to the table and bowing low, 'is for you.'

Standing in the doorway was a young woman wearing a tight T-shirt and little else. Across her exceptionally well-endowed chest were the words: 'Mark Lester – Private'.

Oliver marched his way down the table kicking over bottles and glasses and attempting to explain to the guest of honour how he had acquired the prostitute from a local brothel and wanted Lester to enjoy her services during his first night as a man. By the time he reached the other end Lester had gone 'funny round the eyes' and his birthday present had fled in tears. Surrounded by open mouths and glares of disgust Oliver attempted to salvage the situation – by emptying a bowl of chocolate trifle over his head and frog-marching out of the room like a demented Nazi.

Mark Lester's eighteenth birthday marked not only the end of his childhood but also his acting career. Since *Oliver!* he had made fifteen films, sometimes three a year, all under the guidance of his parents. Coming of age, Lester rebelliously demanded control of his financial affairs. Finding himself with access to his teenage earnings he soon squandered most of it on high living and drugs. '*The Prince & The Pauper* was meant to be my transitional film,' explains Lester. 'Instead it was my last. I never worked as an actor again.' At the age of 27, having kicked his addiction to hard drugs, Lester finally sat his A-levels and went on to qualify as an osteopath.

During a break in filming *The Prince & The Pauper* Oliver flew south to enjoy some Mediterranean sunshine; he found the 'bleakness' of Hungary depressing. Paying for a group of friends to fly in and join him, Oliver hired a villa from Jack Hawkins. Only after allocating the *en-suite* bedrooms did he discover there were not enough to go round. Oliver quite happily spent his holiday sleeping on the floor of a broom cupboard.

All along the French coast east of Monaco, the great, the wealthy, the famous and the talented gathered under pavement parasols to watch and be entertained, fêted and flattered. Sprawled across the outside tables of a Cap Ferrat café, Oliver and his entourage became aware of two suntanned men watching their antics with a mixture of envy and disdain. It was only nine in the morning and the party were already drinking heavily.

'What a bunch of wankers,' commented one of the men. Oliver twitched, but ignored the remark. 'What a bunch of wankers.' This time it was louder.

Oliver swayed to his feet and staggered towards them. 'Wankers,' he hissed. 'You call us wankers, boy?'

'Yep,' said one of the men.

The waiters, sensing trouble, hurriedly began clearing the tables of anything breakable.

'You're absolutely right,' announced Oliver. 'Come and have a drink.'

Fronting up to Oliver Reed earned Stephen Ford his spurs and a lifelong friendship. Ever in search of the perfect practical joke, Oliver had, at last, found a fellow court jester worthy of his attention and loyalty. Over the next 25 years both men would plot and plan and revel in each other's public humiliation. There were no rules, no boundaries of good taste, no statute of limitation on revenge. Like Oliver's sword-wielding exploits on and off the film set, his mischievous sense of humour was always played for real and always drew blood.

Not understanding the game in progress, onlookers watched perplexed at the ball going back and forth between Oliver and Ford. Some thought it was they who were being tested; others vaguely realised they were witnessing some eccentric and lunatic trial of strength between two adolescent grown men. And, as though it were part of some bizarre contest, the ball frequently took on a life of its own: what started as a simple prank would be fielded and hurled back to the confusion of the players and dismay of those within earshot.

Returning to the south of France after a visit to London, Oliver was presented with a T-shirt by his newfound friend. Across the front Ford had had printed: 'Oliver Reed est le plus grand branleur dans le monde.'

'What does it say?' asked a delighted Oliver.

'Well,' translated Ford, 'It says Oliver Reed is the greatest thing since sliced bread.'

'Great,' announced the actor. 'I'll wear it for dinner.' That night Oliver puffed out his chest and strode into his favourite restaurant. 'What are they laughing at, Steve?'

'No idea, Oliver,' said Ford, ignoring the smothered giggles. 'Probably recognising you as a buffoon I suppose.'

By the main course people were stopping at Oliver's table and pointing. 'What's going on?' demanded Oliver. 'Is it something to do with this fucking T-shirt?'

'No idea,' said a stone-faced Ford.

'Well I'm going to find out,' said Oliver heading for an attractive young French woman drinking at the bar. 'Have you read this?' he asked, puffing out his chest. The woman grinned and nodded. 'Why is it so funny?'

The woman swallowed a snigger: 'It is difficult to say, but . . .'

'Come on girly, tell me.'

'OK,' she said. 'It says, "Oliver Reed is the biggest wanker in the world." '

For more than a century the Corniche Infériure has attracted a unique selection of heroes and heroines. The Rothschilds, Somerset Maugham, Otto Preminger, Napoleon and Leopold II, the King of the Belgians, have all found sanctuary between Beaulieu, St-Jean-Cap-Ferrat and Villefrance-sur-Mer. Oliver Reed, hovering between visitor and tourist, found the scenery and climate 'seductive and exciting'. To the east, the promontory and steep mountain backdrop keep Beaulieu so sheltered that it remains one of the hottest towns in France, while to the west the Corniche overlooks the deep-water port of Villefranche. Striding through the narrow lanes and stairways and the brightly coloured houses of Villefranche, Oliver sought out quiet bars and noisy, food-scented restaurants and bistros.

Alexis Camus – a distant relative of the existentialist writer and philosopher Albert – introduced herself to Oliver one night in a side-street bar. His mind, she recalled, was 'wonderfully bright – illuminating'. Talking to the 38-year-old actor, she soon discovered there was a frightening difference between his sober and intoxicated personalities. 'Without a drink he could take your breath away,' said Camus. 'He was interested in so much: politics, the state of the world, a person's character. But give him a drink and he was a juvenile, a child with his little boy's mind on mischievous things.'

Oliver's physical side was far less attractive. He never seemed quite clean to his French acquaintance, who got the impression he wore the same clothes for days on end. But, when he dined out with Stephen Ford, it was Oliver's lack of patience and not his clothes that attracted the attention.

One favourite restaurant was on a street corner, with a bar at ground level and the dining room on the first floor. The restaurant was full but there was no sign of any waiters. When Oliver attempted to leave Ford persuaded him to stay. Half an hour later and their order had still not been taken. 'Right,' announced Oliver, 'I'll show you how to get some service.'

He picked up a chair and hurled it through a window and into the street. Within seconds an irate manager and five waiters had surrounded Oliver's table. 'Ah yes,' he said with a smile, 'I'll have fish soup please . . .'

On another occasion Oliver arrived with four or five friends at a Beaulieu restaurant. The dining room was full so the party agreed to eat at the pavement tables. There was a sudden and vicious clap of thunder and what had started as a cloudless evening turned into a monsoon. The entire party took its lead from Oliver, who continued to eat and drink and chat as if it were all quite normal. With food floating in the serving dishes and water running off the tablecloth the party summoned the waiters and ordered and ate their dessert. Inside the restaurant the service ground to a halt as the entire company pressed its collective nose against the window to watch the pavement spectacle.

Oliver returned to England suntanned and enthusiastic about working with Michael Winner again. *The Big Sleep* was the director's nineteenth film and his fifth with Oliver in a principal role – this time as Eddie Mars, a deep and dangerous London casino owner. For the first time Winner noticed his friend's drinking was beginning to impinge on his professionalism. 'He was certainly drunk some of the time,' recalls Winner. 'And he occasionally came in a little late and a little drunk from the night before.'

While shooting in Chorley Wood, an up-market London suburb, Oliver arrived and announced to Winner and fellow star Robert Mitchum that he had been sitting on a pole the previous evening and 'damaged my balls'.

'I must show you,' said Oliver, eagerly removing his trousers.

The two other men glanced at each other and then at the crowd who were watching the shoot. 'We really could live without this, Oliver,' said Winner. 'Honestly, we could.'

But Oliver, by now trouserless and pantless, began to examine his testicles. Amazingly, recalls Winner, no one seemed bothered by the potentially criminal display. 'There we were sitting in this very po-faced part of London on a hot summer day and not one person gave a shit. Not even the locals. It was the first time Oliver misbehaved on set.'

Oliver Reed had not seen Keith Moon for more than two years. Since his friend's devastating and expensive outburst at David Reed's Los Angeles birthday party, Oliver had read some contradictory accounts of Moon's mental state.

Jack McCulloch, whose younger brother Jim was lead guitarist with Paul McCartney's band Wings, told one British newspaper how Moon arrived at a US concert. 'I didn't believe it was him,' says McCulloch. 'The brain had gone. There was not the same joviality there, it became a chore to do all the little tricks, and the jokes were not free flowing, and they weren't funny, they were getting nasty – and the comments were getting nasty.'

Returning to England in September 1977, Moon appeared far more rational. 'I had a lot of fun in California, but it was superficial fun,' he admitted to open-armed tabloid press. 'I miss this country too much. I missed my mates, my mum and the lovely ordinary things that make Britain great.'

On Thursday, 8 September, Oliver awoke to be confronted by the news he had long known was inevitable. The front page of the *Daily Mirror* contained just one headline: DRUGS DEATH DRAMA OF POP WILD MAN MOON.

Keith Moon – the man forever responsible for Oliver Reed's sense of the bizarre – was dead. 'His shadow is always on the sunny side of the street with me, because of that path he showed me,' Oliver was to say.

To Oliver it was a wasteful, frightening, self-deprecating death and, for the first time, sowed within the actor thoughts of his own mortality. 'I had been beaten before; I had been shot at; I had nearly died before; but that morning I wondered what it would be like to know you were going to die. That whatever you did or said or tried to do made no difference – you were just too far gone.'

By the late 1970s Ian Ogilvy had taken over from Roger Moore as television's Simon Templar. The locations had also moved on: instead of building back-lot replicas of European towns and cities most of the episodes were shot abroad. In 1980 the *Return of the Saint* crew were in the South of France. So, too, was Oliver Reed.

One evening Ogilvy and the producer Robert Baker were joined in their Cap Ferrat hotel by the *Saint*'s elderly creator Leslie Charteris. Born Bowyer Yin, the son of an English woman and an Oriental doctor, by the time the first Saint novel – *Meet the Tiger* – was published in 1928 the author had legally changed his name to Leslie Charteris. And as Leslie Charteris he wrote more than forty Simon Templar adventures.

The trio were enjoying a drink when Oliver lurched into the bar. The barman, experienced in the ways of the drunken actor, promptly disappeared.

'This,' Baker said, 'is Ian Ogilvy, the new Saint.'

Oliver studied Ogilvy for longer than was comfortable before leaning forward to ask, 'You a poof?'

Baker realised he had to cool things down. 'Oh, and this is Leslie Charteris, who invented the Saint.'

Oliver was visibly impressed and informed Charteris how much he admired him and that he had read all his books. An obvious lie.

Suddenly Oliver grabbed at the bar knife used for slicing lemons and ran it across his wrist. All three watched open-mouthed as the cut filled with blood.

'You and I have got to be blood brothers,' Oliver announced making a second grab for the writer's wrist.

Unmoved and unimpressed Charteris coolly placed his hands behind his back and picked up the conversation from where it was interrupted.

Oliver eventually mumbled his way out of the bar, leaving a trail of blood across the carpet.

Even without the alcohol – and sometimes Oliver could go days without demanding or taking a drink – his complex and confusing character could swing through a range of emotions – anger, remorse, self-pity and jealousy – and all in less than an hour.

Jack Hawkins's villa was situated on a cliff top overlooking Cap Ferrat. It was built on stilts with a magnificent sea view, and the literal translation of its French name was Garden on the Sea.

Embarrassed by Oliver's unnecessary and hurtful behaviour in a Beaulieu restaurant the night before, Stephen Ford decided to remonstrate with his friend. 'Yeah, yeah, whatever,' said the actor, unconcerned.

'No, Oliver,' continued Ford, 'you were absolute crap. You have got to get to grips with yourself and realise that you are supposed to be a human being.'

Oliver's body language was showing signs of irritation. 'Yeah OK, Stephen. You've made your point.'

'You've got to stop thinking that just because you're a big film star you can behave any way you want and get away with it.'

Ford suddenly noticed Oliver coming towards him, his face distorted with anger. With Oliver in pursuit the businessman, wearing only a pair of swimming trunks, circled the garden gazebo a couple of times before attempting to escape through a rose bed. As he emerged the actor was waiting. Picking up his friend, Oliver hurled him back among the thorns before throwing himself across Ford's gashed and bleeding body. Ford wriggled free and the chase continued until Oliver managed to trip his prey over the edge of a giant rock at the bottom of the garden, once again hurling himself on top of Ford.

'You are a cunt, Stephen Ford,' hissed Oliver. 'You're such a cunt.'

'Oliver,' said Ford, as convincingly as he could. 'Please don't move.'

'What do you mean, don't move? You're always telling me what to do.'

'Just don't move, OK?'

'Why?' asked Oliver.

'Because we're just about to go over the top.'

Oliver peered past his friend and down the 30 yard drop to the rocks below. 'Oh, fuck . . . Oh, fuck . . . Oh, fuck.'

'Keep calm, Oliver,' pleaded Ford. 'Please keep calm.'

'Oh, Stephen. Oh, God, you know I love you.' Tears were streaming down Oliver's cheeks. 'I'm sorry, but you just wind me up so much.'

'I know I do, Oliver,' said Ford, fingernailing his way upwards. 'But you know it's for your own good.'

'Yes, I know,' said Oliver as he dragged his friend to safety. 'God, look at you. You're covered in blood. I'm so sorry, I'm so sorry.' The tears had dissolved into deep, breathless sobbing – the inevitable aftermath of being a naughty boy.

Alerted by the ruckus, Jacquie was shocked to find Ford dripping blood on the manicured lawn. 'For God's sake, Oliver. Leave Stephen alone.'

'But he needs some antiseptic or something.'

'I'm going to take him upstairs,' said Jacquie. 'Don't you think you've done enough? Just sit down and shut up you stupid little bastard.'

In the bathroom Jacquie began examining Ford's wounds. 'You're going to have to take your trunks off,' she said. 'You're bleeding in there as well.'

Before the swimming costume had hit the floor the door burst open and Oliver, the anger back in his eyes, screamed, 'What are you doing with my woman? What's going on? Why is she giving you a blow job?'

Pushing her lover out of the bathroom and locking the door Jacquie continued with the first aid. 'Come on out, Ford.' Oliver hammered at the door. 'Fuck you, Ford. Come on out.'

Oliver's relationship with women – his ownership of women – was uncompromising and dictatorial and total. He would exercise a kind of long-distance control over his former mistresses, often telephoning at odd hours to pass judgement on a dress or outfit or to 'tut' disapprovingly at the woman's choice of new boyfriend. One actress with whom Oliver had an affair during his marriage to Kate returned to her hotel suite from an award ceremony. A few minutes later the telephone rang. It was Oliver and it was three in the morning. 'He had seen me on the television news with a certain man on my arm and called to warn me off,' recalls the Swedish-born actress. 'After I had put the phone down I suddenly realised that this wasn't an ex-lover calling, it was a father or grandfather giving gentle advice to his favourite daughter – and this was fourteen years after Oliver and I had broken up.'

Long after his first marriage ended, and despite ongoing legal wrangles, Oliver continued to carry a torch for Kate. Somewhere, deep inside, a part of him was still in love and demanded loyalty. When a friend hinted – falsely – at having slept with his ex-wife, Oliver chased him from the house and hurled oaths and bricks at his escaping car. 'Oliver was insanely and intensely jealous of his women,' says Stephen Ford. 'To the point of madness in some cases.'

To an individual woman Oliver could be charming and attentive and demanded the same courtesy from his male companions, once publicly reprimanding his teenage son for not lighting a female hotel guest's cigarette.

He was developing a loathing for women as a gender, which frequently got him into trouble and only intensified with age. Unlike his public drunkenness, which he learned to turn on and off at will, Oliver's hatred and intolerance of women never wavered. Like the Victorian monument in which he lived, his chattel mentality was lost somewhere in the dark corridors and stairways of a discredited age and he could see no sane reason why he should attempt to find his way out.

The woman with whom Oliver shared Broome Hall had come to her own understanding: 'If I heard he'd run off to Siberia with Brigitte Bardot, I wouldn't bat an eyelid. What's the point? If he wants to do that, there seems no point in trying to stop him. I realise I don't think in conventional terms about marriage, but then, I suppose I'm not normal in so far as no normal female would ever get involved with Oliver.'

Whatever Jacquie was saying – whatever any woman was saying – Oliver refused to listen: 'I understand they have their moments of importance, which is fine for them and fine for their jobs and fine for their relationships. But beyond that I will not listen. And upon that my relationship with any woman is conducted. For conversation, I will go to my local and talk to a lot of drunks.'

Others, however, were only too willing to listen to Oliver's opinions. By the late seventies his performances on radio and television programmes, notably in America, were legendary. Oliver's first appearance on Johnny Carson's *Tonight* show produced sky-high ratings but earned the actor few friends.

The veteran presenter had already interviewed Shelley Winters, who remained on the set while Carson introduced and then spoke to his second guest. When Oliver began expounding his attitude to women Winters became visibly agitated. 'Use women as a sex object,' continued Oliver. 'Maybe I'm kinky.' It was too much for Winters, who stood up and poured a drink over Oliver's head. His comments were bleeped out, in order not to offend viewers, but were quoted in full in a studio press release.

After the show Oliver added another comment: 'My row with Shelley Winters was caused by her abominable lack of manners. She is getting old now and probably a little crazy.'

Back in England, the BBC switchboard was jammed with thousands of complaints after Oliver took part in a Monday-morning chat show, *Start the Week,* and announced: 'I think ideally a woman should behave like an angel to my friends, a nun in the street and a whore in the bedroom.'

On one extended visit to the South of France Oliver was persuaded to invest in a 'yacht'. To his delight he discovered the *Ding Hao* was a sixty-foot Chinese junk and the only vessel of its kind sailing the Mediterranean.

The *Ding Hao* was owned by a French-Canadian business-man called Cornel Demere. The preliminaries of the sale were concluded by telephone and Demere agreed to send his daughter, Susie, to Europe to sign the deal and collect the cheque. Ever the gentleman, Oliver offered to put her up at the Hawkins villa. Susie, recalls Ford, was 'much smitten' with her host and insisted he return with her to Canada – an offer Oliver did not want to accept.

Backed into a corner, he blustered to the last. On the morning of Susie Demere's departure the telephone rang in Ford's nearby house. It was Oliver. 'Steve, as you know I'm going to Canada to meet Susie's father.' Oh, yes, thought Ford suspiciously. 'And we are at the airport and I've left my passport and ticket at the Hawkins's house.'

'Really, Oliver.'

'Yes, and of course I need them to travel.' It was obvious Demere was listening to the conversation. 'Can you go to the house and bring them to Nice airport?' A pause. 'It's OK, Steve, she's left the booth. Ignore this phone call.'

'Ignore it?'

'Yes, ignore this . . . You haven't got a key? Oh shit, well you'll have to drive the car through the glass front door. It doesn't matter, I need to go to Canada.'

'OK, Oliver.' By now Ford was convinced he was being suckered. 'I'll be right over.'

'Ignore it, you bastard, just ignore it.'

Slipping his own passport and a spare airline ticket into an envelope, Ford arrived at the airport to find his friend already making excuses. 'He's never going to make it,' Oliver was telling Demere. 'If the plane goes without me, I'll follow on later.'

'It's OK, Ollie,' yelled Ford across the crowded departure lounge. 'I've got your ticket and passport. You can go to Canada.'

'Fuck,' mouthed Oliver. And then: 'Steve, thanks so much. What a great pal you are. I'll just go check in.'

Thirty minutes later, and with the flight being called for the final time, Oliver had still not reappeared. He was eventually found sitting in a corner with his head in his hands pondering his next move.

In an omen-riddled industry boasting more than its fair share of superstitions, Oliver Reed's third and final pairing with Glenda Jackson should have sounded alarm bells long before shooting started.

Jackson had been hired by the writer-producer Judd Bernards to play the title role in *The Class of Miss McMichael* filmed on location in Bethnal Green in October and November 1978. Oliver would be her authoritarian and hypercritical slum-school headmaster. It was written as a black comedy and directed by Silvio Narrizzano, who in 1966 had a hit with *Georgy Girl*, and it soon became apparent to everyone concerned that the project's budget was as stricken as the battle-scarred East End school in which it was shot.

'They cheapskated it,' Oliver complained. 'Even in the most complicated scenes there was no time for rehearsals. It was "turn on the lights and fucking shoot it".'

For Jackson the tight schedule and low budget almost ended her career. After a bitter clash with the headmaster, Jackson's character, a liberal but dedicated teacher, systematically destroys his office around him. In a climactic frenzy she pulls down a huge glass-fronted bookcase. Unknown to the actress the props department had not been given enough money to replace the real glass with stunt sugar glass and, as the panes shattered, her face and head were showered with razor-sharp splinters.

The antipathy between Oliver and Jackson – which smouldered throughout *Women in Love* and started to smoke during *Triple Echo* – finally burst into flames during *Miss McMichael*. Their meetings were professional and perfunctory and restricted to the set. 'I only saw her during working hours,' admitted Oliver. 'We acted together and then I went to my room and she went to hers. We didn't socialise, ever. She certainly never went to the film unit's communal lunches.'

Jackson has similar memories: 'Oliver and I had absolutely nothing to say to each other,' she said. 'As people we were as different as chalk and cheese ... I neither like nor dislike Oliver on a personal level.'

The film itself fell despairingly between two identities: resembling an updated but less funny version of a 1950s *St Trinian's* caper and never quite possessing the gritty punch of *The Blackboard Jungle* or *To Sir, With Love*. *Variety* remained unimpressed: 'Poorly mannered, simple minded, badly disciplined ... gives social science a bad name.'

The disastrous collapse of *The Mad Trapper* – and its star's out-of-hour antics – were giving David Cronenberg second thoughts. The writer-director had sent Oliver Reed an early draft of his latest script just as the actor's Toronto shenanigans were hitting the headlines. Oliver, eager to make a second film opposite Samantha Eggar, promptly lauded it the 'finest script I've read since *The Devils*'.

Convinced by his would-be star's enthusiasm and promise of propriety, Cronenberg duly contracted Oliver to play the psychoplasmics guru Dr Hal Raglan in *The Brood*. 'I must admit I wasn't looking forward to Ollie's arrival,' admitted Cronenberg. 'But on the set, at least, he behaved impeccably and the film came together very well.'

'I distrust people that write books and people that read books,' Oliver Reed once confessed. 'I cannot understand people who have enough time to sit down and read about other people's experiences. I find myself far too busy talking or lying in wet fields drunk.'

By 1978 the actor had mellowed his opinion – influenced no doubt by the promise of a publisher's cheque – enough to work on his own autobiography. The book was written on the run with Oliver remembering and dictating memories and stories in pubs and restaurants and on the film set, his ghostwriter transcribing and polishing and believing. Full of himself, expansive, joking, shadowed by an unquestioning ear, Oliver was riding an emotional tidal wave. In such a mood he could embroider and fabricate almost anything. None of the autobiography was true in the sense of having taken place: it was true only in the sense that Oliver wished it had happened in the way he wanted it to.

For years, in bars and at parties and during interviews, he had unwittingly and unknowingly rehearsed his autobiography: Oliver the neglected child who grew into the teenage rebel; the victim pupil shunted from school to school; the virgin soldier; the struggling actor; the mistaken marriage and the compulsive affairs. His laddish storytelling now became legendary, modifying here, exaggerating there – leaving a trail of truths, half-truths and outright fantasies. What better way than to open his own memoir than with a complete fiction?

At the time he was working with Samantha Eggar on *The Brood*, Oliver Reed was dictating and revising his autobiography. When the book appeared the following year it contained one of his most puzzling 'fibs or fantasies'.

On page one of *Reed All About Me* the actor describes his first fumbling sexual encounter with a four-year-old girl called Vicky, whose parents owned and ran the pub at

Bledlow, the Buckinghamshire village where Marcia Reed lived with her lover:

> I had already found out the amazing difference between a boy and a girl ... It was but a fleeting glimpse ... I was five years old and we had gone upstairs in her father's pub to play doctors and nurses and no sooner had I pulled down Vicky's knickers than her mother walked into the room.
>
> But as the song says, 'thank heaven for little girls'. Vicky of the red hair and green eyes grew up in the most delightful way as Samantha Eggar – Victoria Samantha Eggar.

Amusing and innocent as the story appears there is slender evidence to suggest it ever happened. No 'Eggar' appears on any county or licensed trade record for the Red Lions at Bledlow – nor anywhere else in Buckinghamshire – during the early years of the war. It would be even more surprising if the family did. Ralph Alfred J Eggar was born nine days after the start of World War One and commissioned into the army 21 years later, ultimately rising to the rank of brigadier. In the spring of 1937 the young officer took a Dutch-Portuguese bride who, two years later, gave birth to their first daughter, Victoria Lucy (not Victoria Samantha as Oliver claimed). It is highly unlikely that a career officer such as Ralph Eggar, or his wife, would have taken time off from the war to own a rural inn.

Just why Oliver should fabricate such a childhood memory, knowing the facts could easily be verified, is a mystery. Even more puzzling is Samantha Eggar's continued silence over what would appear to be nothing more than mischievous gossip.

Among his friends at the launch of *Reed All About Me* was David Ball, the accountant Oliver had first met five years earlier while working on *The Great Scout and Cathouse Thursday* and who was now a producer in his own right.

'So this is your book then?' asked Ball.

'Yeah,' shrugged Oliver. 'Load of old bollocks really.'

* * *

Few men frightened Oliver Reed. In Stringfellow's nightclub Oliver would search out suitably drunken opponents for one of his more dangerous sports – head-butting. Each contestant would smash his head against his opponent's until one collapsed or surrendered. A regular victim was John Entwistle, the Who bass player, who – after being knocked out three times – asked the club owner, Peter Stringfellow, to either ban the game or suspend Oliver. In 1980 Oliver came face to face with one man he dared not cross.

A suspense thriller with pretensions of Hitchcock, *Venom* rises little further than a fifties B-movie. A ten-year-old boy is kidnapped and held hostage. The gang – including Oliver as a chauffeur, Dave Connolly – and their victim are trapped when the police besiege the family's London home. Inside, a deadly black mamba, mistakenly shipped to the boy instead of a harmless African house snake, has escaped from its cage and is stalking its prey. The mistake is noticed by a toxicologist, Dr Marion Stowe, played by Sarah Miles.

Joining Oliver on the Piers Haggard-directed film were Sterling Hayden and Nicol Williamson. 'All magicians in their own way and all drunks in their day,' recalls Sarah Miles. 'But neither Stirling nor Nicol was as incorrigible as old Ollie Reed.'

Leading the kidnap gang is Klaus Kinski, the Polish-born actor with a gelignite temper and an irritating habit of stomping off the set for the slightest provocation – including his jacket being hung on a wire and not a wooden coat hanger. In the third and final part of her autobiography, *Bolt from the Blue*, Miles claims Kinski's inclusion in the cast only exacerbated the gloom over what was increasingly seen as a 'doomed' project. 'The film was appropriately called *Venom* and Klaus seemed determined to live up to its name,' she says. 'From what I was able to glean, the only excuse for his domestic outbursts sprang from his daughter, Nastassja Kinski, being on a roll. After Polanski's *Tess*, she became the new darling of Hollywood, courted, caressed and cast wherever she went. I believe Klaus was actually envious of his own offspring.'

More baffling was why Oliver and Williamson – 'smiling sweetly on tippy-toes', according to Miles – should ignore Kinski's arm-waving, high-pitched rantings.

At the end of one obnoxious outburst Miles asked Williamson, 'Why don't you give him one?' The actor turned physically pale and shuffled off.

Cornering Oliver, with whom she had worked on *The Big Sleep* twelve months earlier, Miles demanded, 'Why do you stand for it? You're big enough to sort him out.'

'Because,' whispered Oliver, 'I'm no bloody fool.'

They had been together as a couple for thirteen years – the first three clandestine, the next ten as all but a married couple. Their affair, begun on the set of *Oliver!*, had been an exhausting experience. In recent years their life at Broome Hall had degenerated into a Jekyll-and-Hyde 'marriage' which neither Oliver nor Jacquie nor anyone else understood very well. Apart, they telephoned each other weekly. Together in the same house for more than a month they embarrassed themselves and their friends with long and loud arguments.

Sarah had not yet reached her tenth birthday and accepted the disagreements the way children always have: with confusion and split loyalties. Mark, who recently announced he wanted to follow his father into films, had seen it all before in Wimbledon when his parents' marriage was coming to an end. There was no easy answer to his father's drinking, nor his irrational quarrels with Jacquie. Only this time there was no other women. His father was of an age when the company – the admiration – of men was more important than any sexual conquest. Women, recalls one friend, simply did not interest Oliver any more.

For Jacquie the acceptance had worn tissue thin – so thin she could now see clean through the majority of freeloaders and hangers-on who descended on Broome Hall each weekend for free food and booze. Having been born with a motherly, tolerant nature, she now found she possessed a built-in bullshit detector, very often smelling it before a person opened their mouth. 'You're small-minded about people,' Oliver would berate her. 'You don't like my friends.'

It took one of Oliver's 'friends' to put an end – if only temporarily – to the ritual draining of the actor's already precarious personal finances.

Each Sunday Oliver ferried his assorted collection of guests to one of the nearby public houses for pre-lunch drinks. This time, possibly because of Stephen Ford's presence, Jacquie agreed to accompany the party to the Cricketers Arms in Ockley. Within minutes the group had swollen to more than twenty. 'Right,' announced Oliver, 'whose for a curry?'

The fleet of cars set off for Dorking. At Oliver's favourite Indian restaurant the group, seated at two long tables, began ordering top-of-the-menu dishes and expensive bottles of wine. Ford could see Jacquie rolling her eyes as the tab clocked up.

When the £200 bill arrived the host reached for his wallet. 'Hang on a minute,' said Ford, snatching the till receipt.

'Don't make a fuss,' muttered Oliver, clearly embarrassed. 'I'm going to pay it.'

'No way,' said Ford. Whipping off Oliver's hat, which he wore throughout the meal, Ford made his way down the tables demanding a pro-rata contribution from each diner.

Oliver was mortified. 'For God's sake, stop it, Stephen. You can't do this.'

'Watch me,' replied Ford, rattling the hat under the nose of another freeloader. 'You can't be a cunt all your life, Oliver. And I'm going to stop this once and for all.'

Some paid up willingly; others needed to be bullied; some claimed they did not have any money on them. 'It was a disgusting display of greed,' remembers Ford. 'But Oliver felt guilty that he earned so much and felt he had to make it up to people who were not earning as much money. Of course, most of them just took advantage.'

In reality, Oliver's expenses far outpaced his income. Broome Hall, now impressively on the way to complete restoration, had sponged up money for years. 'I will never get my money back,' conceded Oliver. 'It was a commitment not an investment. It is my personal contribution to England's green and pleasant land.' By the late 1970s Simon Reed viewed the employment of twenty staff, including fifteen carpenters, as near lunacy. 'It was haemorrhaging money,' says the youngest Reed. As each room was repanelled and reopened the domestic bills soared; heating the eight-hundred radiators was costing £1,000 a week.

There were other extravagances which David Reed, still attempting to balance the books, found it hard to live with. Attempting to see how fast he could drive his green Rolls-

Royce from Broome Hall's gate to the main house, Oliver crashed into the masonry of an old bridge. The car was a write-off. 'I never liked the colour anyway,' shrugged Oliver walking away from the wreck. The hall's painstaking restoration work was dragged out still further when a frequently bored Oliver treated the entire workforce to drinking sessions at the local pub. Even more man-hours were lost when he demanded his craftsmen build two secret bars in the estate grounds. The first was a two-storey tree house where a thirteen-foot ladder led invitation-only guests into a rustic but fully stocked bar; when the drinking got too much they could collapse in the bedroom above. And behind the house a traditional garden shed contained a straw-floored bar and easy chairs and the choice of dozens of types of cider.

Away from home, and when Oliver was not living on a film company's expense account, David attempted to curb his brother's spending with a strict weekly allowance. It never worked. Two or three days into the week Oliver would telephone David to confess he had spent his £200 pocket money and demand a bank draft for more.

By late 1979 Oliver's relationship was also nearing bankruptcy. His Jubilee Day proposal two years earlier had been turned down because, Jacquie explained, being married would only make him 'unhappy and responsible'. There had been some good times during the affair, but much of it had been difficult. As a 'husband' Reed had been a mess and, given Jacquie's insecurities, she never learned to disentangle herself from his moods: to stand off and look with some objectivity at what he was doing and how he was treating her and their child.

Oliver fretted and picked arguments. Christmas was a disaster. As New Year approached the individual skirmishes merged into a running battle. Jacquie finally announced her intention to leave as soon as the holiday was over. Breaking his favourite shotgun Oliver loaded two cartridges. Storming into the kitchen he wound the hands of the antique clock forward to midnight – and blasted it with both barrels.

'Now the year's finally over,' he said.

Jacquie moved out the next day taking Sarah and her Mercedes sports car. By the end of January Broome Hall had been sold.

Chapter Fifteen

'Perhaps I am afraid, with scarred face and baker's hands, to confess to the softness underneath.'

BALANCING ON HIS HANDS, HIS BODY PARALLEL to the bar of the Rowhook pub, Oliver Reed watched the three teenagers enter the lounge. Behind the boys was an attractive, dark-haired schoolgirl apparently intent on ignoring the 42-year-old actor's impromptu acrobatics. Oliver had never seen the girl before – but he knew he had just fallen in love.

Josephine Burge was sixteen years old and about to take her O-levels. When her two older brothers started talking about the film star who used their local pub the teenager demanded his autograph. She had never heard of Oliver Reed or, as far as she knew, seen any of his films. Josephine was also unaware that on the 1964 spring day she was born Oliver was on the set of the film that would make him an international star.

The sale of Broome Hall had been swift and profitable. Unlike his first wife, Jacquie was so far making no financial demands after the break-up; they rarely spoke, all she wanted to do was forget. Oliver's search for a new home ended two miles down the A29 at the far end of what the Romans called Stane Street. Pinkhurst Farm, not far from Oakwoodhill, was far less grand than his former home yet contained enough spare rooms to accommodate guests and more than enough grazing for Oliver's horses. The only thing it lacked was a mistress.

Having chosen – if not won – his new bride, Oliver wanted to tell the world. Before breaking the news to his family he sought the approval of friends. Stephen Ford was one of the first. 'I have met this wonderful girl,' Oliver announced on the telephone one morning. 'I see her every day on her school bus.' His friend's reaction was predictably disparaging. 'You must come down and meet her,' pestered Oliver.

That Saturday Ford deposited his bags at Pinkhurst Farm and the two men walked to the King's Arms at nearby Rusper. Before the pair finished their first round of drinks Josephine and her mother entered the pub lounge. 'I couldn't believe how young Josephine looked,' says Ford. 'She didn't even look sixteen. She looked like a very shy fourteen-year-old schoolgirl.'

Ford could smell disaster. At the bar he attempted to warn his friend: 'There's no chance of this, Oliver. Why is this girl going to be interested in a silly old fart like you?'

'There's more to me than meets the eye,' Oliver countered.

'I hope so,' said Ford, 'because she's not going to be very impressed.'

Anne Burge and her family lived in a cottage, less than fifty yards from the village pub. At closing time she invited the pair back for more drinks. Oliver, who was wearing a new and very expensive tweed jacket, asked Ford if he liked the latest addition to his wardrobe. 'No, I think it's absolute crap,' said a grinning Ford.

The comment obviously ruffled the actor, who turned to Anne Burge for a second opinion. 'Oh, it's nice, Oliver,' she said, attempting to field the joke without offending her guest. Oliver let out a pained sigh before ripping off his jacket and hurling it on to the blazing log fire. 'No, no, leave it,' he ordered as she grabbed a pair of tongs. 'I'm never going to wear the thing again anyway.'

Stephen Ford had witnessed the fragmentation and messy destruction of Oliver's relationship with Jacquie Daryl. Not once in the past four years – either at Broome Hall or on the *Ding Hao* – had his friend shown any interest in women. Any offers – some bashful, some blatant – were politely but firmly refused. Sex was no longer on Oliver Reed's agenda. Ford listened to his friend's obsession with the teenager with rising trepidation. 'He had to have her and that was it.'

Still a virgin and with only one 'walking-out' boyfriend, Josephine was unaware of the riptide of charm and flirtation that was about to engulf her. Ever the gentleman, Oliver knew that his first responsibility was to clear the field. When Jospehine's boyfriend turned up at the village pub Oliver felt obliged to reassure him.

It was, recalls Ford, a bizarre scene. Here was this 42-year-old international film star talking man to man with a seventeen-year-old boy about a teenage girl who was younger than both of them. 'I think she's lovely,' Oliver admitted to the youth. 'I don't want you to think I'm just trying to get a conquest here. I am going to look after her and I hope it isn't going to upset you too much.' The pair shook hands and Oliver turned away to resume his courtship.

When he was not working, Oliver made sure that each morning he was close enough to the road to wave to Josephine as her bus took her to Weald Comprehensive School in Billingshurst. He sent flowers or personally de-livered bouquets to her home. Sometimes he would arrive with a leg of lamb, which Anne Burge would cook for Sunday lunch. During the 1980 summer holiday, Josephine picked fruit from the quince tree in her garden; Oliver bought the entire harvest to supplement her pocket money. It was, she later recalled, 'a very lovely courtship. Oliver was extremely gentle and charming'.

By September the teenager returned to her studies in the comprehensive's lower sixth and the majority of her school and village friends had grown to accept their growing closeness. 'Everyone was sweet about Oliver and me,' says Josephine. 'No one in the village minded and even my teachers knew I was seeing him.' When journalists started besieging the school gates or attempting to buy stories or pictures of the couple the village closed ranks: 'Everyone remained loyal to me and my family and that meant an awful lot.'

It was time, Oliver decided, to tell his family.

Simon Reed had been introduced to Anne Burge and her daughter on one of his occasional visits to Pinkhurst Farm. 'We were in a group in the pub and I remember thinking what a nice young girl she was.' His brother waited for the safety of a telephone call before announcing his intention to one day marry a woman – a schoolgirl – 26 years his junior.

The moment will remain with Simon for the rest of his life: 'I flipped, I totally lost it. It was something beyond my comprehension. Beyond anything I thought Ollie had done in the past or would do in the future.'

No matter how compelling his need to remain in Surrey that summer, Oliver never hesitated in honouring his acting and charity schedule. In the middle of August he was in Dublin, freely adding his name to an all-star cabaret guest list raising money for Irish hospitals. As ever he insisted on covering his own travel and accommodation expenses. In the bar of the Gresham Hotel he heard someone say, 'Bloody hell, it's Oliver Reed.'

'Hello,' replied Oliver. 'How are you?'

'Not so bad, thanks.'

Turning back to the bar, Oliver confided, 'I'm just looking at all the shorts and wondering what to have today . . . What's yours?'

When Oliver's triple vodka and his fellow drinker's pint of Guinness arrived the man introduced himself as Phil Kelly, a singer-turned-comedian appearing in *The Al Jolson Show* at Dublin's Olympia Theatre. Discovered by Joseph Locke while busking for the queue outside the legendary tenor's Blackpool show, Kelly turned down a five-year contract with Jo Loss and his band in the early fifties because he thought he could earn more as an Irish-linen salesman than he could as a professional singer. 'Listen,' said Oliver, waving at the barman for a refill, 'why don't you come along tonight and do a few songs?'

There was one problem, explained Kelly. The only outfit he possessed was his bright-green stage suit. 'I suppose I could always borrow a bow tie from one of the lads in the band,' he said.

'Oh no you won't,' said Oliver, downing his newly arrived triple. 'Come with me.' Two hundred yards up O'Connell Street the pair entered a men's outfitters. 'Kindly provide this fellow with a black tie,' requested Oliver. Handing over a £20 note to pay for a £3 tie Oliver nonchalantly informed the assistant he could 'keep the change'.

To repay Oliver's kindness, and several rounds of afternoon golf, Kelly secured a box for the actor at his Olympia

Theatre show. Whenever the Dublin-born performer appeared on stage Oliver bombarded him with complaints that his chair had only three legs and he was in danger of falling over. Unable to compete, and to the audience's obvious delight, Kelly had a spotlight illuminate his truculent guest – who promptly wobbled and fell over. Emerging to a standing ovation, Oliver held his defective chair triumphantly aloft before hanging it on a lamp fitting on the front of his box, where it remained for the rest of the evening.

After the show, and long after the audience had left, the rest of the cast joined Oliver in the theatre bar for a celebration drink. At four in the morning the party showed no signs of breaking up. 'Oliver, when does the bar shut?' asked Steve King, another of the show's stars.

'When the last person falls off their stool,' grinned Oliver.

Of the two films Oliver made during 1980 both proved lucrative but undistinguished. *Dr Heckyl and Mr Hype*, in which Oliver played the title roles, was a sad American attempt to turn Robert Louis Stevenson's classic Victorian horror story into a comedy. His second film won notoriety for an entirely different reason. *The Lion of the Desert*, in which Oliver co-starred with Anthony Quinn, was made possible only through an international scam masterminded by the producer and director Moustapha Akkad.

Quinn and Akkad were putting the finishing touches to *Mohammed, Messenger of God*, a garbled retelling of the life of the founder of Islam. The film, shot in Lebanon, was partly financed by Colonel Mu'ammer al Qaddafi and the Libyan government. To snare a second tranche of Libyan money Akkad needed Quinn's help.

Lion would tell the story of Omar Mukhtar, an elderly teacher who could not ride a horse or shoot a gun but who accepted the role of patriarchal partisan and forestalled Italy's advance into Libya. Mukhtar, who was hanged in 1931, was a hero of Qaddafi, who had amassed a worldwide collection of Mukhtar photographs and artefacts.

To bait the honey trap Akkad had Quinn photographed as the ageing guerrilla leader. 'He used archive material as a guide and hired the best make-up men and costumers he could find,' relates Quinn. When the pictures were ready the producer arranged a meeting with the Libyan leader.

Akkad opened the discussion with several decoy projects. He then 'accidentally' dropped the books he was holding, which spilled out the photographs of Omar Mukhtar.

'What's this?' asked Qaddafi, retrieving a handful of the pictures.

'Oh, that's nothing,' Akkad said. 'Just some pictures of one of your generals. I believe there's a museum here, in his honour.'

'Yes, Omar Mukhtar,' said Qaddafi. 'But where did you get these pictures? I have never seen them before.'

'These I got from England,' lied Akkar. 'These are to help with research for a picture I want to do.'

Qaddafi was getting more and more excited. 'Tell me, you are planning a picture about Omar Mukhtar?'

'I have been thinking about it.'

'I will back it,' announced Qaddafi, waving his hands in the air. 'Make a list of what you need and I will see that you get it.'

The trap had been prised open and set by the Libyan leader. A year later it would snap shut on his own government, netting Akkar several million pounds.

The producer informed his benefactor he wanted to shoot the location scenes in the desert, but could find no place to house his actors and technicians. Qaddafi instantly sanctioned the building of a luxury village complete with swimming pools, tennis courts and air-conditioned bungalows. When the filming was over Moustapha Akkad retreated to Tripoli's Beach Hotel and sold the entire complex back to the Libyan government. The film flopped in Western cinemas but remains one of the all-time highest-grossing Arab pictures.

On Friday, 9 January, and badly in need of a rest after his stint in the north African desert, Oliver flew with Josephine to Barbados. The following Monday, while Oliver and Josephine were enjoying their Caribbean holiday, the teenager's Weald Comprehensive headmaster was informed that his sixth-form pupil was absent with influenza.

It wasn't long before Oliver was spotted in Barbados in the company of a very pretty – and very young – companion.

Within days the British press initiated Oliver's public cruci-fixion as a 'dirty old man'. Anne Burge defended the couple the best she could, claiming the actor was a 'gentleman' and that Josephine was 'lucky' to be offered a break in the sun. The newspapers were less understanding. One columnist insisted: 'Any mother daft enough to let her child go 4,193 miles away with a middle-aged movie star, while allowing her daughter's headmaster to think the child was off school with 'flu is foolish enough to believe anything.'

The hunt was on. The price for an intimate photograph of the couple leap-frogged skyward as picture editors across the world attempted to outbid each other. 'For some reason the French were desperate for a shot of Ollie and Josephine,' claims Steve Berry, a freelance photographer. 'One French magazine was willing to pay anything for a picture of them kissing, or better still making love. For a sex picture I could have named my own price and retired.'

A feeding frenzy of reporters and photographers greeted the couple's return to England. Several years later Oliver, whose relationship with the press had been playful if not always good-natured, confessed even he had been shaken by the 'personal venom' displayed by some journalists. 'I grew up in the age of the paparazzi,' he said. 'I was used to them examining every aspect of my life, but it was all terribly new and frightening for Josephine. She was deeply hurt by some of the vicious attacks on her and her family.'

The day after their return Josephine was summoned to an out-of-hours meeting with her head teacher, Geoffrey Lawes. There was still no thought of the first-year A-level student leaving school. She would, Lawes announced in a press statement, be returning to her desk the following Monday. 'Jo will have the full support of her teachers and friends in resuming her education and in avoiding further curiosity from the press and public about her private life.' There was only a passing swipe at Oliver's still dubious interest in such a young and apparently vulnerable young woman. 'We are delighted that Jo is back in a secure environment.'

It was obvious to Anne Burge that her daughter had fallen deeply and hopelessly in love. The meetings continued, sometimes chaperoned at Pinkhurst Farm or over dinner at the Burges' home, and sometimes alone at obscure country hotels where Josephine found herself shoved into kitchen refrigerators and bedroom toilets or hidden under blankets in the backs of cars to conceal her from tipped-off reporters. When there was nowhere left to hide, the couple took to spending weekends abroad.

'I felt after Barbados I had to be very protective,' explained Oliver. 'I didn't say a thing to the press and, for Josephine's sake, denied everything about a possible romance. But then we became tired of lying and hiding and slinking around.'

On Josephine's seventeenth birthday – 16 April 1981 – they were once again in America. It was the culmination of a hectic four weeks for a teenager one English magazine had dubbed Oliver Reed's 'child–woman': a holiday in New York; another in Dallas; back to New York for a US launch of the £20-million epic *The Lion of the Desert*. By the end of the month they would be in Iraq to start work on *The Great Quest*.

The day had not started well. Oliver had forgotten to get a birthday card or present. While Josephine was still asleep he slipped out to buy a card and wrote in it, 'To my beloved Josephine'. A present would come later. When Oliver got back he told her he was taking her to lunch at an exclusive Park Avenue restaurant, mentioning only at the last minute that they would be sharing the meal with a writer from *Woman* magazine, Alan Markfield.

When they arrived, noted Markfield, Oliver was wearing a smart, grey, double-breasted, pinstripe suit with a forget-me-not buttonhole. 'Meet Josephine Burge,' he said proudly. 'She's the one who has tamed me, she's the one who has put to rest once and for all the demon hellraiser, Oliver Reed.'

Away from the British press, and apparently unnoticed by their American colleagues, Oliver continued to defend what he still stubbornly called his 'old-fashioned' love story. 'Josephine is the person I want to grow old with, my happy-ever-after girl,' he said.

'She has this wonderful, beautiful, pure clarity of vision that keeps everything in perspective for me. I thought I knew it all and had done it all. But Josephine has this extremely unusual gift of suggesting that I'm slipping up without making it seem she's bludgeoning me.'

As the trio left the restaurant Oliver offered Markfield one of what he once described as his 'baker's hands' and announced, 'I'm not ashamed of love and I'm not hiding around any more. I'm lucky to have a girl like Josephine.'

In Britain, the press marked the day with a concentrated and bitter smear campaign. Oliver's ex-wife, Kate Byrne, was reported as describing the relationship as 'madness' and claimed, 'He must be having a brainstorm. He had fads on cars and different ways of getting drunk – but never young girls.' Even Mark Reed, at that moment looking after his father's Oakwood Hill farmhouse, was misquoted as saying, 'I think this is a flash in the pan that became too serious. I don't think he will marry Josephine. I hope not. I don't fancy a stepmother younger than I am.'

Even the headmaster of Josephine's Billingshurst comprehensive school condemned the affair. 'It is,' said Geoffrey Lawes, 'a case of concern for her moral welfare. I should naturally like to see her back at school.' In reality Josephine had never stopped studying. Her luggage always included her English, sociology and history textbooks and, however short their stay, Oliver insisted on hiring a private tutor. 'I may be a lecherous old man, but I'm not cruel,' he said.

The lone voice of support came, not surprisingly, from Josephine's widowed mother. 'Oliver has been a very good friend of the family for a year now,' explained Anne Burge. 'He is not a bit like his wild public image. I am only sorry people have picked up tittle-tattle and turned the friendship into something sordid, which it is not. There is no one I should be happier to trust Josephine with than our family friend Oliver Reed.'

From New York they flew direct to Baghdad. It was Josephine's first time on a film set and her first experience of her lover's all-night drinking sessions with his stand-in and minder, Reg Prince.

The Great Quest was the true story of how a British major and an Indian Army corporal made a historic dash across the Iraqi desert during World War One. There were only two English actors in the film: Oliver played the officer and Albert Moses the NCO. The rest of the ninety-strong cast was recruited from Iraqi tribesmen. Moses, whose diverse film career ranged from *The Spy Who Loved Me* to *Carry on Emmanuelle*, found the seventeen-year-old Josephine 'shy but charming'. His co-star was harder to keep up with.

Each evening after dinner Oliver and Reg Prince would embark on an eight-hour drinking session, challenging all comers to an agonising game of chicken. A lighted candle was placed in the centre of a table and members of the cast and crew and other hotel guests were invited to bend forward, hands behind their backs, until the flame licked their nose. Anyone who backed out too soon was held over the candle until the flame had singed their whiskers and sooted their nose.

'Off duty Ollie was an eccentric, a terrible extrovert, a dangerous drinker and wonderful company,' remembers Moses. 'Most nights he would stay up drinking until four, sometimes five, in the morning.' By eight he was washed and shaved and line-perfect to begin another day's shooting. 'He was an actor's actor,' adds Mosses. 'A true professional.'

Shooting for *The Great Quest* ended in mid-June. Oliver and Josephine just had time to visit relatives in England before they were off again, this time to two of Oliver's favourite locations – the South of France and Canada.

In Monte Carlo – which, like the rest of southern Europe, was experiencing its worst weather for decades – Oliver was hired by Walt Disney to play Commissar Sergei Krokov in a spoof spy thriller called *Condorman*, based on Robert Sheckley's novel *The Game of X*. The film's lead credit went to Michael Crawford and gave Oliver the chance to continue the 'brotherly' pranks he played on his fellow actor when they first worked together on *The Jokers*.

'Michael is the kind of fellow who always jumps to the ready conclusion,' explained Oliver. 'He goes into panic-hysteria before thinking something through. The whole process is funnier than any joke you play on him.'

During the late 1960s Crawford's in-laws were staying at his Clapham flat for a holiday. One afternoon the actor opened his front door to be confronted by Oliver shouting directions to someone below. 'OK, mate. Back a bit. Back a bit ... Oh, hello, Michael. I've got that ton of horse shit you wanted.'

A few years later, when Crawford moved to Wimbledon, Oliver 'inadvertently' dropped some seeds on his lounge carpet. Apologising, he confessed they were marijuana. 'Michael flew into hysterics again, saying he had children in the house and what would happen to his career if the police came round?' laughed Oliver. 'They were simply forget-me-not seeds, but he didn't know that. He was the best victim I knew.'

Like his acting, Oliver's sense of humour relied on seductive and instinctive timing. Crawford recalls: 'For the first few weeks of production he remembered the good old days and every now and then, for old times' sake, he'd give me one of his crushing bear hugs on the set.' Then one day Crawford found himself 'accidentally' locked in his dressing room – with Oliver heading the concerned hunt for the apparently lost actor.

The following night Crawford awoke in his Monte Carlo hotel to find Oliver silently and very professionally turning every piece of furniture in the bedroom upside down. As his fellow actor tiptoed out, unaware he had been spotted, Crawford whispered, 'Thank you, Ollie.' For no readily apparent reason Oliver had also that night decided to hurl his dinner jacket into the Mediterranean. Refusing to write off an expensive addition to the wardrobe, the film's account's manager borrowed a boat and rowed out to retrieve the hand-made tuxedo.

To make amends to Crawford, Oliver invited his co-star to lunch at Monaco's poshest restaurant. Ordering the most expensive caviar and smoked salmon on the menu, he informed the waiter, 'Michael Crawford has asked to pay for this.'

'No, I didn't. No, I didn't,' screamed Crawford chasing the waiter through the crowded dining room.

More scary was Oliver's unique brand of total-immersion method acting. Almost from the first day of shooting, the 43-year-old actor adopted the growling Russian accent he gave his KGB character. Sitting alone in a Swiss bar one night, Oliver spotted his co-star. 'Come here and hafff a dreeenk,' he commanded.

'It's OK, Ollie,' Crawford said. 'I'm meeting someone.'

Oliver slapped his hand on the table. 'Come here and hafff a dreeenk!'

'No, Ollie, really . . .'

Inflating his massive chest as he rose, Oliver glared down at Crawford. 'Cummmm here into Russian Embassy and hafff a dreeenk, you little feathered fart,' a reference to the film's opening sequence where Crawford attempts an airborne escape from the Eiffel Tower dressed as a bird.

For Barbara Carrera, the film's hapless heroine, Oliver's enthusiasm was even more frightening. Held captive in a helicopter, Carrera repeatedly failed to produce the level of panic and fear expected of a defecting Russian agent about to be murdered by the KGB. Oliver's unscripted solution was simple. On the next low-level take he kicked open one of the helicopter's doors and started to push his co-star into the noisy slipstream.

Directed by British-born Charles Jarrott, responsible for another Disney adventure, *The Last Flight of Noah's Ark*, the film never really worked. *Variety* branded it as having 'the look and depth of a fifteen-year-old episode of television's *Wonderful World of Disney* series'. Oliver would, henceforth, refer to the film as 'Condom-man'.

From France Oliver and Josephine flew directly to Canada, this time to work on the film *Spasms* with the *Easy Rider* star Peter Fonda. 'I accepted at once,' admitted Fonda. 'There was no way I was going to pass up the chance of working with this legendary actor.'

Part of the attraction, as far as the American was concerned, was not so much the force of Oliver's on-screen performance as his off-set antics. Two years earlier while filming *The Mad Trapper*, Oliver concluded a four-hour lunch – during which he personally consumed five bottles of wine – by walking back to his Toronto hotel wearing only a shirt, tie and shoes. Rescued from the subzero temperatures by the police, he told them, 'The only way you can cope with life as an actor is to bring a smile to people's faces.' The film folded after just two weeks' shooting.

Fonda, himself no mean drinker, remembers one night with Oliver: 'After an evening of Cuba Libres, he took me on a tour of Toronto. I awoke, wearing my raincoat, lying on my

hotel bed. The $2,500 I had in my pocket was still there.'
Oliver had financed the entire escapade.

The film, as far as Fonda was concerned, was 'definitely
forgettable'. It was first released on cable television as *Spasms*
and later in cinemas as *Death Bite*.

Instead of returning to England, Oliver decided it would be
nice to spend Christmas 1981 in Los Angeles. On Christmas
Eve, while Josephine was shopping, he started drinking with
a former soldier whose singular claim to fame was the kidnap
of Ronnie Biggs. After smuggling the Great Train Robber from
South America to Barbados the mercenary was forced to
abandon his ransom plan after the British government
refused to negotiate a deal.

Fuelled by an afternoon's beer and whisky, the pair set off
for the city's Mexican quarter and the premises of a legendary
tattoo artist.

'I want you to tattoo this,' demanded Oliver, producing his
penis, 'with that,' pointing at a sketch of some eagle's claws.

The man shook his head and backed away.

Suddenly the bead curtain at the back of the studio parted
and the man's wife appeared. 'I do it,' she said. 'Make bigger,
please.'

Two hours later Oliver returned to his hotel bedroom, his
penis wrapped in a wodge of bloodied cotton wool. All he had
to do now was break the news to Josephine.

Chapter Sixteen

'I'm always wondering whether I've got to apologise for my behaviour last night.'

Oliver's patriotism was inbred and uncompromising and, with the help of a little drink, could come dangerously close to causing a diplomatic incident.

While filming *Hannibal Brooks* in the Alps he ended a drunken night out by tearing down and urinating on the Austrian flag. A few years later he was filming in Germany. Calling at one bar Oliver was dismayed to find it festooned with every national flag but the Union Jack. Grabbing the owner by the shirt, he warned him, 'I'm coming back tomorrow night. If you haven't got a Union Jack by then I'm going to trash this place.' The next night there was still no red, white and blue – and Oliver started by hurling the chairs through the windows.

At home his record collection included a complete set of Winston Churchill's wartime speeches and he would frequently whisk house guests away to sit and listen in silence. When Oliver's daughter Sarah telephoned to say she was bringing her new German boyfriend home to meet him, the couple arrived to find Oliver's house garlanded in red, white and blue ribbons and draped with dozens of Union Jacks.

The start of the Falklands War in April 1982 gave Oliver the opportunity to indulge in the kind of jingoism he had witnessed in his grandfather Launcelot Andrews. 'The Falklands was the war Ollie was never given the chance to fight in,' says Stephen Ford. 'He was totally and fanatically fascinated by it.' Every newspaper story and feature was clipped and filed. 'The telephone would ring at two or three in the morning and Ollie's excited voice would shout at me, "We've taken Mount Longdon," or "Quick, quick, switch on your telly. Have you seen what's happening at Goose Green?" '

During location filming in Scotland for *The Bruce*, Oliver took a few days off to tour his grandfather's homeland with Josephine. It was the first time he had been north of the border. At one Highland pub the couple were so moved by the gentle admiration of a white-haired tourist that Oliver gave him a real-horn comb he had purchased a few days earlier.

As the elderly gentleman bowed an exit, Josephine asked where he was from. 'I am from Germany,' he said.

Oliver's teeth clamped shut. 'I have just given my comb to a German,' he growled.

'Right away you could see how violence can erupt out of nowhere,' recalled Sally Vincent, a *Guardian Weekend* writer who witnessed the scene. 'It wasn't so much that Oliver's face bulged and his eyeballs seemed to plop out on his spectacle lenses. His whole body actually swelled up like the Incredible Hulk's. It was a nasty moment.'

In many ways Oliver was a relic of the class he was born into, living by the old standards while desperately attempting to keep pace with the new. To Stephen Ford his friend was 'English, not British'. When the businessman arrived in a new Rover car flying a Union Jack on the front Oliver cooed with praise. But when Ford swapped the Rover for a Mercedes Oliver exploded with rage and hurled bricks at the day-old car. 'What are you doing buying a fucking German car?' ranted Oliver. 'What's wrong with English cars?'

A few minutes later Ford discovered an American-built Jeep parked at the back of Pinkhurst Farm. 'What's this?' he demanded.

'That's not a car,' blustered Oliver. 'That's just a thing for the land. Different thing altogether.'

'So what's wrong with a Land Rover or Range Rover?'

When he wasn't defending his country's honour he was marching, another fixation Oliver blamed on his time as a boy scout, but, more likely, he inherited from his time as a squad corporal at Church Crookham.

By the mid-1960s Oliver had already amassed an impressive arsenal of antique weapons. One summer night after the pubs had closed he equipped seven of his friends with an assortment of swords, pikes and blunderbusses and formed them up in the garden of his Homefield Road flat. 'Right lads,' he informed his improvised squad in a Colonel Blimp voice, 'we're going to take over the police station.' With unquestioning loyalty the heavily armed raiding party was marched down Wimbledon Hill Road and brought to a halt beneath the blue lamp of the town's police station. Oliver strutted in and emerged a few seconds later with a stern-faced sergeant. ''Shun,' ordered Oliver. 'Left-turn. Quick march.' In the station yard a constable was holding open the doors of a Black Maria, into which the actor counted his squad. They were driven back to Homefield Road like naughty schoolboys and the sergeant warned them: 'If I see you lot out again with those guns I'll have them confiscated.'

At a scouting event on the village green at Ockley, Oliver suddenly announced he wanted to show a pack of cubs how to march. The sight of an international film star swinging his arms and ordering a troop of seven- and eight-year-old cubs around the field delighted the parents – until Oliver marched straight through the village pond. Not one cub broke ranks. Splashing through the waist-high water they emerged on the other side dripping and smiling.

Stephen Ford was frequently press-ganged into marching Oliver around the seafront of a French resort to provide a picture for the actor's fans, 'or sometimes because he was bored and wanted something different to do'. On one occasion Ford commanded Oliver to march across the town square, down a flight of steps, around the harbour – and straight off the end of a pier into the sea. Oliver, like his cubs, never faltered. An order was an order. When mischief took over the pair would march in and out of the promenade bars and restaurants. 'He loved to march,' recalls Ford, 'especially if there were a lot of people around. He was good at it and he loved to show off.'

Playing soldiers in public was fun. Dodging bullets on Oliver's private estate was a little too realistic for most of his friends.

One afternoon at Broome Hall Oliver suddenly announced, 'Some of the boys are coming round later and I think we should play soldiers.'

'That sounds dangerous to me,' opined Stephen Ford. 'What does this entail, Oliver?'

'There will be about four of you and about eight of us,' explained Oliver, 'and when it gets dark you have got to try and capture the boathouse beside the lake without us getting you.'

Ford's lack of enthusiasm deepened when Oliver reappeared a few minutes later dressed in full combat gear, his face blacked, and carrying a .303 Lee Enfield rifle.

When Oliver's platoon, which included his son Mark, set off for the boathouse one of the attackers admitted that a suspicion about his host's war games had prompted him to bring some railway maroons, detonating devices used to warn train drivers of danger on the line. As they crawled on their bellies towards the lake, Ford waited for the first of the diversionary explosions. In response to the first ear-splitting blast Oliver opened up with his rifle. 'Ollie was using real bullets and firing at anything that moved,' says Ford. The second explosion set light to a nearby tree. 'Through the darkness we could hear him shouting at us to call the fire brigade and then as soon as we started to get up he would loose off another bullet.'

Late at night Oliver would invite his guests to live out another equally dangerous fantasy. Having collected armfuls of swords and medieval weapons from the Broome Hall walls he would distribute them to his unsuspecting audience. 'Right, let's have a fight,' announced Oliver, brandishing a broad sword above his head. 'He knew what he was doing,' recalls one scarred survivor. 'We didn't and it was pretty terrifying.'

For a young woman in her late teens living with a man almost two and a half times her age it was an equally daunting experience. Unlike Kate, whom he failed to tame, and Jacquie, who had given in for the sake of peace, Josephine willingly accepted her lover's petty rules and monumental blunders with amazing equilibrium.

On location or on holiday, Oliver kept a possessive and puritanical eye on his woman. Jacquie, startlingly beautiful, who never lost her dancer's figure, was allowed to wear only a one-piece bathing costume, never a bikini. When she came out of the water a towel or sarong would be waiting. A display of cleavage produced a splutter of indignation: 'Cover up, cover up, why is your blouse undone?' From the start Josephine's wardrobe fell within a set of clearly defined ground rules: her clothes would be stylish and expensive; loose-fitting and long; mumsy; and with definitely no hint of sex. 'She was happy to go along with it,' explains one close friend, 'because she loved him so much.'

Filming real storms at sea had long been a problem for postwar directors and producers. Special studio storms could be shot only in close-up and remained unconvincing. And waiting for the weather to worsen on location itself was, by nature, unpredictable and uncontrollable.

By the mid-1960s film studio bosses on Malta realised it was not the island's cloudless skies and long hot summers that would win them a place on the world filmmaking map – only the ability to deliver storms on demand could achieve that.

In 1966 *A Twist of Sand* – starring Honor Blackman and Richard Johnson – was the first film to use the Rivella film studio's new storm tank. A 600-by-400-foot 'lake' was built only yards from the sea, using the Mediterranean as a natural backdrop. What made the facility unique was the addition of a giant tip tank, designed by a British special-effects expert, and capable of unleashing fifteen-ton waves on command.

Oliver Reed's turn to face the full force of the world's fiercest man-made storms came in 1983, when he arrived to recreate Christopher Columbus's epic discovery of North America almost five hundred years earlier. Financed by American money, *Christoforo Colombo* was a six-hour Italian television mini-series written and shot in English. The Italian would be dubbed on later. Although the explorer's landfall would be filmed on location on the far side of the Atlantic, all the European and voyage sequences were to be shot in Malta during October and November.

It was Oliver's first visit to Malta. He was hired to play Martin Pinzon, the captain of the caravel *Pinta*, one of the ships in the Columbus flotilla. 'Ollie was fascinated by the mechanics of the tip tanks,' remembers one of the studio hands. 'He wanted to know exactly how it worked and, during rehearsal, asked if he could release the water himself.' Refusing a stand-in, Oliver remained on deck for two nights filming, soaked to the skin and battered by freezing water. 'Ollie loved it,' adds the studio hand. 'It was like watching a small boy, all smiles and sparkling eyes, playing grown-up pirates.'

Another member of the studio staff impressed by Oliver's performance was Rivella's managing director, Lino Cassar. 'Anyone who can withstand fifteen tons of water, first from the left and then the right, every few minutes and still deliver his lines is a true professional actor,' says Cassar. 'It was a spectacle I will never forget.'

For the first time in almost thirty years Oliver Reed was considering quitting the film industry. He was depressed by a series of health problems and his acting, Oliver felt, had become little more than 'emotional prostitution – I say "I love you" and don't mean it. I smile when I don't feel it. There's a whole new generation watching movies and they have no idea who I am,' he admitted. 'They see this old chap on the screen and they read about my punch-ups in pubs. But they don't know what I've done.'

The *Guardian* writer, Andrew Rissik, has his own theory on the actor's apparent decline. 'Perhaps Oliver himself took too light a view of his own stardom; the dyslexic boozy practical joker inside him may always have bridled at the "serious" pretensions of straight acting. As an artist – as a screen presence – he was in decline not because of any innate lack of capacity, but because directors could no longer be bothered to put him to the test.'

It was one of Oliver's heavily publicised 'punch-ups' the following year – this time with two police officers – that landed him three nights in a police cell and a £100 fine.

Two Guernsey policemen arrived in Berthelot Street on the last Sunday in August 1984, to find Oliver dressed only in his underpants and smeared with dirt and blood and walking in circles in the centre of the St Peter Port side street.

Overlooking the road was the staff quarters of the Duke of Normandie Hotel and, despite Josephine's desperate attempts to calm her excited lover, the drunken actor had spent the previous half-hour trying to open and clamber through a ground-floor window while demanding to see 'the General', one of his Ulster drinking partners. Frustrated by the window's lack of co-operation, Oliver punched a hole in the glass, gashing the back of his hand.

Attempting to calm the island's most famous resident proved hazardous and futile. When the officers suggested Oliver, who had spent the evening consuming two bottles of rum, should return to his hotel he clenched his fists and began throwing hefty but off-target punches. 'Come on,' he shouted, 'Come on, have a go if you dare.'

Pacified by Josephine and shepherded by the policemen, Oliver was eventually returned to his seafront hotel. As the officers turned to leave the 46-year-old actor plunged head first out of the front door and collapsed spread-eagled across the pavement. He was arrested and dragged comatose to the capital's police station.

With the next day a Bank Holiday it was 43 hours before Oliver appeared before Guernsey magistrates' court. Silent and 'remorseful', he admitted the charge of damage and 'acting in a disorderly manner while drunk' and was fined £100.

An exploit at another Guernsey hotel was less criminal, but equally dangerous. Oliver was occupying a first-floor hotel suite overlooking the swimming pool. One night – and without apparent encouragement – he began speculating if it was possible to dive into the pool direct from his bedroom, a distance of several yards. Having opened the window, he charged across the bedroom and dived head first through the window, sailing over the tiled terrace and into the pool. To prove his escape from almost certain death was not a fluke he repeated the experiment.

The child within Oliver Reed – the child that never left him – had but one fear: that he should become boring. 'He suffers from a low threshold of boredom and irritation,' announced one interviewer. 'Frankly he likes to make things happen.' And usually at the most unexpected moments.

Cristoforo Colombo was finally ready for release. To launch the mini-series the producers hired the Italian cruise liner *Achille Lauro* and invited scores of international critics to join the cast for an extended screening. The ill-fated liner – which was hijacked by terrorists the following year and later caught fire and sank – would remain at its north Italian home port of Bologna while the guests were wined and dined and treated to three two-hour screenings over as many days.

The final night was marked with a black-tie dinner in the luxury liner's main dining room. By coincidence Lino Cassar, the managing director of the Rivella film studio in Malta, found himself on the same table as Oliver Reed and his companion Josephine Burge. All went well until the pre-screen interval. Oliver excused himself and left, presumably, Cassar thought, to visit the toilet. A few minutes later Cassar caught sight of the actor nodding to the guests as he nonchalantly returned to his table – minus his trousers.

'It was a very surreal situation,' recalls Cassar. 'Ollie was taking his time, sauntering through the tables trouserless and nobody had the nerve to say anything. It was like a scene from *The Emperor's New Clothes*. The only person who seemed to mind was Josephine, who became very agitated and embarrassed and tried to cover Ollie up with a tablecloth.'

Removing his trousers, claims another friend, had long become an instinctive reaction for a bored Oliver. 'He was a great trouser remover,' says Stephen Ford. 'Ollie would remove his trousers – and sometimes other people's – simply to spark a reaction.' Not always the reaction he wanted. When he dropped his trousers in a Caribbean hotel the tattooed image on his penis was mistakenly interpreted as an involvement in voodoo and Oliver was chased from the bar.

Making things happen in a London television studio produced a predictably bigger reaction than Oliver imagined and, unlike his later on-air exploits, this was one he could never convincingly pass off as a prearranged stunt.

Oliver was booked to make a surprise live appearance at the end of a London Weekend Television programme called *All Star Secrets*. The show's subject was the boxer Henry Cooper, with whom the actor had clashed while filming *Royal Flash* ten years earlier. Psyching himself up in the green room, Oliver ended a spontaneous shadow-boxing session by shattering a mirror with a left hook. His hand hastily bandaged, he signalled his off-camera arrival by punching a hole in a screen on the studio stage. And, when the show's host, Michael Parkinson, asked him how many rounds he would now like to go with Cooper, Oliver failed to reply with the prescripted line: 'As many as he will buy.' Instead, he took a powerful but aimless swing at the boxer. Oliver was, as one crew member put it, 'like a hurricane that blew through but did not kill anyone'.

Forty-eight years old and ageing quickly, his hairline receding and greying, his internal organs slowly betraying him, Oliver Reed had not starred in a critically acclaimed film for more than twenty years. By the end of the sixties his annual income had been rising in direct proportion to his international status as an actor. Thirty years later he was fast becoming a grotesque relic of the British cinema, too often hired to ensnare investors or add a whiff of respectability to a lightweight script or cast.

By 1986 the qualms Oliver once possessed after appearing in *Women in Love* – 'I haven't been offered a nude scene since . . . and I don't want one' – had been dispelled by numerous and questionable public performances. When he was offered the role of Gerald Kingsland the prospect of prancing bare-arsed in front of a film crew was more exhilarating than Oliver cared to admit.

For the last five years Oliver had enjoyed the feeling of walking into a crowded room with his beautiful, young and very often frightened lover. At these times he was always considerate, always careful to include Josephine in the conversation, squeezing her hand and smiling his tight-lipped but secret smile. Josephine never felt pushed into the background because she was never a threat; she was never in competition with him. At moments like these Oliver was at his sober, intelligent and funny best. High on the prospect of *Castaway*, it was time, he announced, to get married.

The marriage surprised no one. Early in their relationship Oliver tried to get Josephine to accept a philosophy that might hold her together – hold them together – through the bad drunken times. He confessed, 'I'll do some things you will hate, and things that I will hate, but I just want you to know it is not really me and that it will be all right in the morning.'

On 7 September, 21-year-old Josephine Mary Burge became the second Mrs Oliver Reed.

Castaway – next to *Lion of the Desert* – was Oliver's favourite film. He had fun making it. To anyone who knew Oliver Reed personally – and for a good many who didn't – Gerald Kingsland is Oliver Reed. Just like Oliver, the would-be writer is virile and handsome and insolent and smoulderingly dangerous and it is all too easy to imagine Oliver, propped against a remote bar somewhere, announcing, 'You could found a whole new religion on this island with a screw and a cold beer.'

To accompany Kingsland to his tropical island and to play Lucy Irvine, on whose book the film was based, the director Nicholas Roeg chose Amanda Donohoe, a beautiful but relatively unknown actress. Faced with the prospect of a few weeks' filming in London, during which he could look up old friends, followed by several more in the Seychelles sunshine, Oliver was rapturous. 'It is a dream film,' he predicted before shooting started. 'I am really going to enjoy myself.' His gusto was soon lost on his co-star.

After answering his advertisement for a fellow castaway, Irvine meets Kingsland for the first time in London's Bloomsbury Hotel. For the film Roeg – who had been in charge of photography 22 years earlier on *The System* – decided to use a Bayswater hotel in Inverness Terrace. 'You're just down the road,' Oliver told his friend Stephen Ford. 'Why don't you come down and see gorgeous Amanda?'

It was a trap. When the businessman arrived they were in the middle of a take. Oliver caught sight of his friend in a mirror and demanded a 'cut'. Ford, who had so far failed to sniff out a classic public-humiliation manoeuvre, was unprepared for what came next. 'This is my friend, Steve,' said Oliver, introducing Ford to the director. 'He is a pimp and he makes his living by pimping for people. I don't really approve of his way of life, but he is a good friend.'

Ford was suddenly aware how quiet the hotel lobby had become, but quickly recovered. 'That's absolutely correct,' he declared. 'I am a homosexual pimp and Oliver asked me down because there's a very nice boy on the set and he wants me to try and fix him up.'

'You fucking bastard,' exploded the actor. And then, just as quickly: 'Do you want to meet Amanda?'

The actress was waved over. 'I want you to meet my close friend Steve,' said Oliver politely. 'He wants to give you one.'

'And fuck you too,' snapped Donohoe, turning her back on her co-star.

It was a gesture that could well have summed up their working relationship for the rest of the shoot. Oliver was already describing Donohoe as a 'pain in the arse'. It was a description he later justified to another friend by claiming the actress had 'started off as an unknown, but quickly realised she was being turned into a star – and wanted everyone to know it'. Allegations that Oliver had deliberately exposed himself to his co-star rumbled around the Seychelles film unit and were, inevitably, leaked to the press. Unknown to Oliver Reed his trip to the Indian Ocean would sow the seeds of a series of bitter and more costly accusations.

It took almost two weeks to ship the cast and crew and equipment the 5,000 miles to the Seychelles. Each day Oliver and Amanda Donohoe attempted to deliver their best in extraordinarily hot and humid conditions that dulled their enthusiasm and sharpened their tempers. Several scenes had to be reshot.

Oliver, despite Josephine's best efforts, was by now drinking copious quantities of locally brewed beer and imported spirits. Another obstacle to keeping her husband's mind on what they both knew was an important film was the presence of Reg Prince. One member of the film crew decided to use the Indian Ocean assignment to get married. Oliver and Prince arrived at the reception drunk and aggressive. When the actor unzipped his shorts and offered his tattooed penis for inspection to a group of male guests Prince was forced to step in and escort his friend to safety. Josephine's disapproval only made things worse. The next morning other guests at the chalet complex awoke to find her clothes scattered across the balcony and lawn.

With shooting almost complete the stars were given a week off to enjoy the island resort of Praslin. John Hughes, a friend of Oliver's, was also on holiday in the Seychelles and the actor invited him to make up a threesome with Prince for lunch at La Reserve, a restaurant owned by the Seychelles Minister of Culture. The trio began drinking heavily and early. By the time they reached the seafront restaurant Prince had taken offence at something Hughes had done or said. 'Don't behave like a bloody fool, Reg,' warned Oliver. Both men squared up to each other, snarling like dogs through their bared teeth.

Exactly what happened next depends on who tells the story. According to Oliver the atmosphere between himself and Prince got more and more agitated. 'He then took up the table knife and started round the table towards me. I decided to withdraw and try and calm things down.' Backing on to the restaurant jetty, 'I kept Reg within my sights. Then I heard the thundering of feet and a blasphemy. Reg came at me and I deflected him and he went over the balustrade and on to the beach.'

Prince's version of events is somewhat different. He claims he was leaning on the restaurant balustrade looking out to sea when Oliver grabbed his ankles. 'I laughed. I called out. It was basically a joke – on previous occasions he had pushed me into swimming pools,' recalled Prince. 'I did not believe he had any intention of flipping me over and, if he had, he would have believed the tide was in.' After tumbling fifteen feet through the air, Prince landed on a coral beach below and momentarily lost consciousness. When he came to his lower back hurt – it was broken in two places – and he staggered back to the jetty restaurant. Concussed and in pain, Prince pulled a diver's knife from his belt and waved it at Oliver.

The lunch had gone flat and all three decided to transfer the celebration to the home of Oliver's native driver, whose wife had a reputation for making 'atomic cocktails'. Late that night they moved on to out-of-hours champagne scrounged from their hotel manager. When filming resumed the next day the actor was informed Prince had consulted the company doctor about severe pains in his back.

A month after his return, and just as the *Castaway* publicity was beginning to wind up, Oliver got a telephone call from a friend on the mainland suggesting he should buy a copy of the *Daily Mirror*. The front page headline read, OLLIE CRIPPLED ME.

Prince, for whatever reason, had lost no time in selling his story to the tabloid. Luckily Oliver's diary of television and radio appearances kept him busy and his mind off the *Mirror* allegations. When he wasn't travelling, a stream of writers and journalists, some chaperoned some alone, arrived for prearranged interviews at Pinkhurst Farm. The conversations invariably strayed to his drinking exploits and his year-old marriage. Oliver defended himself by telling the truth – and lying to himself.

'I've seen all the pubs around the world and met some charming people. That I wouldn't have missed,' he told one questioner. 'But they're just explosions. That's what I'm like. It bothers me when I'm blagged for those explosions because it hurts the people I love. But I'm only an actor, not a priest beyond reproach. I'm not a villain, I've never hurt anyone. I'm just a tawdry character who explodes. The justification for that I can't begin to assume. But I do know that society needs its goodies and baddies.'

He was, as another of his questioners recalls, on his best behaviour. Six months earlier, just before Christmas, a national reporter had arrived uninvited at the Horsham Road property and demanded an audience. Oliver, already preoc-cupied with a houseful of guests, escorted the man from the property only to find himself accused of causing the journal-ist actual bodily harm. The charge was eventually dropped at Dorking magistrates' court.

Not for the first time was Oliver compared to the American novelist Ernest Hemingway. Commenting on Oliver's *Cast-away* performance one US reviewer said, 'Oliver Reed is a strange actor, and his barrel-like physiognomy and menacing eyes often seem best suited for the gargoyle roles British director Ken Russell gives him. But here Oliver gives a vulnerable, deeply human performance. One of the best of his career. As Gerald, he reminds you of an ersatz Heming-way with his pants down, besotted on mortality.'

In November 1986, *Castaway* was selected as the opening event at that year's London Film Festival. Oliver started celebrating early. As the rest of the National Film Theatre audience took their seats they were treated to piercing whistles and, according to one reviewer, 'choice samples from the Oliver lexicon of invective'. Three months later a second *Castaway* promotion, this time on London Weekend Television, triggered protests from scores of viewers – and delighted Oliver.

It was not the first time Michael Aspel had interviewed Oliver, 'but nothing prepared us for the apparition which lurched on to the set that night,' recalls the veteran presenter. Booked as the final *Aspel & Co.* guest, Oliver had still not arrived at the LWT studio by the time the live show went to air. When the actor finally appeared his hair was ruffled, his shirt was half open and hanging outside his trousers and he was carrying a large jug of what Aspel and his other guests, the comedy actress Sue Pollard and Clive James, the writer and broadcaster, assumed was gin and orange. Watching Oliver stagger towards him Aspel remembers thinking, How the hell am I going to handle this? For one thing I can't take the mickey because the man is incapacitated and vulnerable. On the other hand this is going to make great television and that is what we're here for.

Things only got worse. After slurring his way through the interview, during which he apparently forgot the *Castaway* plot, Oliver insisted on singing a version of 'Wild Thing' with the studio band. 'It was hideous to watch,' recalls Simon Reed. 'It was almost like going back to preteen days of hiding behind the sofa and thinking, Goodness me, what is he going to do next? But Ollie thought he was great, he thought he was sensational. He didn't care. I think he actually thought he was better than he was.'

Watching his father, Mark Reed was more philosophical. 'Of course there were times when he overstepped the mark, when you thought, I wish he hadn't done that. But I don't think I ever felt embarrassed by what he did or got up to. That's who he was and that was part of his character.'

As with *Castaway*, Oliver had delivered his best acting performance for years. The whole thing had been a prank.

He had fooled a show's entire production crew and millions of prime-time viewers. Unfortunately he had also hoodwinked the very people he had spent a lifetime trying to impress.

Producers and directors who, after *Castaway*, had considered Oliver for various roles once again turned their backs on him. Grapevine interest would equally rapidly be denied. 'Because of some of his raucous behaviour people were afraid to employ him,' said Michael Winner, one of Oliver's most loyal directorial patrons. 'To some degree he chose lifestyle over professional advantage.'

Oliver's 'raucous' behaviour not only endangered his own life, but frequently infuriated those forced to repair his wounds. At Pinkhurst Farm Stephen Ford was spending an early Christmas holiday with Oliver and Josephine Reed. They had all been drinking the night before and Oliver shuffled bleary-eyed into the kitchen. 'Those fucking spotlights are too bright,' grumbled Oliver. 'Where's the switch?'

'It's your house,' said Ford, eating his breakfast. 'How am I supposed to know where the switch is?'

None of the obvious switches had any effect on the overhead spotlights. 'I know how to turn the fucking things off,' growled Oliver, clambering on to the kitchen table and punching out each bulb in turn. A spurt of blood shot across the tiled floor. 'No problem.'

The glass had shaved the skin from the back of Oliver's hand and it was hanging around his fingers like a tattered and bloody shirt cuff. 'Jesus Christ,' said Ford. 'You've got to go to casualty.'

'I'm not seeing a doctor for a silly little thing like this,' protested Oliver, wrapping a tea towel around the wound.

Half an hour later, with his blood running out almost as fast as the supply of towels, Oliver allowed himself to be driven to a local doctor. The surgery was shut. Stephen Ford leaned on the doorbell. 'Yes?' said the stone-faced general practitioner, catching sight of Oliver in the car.

'Quick,' pleaded Ford. 'Oliver needs stitching up.'

'Oh, fucking great,' mumbled the doctor, making no effort to hide his irritation. 'Bring him in.'

Leading his patient into the surgery, the doctor turned on Ford. 'You,' he barked. 'Stay there.'

There was no sound from behind the surgery door. Eventually it opened. 'Not bad,' grinned Oliver. 'Seven stitches and no anaesthetic.'

'Great, can we go now?' asked Ford.

'Yes, fuck off,' snapped the doctor. 'And don't bring him back.' As the pair turned to leave the doctor punched Ford on the back of the head.

The next week Oliver bought the doctor a £100 pair of professional boxing gloves as a Christmas present. The note with them said, 'Next time you hit my friend, use these.'

After his move to Guernsey the local doctors became so exasperated by his self-inflicted injuries that Oliver turned to his drinking partner and vet Maurice Kirk to stitch up his cuts and gashes – a kindness the actor repaid with the gift of a knickerbocker suit and, when Kirk was facing a disciplinary committee of the Royal College of Veterinary Surgeons, a written testimonial. 'The treatment he offered was so successful,' claimed Oliver, 'that I hardly show the scars.'

Two childhood imprints remained with Oliver Reed for the rest of his life. The sight of Nanny Morgy skinning and butchering off-ration rabbits in the Bledlow kitchen left him queasy at the sight of blood and the thought of any kind of physical injury to an animal. One friend remembers driving Oliver through Hampshire on their way to a film location when they came across a deer lying in the middle of the road. The actor refused to get out of the car to help drag the dead animal on to the verge. By the time the man returned to his car Oliver was sobbing tears.

During filming in Mexico in the mid-1970s, the studio accountant, David Ball, reluctantly persuaded the star to attend a Sunday afternoon bullfight. The pair took their seats. Less than five minutes into the spectacle Ball noticed Oliver 'fidgeting and quite literally turning green'.

'I can't watch this,' Oliver mumbled through the hand over his mouth. 'This is fucking barbaric. I've got to get out of here.'

As he grew older Oliver's affection and respect for animals, something he openly attributed to his prep-school headmistress and her house of cats, began to take over. His two sadnesses in life, Oliver once admitted, were 'not having made love to every woman on earth, and not having kissed the wet nose of every dog on earth'.

While he was filming *The Misfit Brigade* in Italy a scruffy, half-starved pointer – Oliver would snobbishly claim it was an Italian truffle hound – began foraging for scraps around the canteen wagon. He first fed it from his own plate and then ordered a daily bowl of food for the stray. By the end of the shoot he was so attached to the animal that he paid for it to be flown back to Britain and quarantined. Oliver named the dog 'the General' after his part in the film.

On another film the Mexican crew gave him an orphan piglet as a pet – not through any sense of mischief, but simply because it needed a home and they knew Oliver would take care of the animal. Within days he taught the pig to play hide-and-seek. 'Oliver would hide in a cupboard or under the bed and call its name,' recalls David Ball. 'You would sometimes walk into his apartment to hear this muffled voice calling out and the pig frantically racing around trying to find him.'

Another long-time friend, Stephen Ford, will always remember the actor's knowledge and understanding of nature and animals. Hung over and walking back to his villa or hotel with his friends, Oliver would suddenly stop and demand silence to listen to the dawn chorus. 'He could identify a particular bird by its song and knew the names of most wild flowers and plants,' says Ford. At home, in Guernsey or Ireland, Oliver would take himself off for long solitary walks with his dogs. Even out shopping Oliver never passed a dog or cat without stroking it. Above all he possessed that special kind of magic – not of being able to love animals, but of making animals instinctively love him.

Chapter Seventeen

'Like all thinking adults, I refused to grow up – and it is too late now.'

THE STEEL BLADE WAS COLD AGAINST Oliver Reed's neck. As he started to turn he felt another knife – or was it the barrel of a gun? – jabbed into the small of his back. 'You know I've come here to kill you,' a voice hissed in his ear.

'I would much rather you had a drink, Reggie,' said Oliver. From behind him came a familiar grunt of resignation. In a final act of intimidation the knife at his throat was drawn slowly across Oliver's two-day stubble. He turned and offered Reg Prince the tumbler of gin.

A few minutes earlier Oliver's agitated gardener Bill Dobson had informed his employer of Prince's arrival at Pinkhurst Farm; Prince was spotted resolutely marching towards the main house carrying a large knife. Having talked the intruder into parting with his weapon, not an easy task considering Dobbo's slim build and Prince's reputation, he placed the knife in a drawer for safety and set off in search of Oliver. 'He's come looking for you and he's brought a bloody big knife,' warned Dobbo.

When the actor reached the kitchen Prince and the knife were exactly where the gardener had left them. 'Come through and have a drink,' said Oliver. 'You look as though you could do with one.'

The attack took the actor by surprise. Oliver had not seen his one-time friend and minder since their return from the Seychelles. Rumblings of a damages claim, which first surfaced after Prince's *Daily Mirror* allegations of a broken back and a ruined film career, had so far come to nothing. Looking at Prince now, his hair greyer and face puffier, Oliver could see that the past few years had widened the two-year difference in their ages.

The two men talked awkwardly. In the silences Oliver tried to pinpoint the moment their friendship started to go wrong. It was difficult. In 1975 Prince announced he wanted to retire; Oliver gave him £21,000 as a present and lent him another £6,000 to buy a share in a nightclub and bar. The venture failed but the loan was never called in. Two years later when Oliver flew to Hungary to film the *The Prince & The Pauper* his minder was once again on the payroll. Prince's short temper soon began to show through and his behaviour became erratic and unbalanced. During a drinking session at Broome Hall he started arguing with another of Oliver's friends before beating him across the face and head with a cosh. At first Prince blamed his stomach ulcers. When his own 'medicine' – a pint of milk laced with a quarter-pint of brandy – failed to ease the pain Oliver willingly paid for medical treatment.

Watching Reg Prince trudge away down the gravel drive, Oliver thought it was time to find a new home – if not for his own sake then at least for Josephine's.

For years Oliver had arranged his films and holidays abroad in such a way as to allow him to trim his time in Britain to less than sixty days and successfully avoid a massive annual income-tax bill. Technically a British resident, he could also claim that the bulk of his income had been earned, and paid, abroad. As a younger man he defended his peripatetic lifestyle by claiming, 'I just couldn't be a tax exile. I must live in Britain, it's my culture, my heritage. A lot of people have said the same and then left. Not me, I'm staying.' Approaching fifty and determined to make his second marriage survive, he was at last ready to compromise – by moving to the tax haven of Guernsey.

Petit Houmet was a redbrick property built on the floor of a Victorian quarry and protected on three sides by vertical rock faces. Like Broome Hall, it was once owned by a religious order. In this case, two years after the end of German occupation, the order sold the nunnery for conversion to a private house. Ten miles north of the capital St Peter Port in the island district of Vale, the Reeds' new home offered the privacy they craved and the security they obviously needed.

When the furniture had been shipped and the pets – General the pointer, Twig the lurcher, Biggles and Jenny the two terriers and Kilo the ginger tom – had been safely transported Oliver set about redesigning and rebuilding the interior. First to go were the doors – 'I only fall into them when I'm drunk.' The kitchen was modernised and, at the far end of the house, the walls surrounding an impressive wrought-iron staircase were resurfaced in Spanish tiles. Behind the house the couple installed a sauna and Jacuzzi and a conservatory, which Josephine filled with plants. For the forty-by-eighteen-foot loft space above the double garage and utility room Oliver had special plans: the attic was gutted and rebuilt as a replica pub, complete with fully stocked bar and tables and chairs, and renamed the Garage Club.

Dozens of entertainment and sports personalities became Garage Club members. With David Copperfield, the British-born television comedian, Oliver wrote and recorded bawdy drinking songs. When the snooker player Alex Higgins flew in from Ireland the pair embarked on a two-week drinking binge, which nearly ended the world champion's career – and his life.

Pouring his wife's £200-a-bottle Giorgio perfume into a half-pint glass, Oliver dared his friend to down it in one. Higgins obliged and was violently sick for two days. By the weekend the 42-year-old snooker star had recovered and was bent on revenge. Faced with a pint 'cocktail' of crème de menthe and Fairy Liquid the actor accepted the challenge – 'He was burping bubbles for a week.'

When the drinking finished, at three or four in the morning and usually long after Josephine had gone to bed, Oliver would stagger alone to his study and attempt to make some sense of the words – the sounds – sloshing around in his head. To a drunken dyslexic they were epic poems. To a brother, on the far side of the English Channel and woken from a night's sleep, they were 'garbage'.

When the telephone recitals became too frequent Simon Reed took to leaving his answering machine switched on overnight. 'Bearing in mind how intelligent and innovative his thinking could be you would have thought Oliver's poetry would have at least made some kind of sense,' explains the younger Reed. 'But his poetry was like someone who had been on LSD every night of their lives.

'It was just a collection of random words, no connection at all really. Sometimes he would be pissed, sometimes he would be very pissed, just occasionally he would be relatively sober. It didn't make any difference to the quality of his poetry.'

As the years went by Oliver tried his 'poetry' on a wider audience: he would demand a subject from a friend or visiting journalist and, with his eyes closed, deliver an instant verse. Few examples remain. Interviewing Oliver for *Weekend Guardian*, Sally Vincent recorded one equally baffling offering:

I see was the icing I met
   on a plum cake,
One Christmas,
   one bright and sunny morn,
I saw the sandwiches
   and the sardines,
Lay down
   so deep and crisp and evening,
Lay down with Grannie
   who wore her hair wound,
Woo-ed and fell asleep,
   Oh dear,
   Oh dear,
   Oh dear.

'Mercifully there is no connection between my acting and my verse writing,' Oliver confessed. 'One is a completely manufactured performance, the other is a performance that has at least a slight understanding of soul.'

Early in 1987 Pierre Spengler invited the actor Michael York and his wife Pat to dinner in Los Angeles. After reminiscing about the filming of the *Musketeers* films in Spain fourteen years earlier, Spengler jokingly asked the actor if he would ever consider doing it again. 'I would be enchanted,' replied York.

The next morning the forty-year-old Spengler made six international telephone calls from his hotel suite. The first was to Oliver Reed in Guernsey. 'He would be the hardest nut to crack,' recalled the producer. 'If I could persuade Ollie, I could get the rest.'

With two Musketeers down and two to go, Spengler called Richard Chamberlain and Frank Finlay. By mid-morning the producer made contact with Richard Lester, with whom he had since made two *Superman* movies. The director was also enthusiastic. Spengler's final call was to the best-selling novelist and *Musketeer* screenwriter, George MacDonald Fraser.

Eighteen months later, in the summer of 1988, the cast and crew began to assemble north of London. Unlike its two predecessors, several early – and out-of-sequence – scenes were shot in England. Installed in the impressive King's Room at the Hartwell Hall Hotel near Aylesbury, Oliver was back amid the lanes and countryside he knew as a child. Each morning and evening as he was being driven to the location shoot signposts and village names flashed past his car and through his memory: Stone, Upton, Dinton, Ford, Aston Sandford, Haddenham and Thame. One afternoon, when filming had finished early, he asked his driver to take him to Bledlow.

On the last Friday evening of the shoot the Reeds called at the Angel Inn at Long Crendon, southwest of Aylesbury. Among the regulars were the journalist Jane Parsons and her husband John, whom Oliver, sensing a fellow binge drinker, adopted and christened 'Curly'. It was the start of a bizarre weekend in which her so far untested image of the actor swung from kindness and generosity and charm to outrageous rudeness and grotesque snobbishness, recalls Parsons, 'with a tongue charged like an Exocet missile'.

As the evening degenerated so, too, did Oliver's behaviour. Left at their table while Oliver attempted a drunken and unco-ordinated session on the dance floor, Curly commented to Josephine, 'My God, he's going absolutely bananas.'

'Yes,' said Josephine softly, 'but it is fun, isn't it?'

At the bar a deep and appreciative cheer erupted from a scrum of male drinkers. Oliver, having boasted of his various tattoos, was finally persuaded to place his penis on a stool for public examination.

Before leaving the Reeds accepted an invitation to Saturday morning breakfast. It was a hot and sunny day and the Parsonses' three-year-old daughter, Casey, had already shed her clothes. When Oliver and his wife finally arrived it was almost 11.30. The young girl, bubbling with the prospect of meeting a real film star, raced to open the back door. 'Hello,' she said. 'You must be Ollie, you must come up and see my bedroom.'

'Bloody marvellous,' grinned Oliver. 'I've just arrived and already I've been propositioned by a naked woman.'

In the quiet of the family kitchen or chatting with her alone, Jane Parsons found Josephine a 'very sweet and angelic' young woman. Not once, no matter how outrageous her husband's behaviour, did she raise her voice in protest. 'It was an incredible relationship,' admits the journalist. 'There was no doubt in our minds that she totally adored him and everything about him and her whole purpose in life was to be with him and help and guide him until the moment he died.'

Oliver had already arranged a family lunch with Josephine's brother and friends at the Sir Charles Napier pub at Chinnor, less than a mile from Bledlow. The Sunday lunch was quickly extended to include the Parsonses. Arriving in 'rolling form', Oliver astonished the Parsonses, and fellow diners, by introducing and shaking hands with the entire restaurant. Within minutes his confidence had evaporated as quickly as the wine and, 'after several petulant demands and outbursts of temper', he disappeared into the toilet, returning only after long patient coaxing from Josephine.

Unaware just how deeply Oliver had plunged – and exactly how much alcohol he had consumed in the past 48 hours – the Parsonses agreed to have dinner that night at Hartwell House. What they thought was to be an intimate farewell meal very quickly degenerated into a snobbish verbal mauling. There was no warning. Pointing at John Parsons's wedding ring, Oliver asked, 'Why are you wearing that crap on your finger?'

'What?'

'I said what is that fucking rubbish you've got on your finger? It's crap.'

John Parsons was still unsure if Oliver was joking. His wife was not: 'Hang on a minute, Ollie. I gave him that. You may think it's crap, but I don't.'

The response, coming from a woman, was as sharp and humiliating as a slap across the face. White-hot fury rose behind Oliver's eyes. 'That's the trouble with you fucking people, you have no fucking breeding, no class, you're just common fucking rubbish.' Poking his own signet ring in Jane Parsons's face, he shouted, 'This is proper fucking class, proper fucking breeding. You've got no right to wear a signet ring like that . . . You're a fucking nobody.'

Twelve years on, and only after Oliver's death, has Jane Parsons attempted to rationalise his mercurial and frightening change of mood. 'When he was sober he was absolutely fascinating and very inspiring, full of charisma and star quality,' she says. 'When he drank he became very, very dangerous and probably the nearest thing you could get to being a woman hater. Looking at the signs – which you don't do at the time – I would guess he loathed women, and particularly any woman who had the nerve to stand up and face him.'

To David Reed and his wife, Mickie, the incident was far from exceptional. 'He didn't like women to contradict him,' says Mickie. 'If they did he would get very abusive and very nasty. In that situation he was a very frightening man.' David Reed is convinced his brother's 'hatred of women' intensified as he grew older 'Over the years he changed from being happy to being verbally and physically aggressive, and in the hands of an actor the size of Ollie that could be quite an intimidating experience for a woman.'

With the Buckinghamshire location work complete, the cast and crew moved to Spain. Shooting proper would start on 22 August in the Castillian Mountains near El Escorial.

Once again William Hobbs found himself hired as sword-master. On the first day's shooting the fight arranger found himself standing next to Roy Kinnear and two of the stars. 'Boy, it's weird seeing everybody back again after fifteen years,' said Hobbs.

'No,' said Kinnear, 'the weird thing is everybody's still available.'

Richard Lester viewed the project with equal good humour. 'It would have been unwise to make a sequel very soon after the original films,' he said. 'But the thought of all of us rendezvousing to examine our operation scars and to discuss our arthritis was too good to miss.'

Despite its international cast and the inclusion of 3,000 extras, 750 stuntmen and more than 1,500 specially commissioned costumes, *The Return of the Musketeers* was a lacklustre attempt to adapt Dumas's own sequel, *Twenty Years After,* in which the daughter of Milady de Winter vows vengeance on the Musketeers responsible for her mother's execution. For Christopher Lee, one of the original stars, it was a film that should never have been made. 'They attempted the impossible,' he recalls, 'and tried to shoot a twelve-week picture in eight weeks.'

For Hobbs the biggest surprise was the change in Oliver Reed, this time playing Athos as a drunk and disorderly recluse. Oliver's blustering self-confidence was still evident but, noted Hobbs, he was far more thoughtful about his acting, far more forgiving. Off duty Oliver was a different man. 'As far as I know he never touched a drop of alcohol the whole time,' recalls Hobbs. 'When he wasn't working he was sitting quietly reading a book.'

Since the pair last worked together in 1974 – on *Royal Flash* – Oliver had put on several pounds. The script included a fight scene in which Oliver kicks his opponent in the stomach before escaping. To accommodate the 51-year-old actor's new build, Hobbs agreed the fight should be shot without the kick. Oliver was obviously unhappy.

That night the telephone rang in Hobbs's bedroom. 'Ollie here,' said a gruff but calm voice. 'I am sitting in my bath and I know why you didn't want me to do that move. I'm a fat cunt and I'm sorry.'

On 21 September while walking through Toledo, Roy Kinnear confessed he was terrified of a forthcoming scene.

'Oh, God, this afternoon I've got to go on a horse,' he told Christopher Lee's wife, Gitte. 'I'm not looking forward to that. I don't know if I can stay on.'

Kinnear's lifelong fear of horses soon spread to the stuntmen preparing the shot. As they spread straw and earth on a cobblestoned bridge leading to Toledo castle they doubted if Kinnear was fit or experienced enough to control his horse on the sharp bend. During the first take, with Kinnear following the Musketeers across the bridge, he slipped from his horse and crashed to the ground.

Kinnear suffered severe brain damage. He was taken by ambulance to hospital in Madrid, were he died later the same day. 'Roy's death spread such a pall of misery that it was surprising the film was ever finished and, in truth, the world would have lost nothing much if it hadn't been,' added Lee.

One obituary said of Kinnear, 'A Hardy who never found his Laurel, he will be as much missed by producers looking for a reliable leaven of laughs as by the audiences who knew he guaranteed them.' Even before filming ended in October 1988, it had been decided that the third *Musketeer* epic should be dedicated to Roy Kinnear.

Any peace the Reeds hoped for was short-lived. Once again a telephone call warned that feature writers from a British tabloid were 'collecting dirt' for a series of revelations. The next day the *Sun*'s front-page headline claimed, OLIVER REED BEATS WIFE. Based largely on an interview with Reg Prince – who later admitted receiving more than £20,000 for his co-operation – the story claimed Oliver frequently assaulted his wife, once giving her two black eyes, and treated Josephine like a skivvy. For Oliver his long-standing and unique bargain with the press, that neither should take the other too seriously, had at last broken down. Within hours the newspaper and its editor were served with writs for libel.

In 1990 Oliver was introduced to Richard and Ivy Hall, a retired Hampshire couple living on the edge of the New Forest. They were in Guernsey staying with a relative who owned a pub and restaurant a short drive from Petit Houmet. 'He was sitting in the corner of my brother's pub when someone came in collecting things for charity,' recalls Ivy Hall. 'Ollie took his jeans off and tried to give them to this startled woman. Ollie couldn't understand what all the fuss was about – he thought he was just doing his bit to help.'

The next time they met, at a charity golf tournament on the mainland, Oliver cornered the Halls and asked, 'Why don't you come and work for me?' While he and Josephine were away they needed somebody to look after their Guernsey home and feed and exercise the menagerie. 'Treat it like your own home,' Oliver announced after showing the couple around. 'Anything you find, use it. Anything you need, buy it.' While they settled in at Petit Houmet, Oliver was busy making a film of one of Richard Hall's favourite childhood stories.

During his last week in Spain Oliver had received an invitation to make his American television debut. A familiar face to chat-show viewers, he had never before appeared in a US small-screen drama. Fraser Heston, the son of Charlton Heston and with whom Oliver had worked on the first two *Musketeer* films, was writing, directing and producing an adaptation of *Treasure Island* and wanted the British actor to play the cantankerous Captain Billy Bones.

Oliver hesitated. 'At first I was a little concerned,' he admitted. 'It was a very big project and I was not sure it would work on television.' When Heston explained that the film was slated for a world premiere on America's TNT network, to be followed by a cinema release outside the United States, Oliver relented.

Conceived on a grand scale, the film was shot on location in England and Jamaica on board the *Bounty*, an authentic re-creation of an eighteenth-century three-master originally created for the 1962 version of *Mutiny on the Bounty*. Joining Oliver on the set as a hideously made-up and scarred Blind Pugh would be Christopher Lee, another *Musketeer* regular.

In his autobiography, *Tall, Dark and Gruesome*, Lee recalls, 'In the famous scene where Pugh hands over the Black Spot to Bones, Oliver's greeting, "Pugh! Pugh!", sounded fierce and contemptuous as if he were reacting to a bad smell. This was because for reasons of his own he'd decided to play the part with a strong Glaswegian accent. I had to say, "Gimme his hand, boy, or I'll break your arm – the Black Spot, yiss, yiss, yiss!" That was the moment Oliver chose for his [character's] heart attack. I was trying to get this vital sentence over above the incredible volume of Oliver's subterranean noises.'

News of Oliver Reed's move to the Channel Islands triggered a series of rumours, most of which found their way into print. After three quiet years – just three films and a television mini-series – the press speculated that he was considering retiring on the *Castaway* high. The actor responded by rattling off a list of five more films he was contracted to make in the next eighteen months.

More difficult to defend against were claims, after a lifetime of drinking, that he was suffering from a serious liver disease. Oliver was ill, but it was his kidneys that were causing concern, not his liver.

Aged 49, a heavy drinker and moderately overweight, Oliver was a textbook candidate for gout. Years of alcohol and rich food had upset the chemical processes in his body, causing his kidneys to produce excessive amounts of uric-acid salts. Not only was Oliver at risk from kidney stones, but the urates could lodge in various parts of his body causing inflammation and severe pain. For some reason, as Oliver knew from personal experience, the big-toe joints are the most likely and painful to be affected.

Oliver's doctor ordered an immediate change of diet and a drastic reduction in his alcohol intake to reduce the production of urate crystals. Although Oliver was likely to suffer acute attacks for the rest of his life, a change of lifestyle was the only way of avoiding kidney damage and coronary disease and ultimately heart failure.

The months of strict diets and even stricter alcohol consumption left Oliver scratchy and depressed. For a man with few psychological hang-ups he suddenly found himself with a morbid and unshakable fear of a lingering illness – even worse, the prospect of a slow dishonourable death. 'I cannot bear the thought of slowly wasting away in bed.' Out of Josephine's hearing his friends noticed he was invoking the word 'suicide' far too often, embarrassing them with detailed directions on how he would do it and taking undue pleasure in their discomfort. Drinking himself to death would have been the preferred option, according to one Vale publican, 'but Ollie thought his body was ailing and needed a quicker way out'.

In the 1980s Oliver confessed his nightmare to his son Mark, who reluctantly swore to perform 'his sacred duty and put a shotgun in my mouth and pull the trigger'. It was a solution Oliver still seriously considered, but one he could hardly expect of his wife. 'If I knew I was going to be a responsibility to Josephine I would drink a bottle of brandy, swallow a bottle of sleeping pills and just go quietly to sleep,' he admitted. 'I would tell her when I intended to do it and I hope she would kiss me goodbye, but if I thought it would distress her I would wait until she went shopping and do it alone.'

The manner of his going was an irrelevance. Oliver was far more concerned with his mortal departure. 'When I go I want it to be a good excuse for the best party you have ever seen,' he said. 'I want everybody to have a good drink and to cry. If they are not crying, I want them to pretend to cry – a load of them are supposed to be actors, for God's sake.'

Chapter Eighteen

'We all love a baddy, but not an evil man.'

B
Y 1991 OLIVER HAD BECOME SO GOOD at his art – so
consummately capable of switching his drunkenness
on and off – that he not only fooled the nation, he also
fooled his family. First he had to convince a High Court judge.

The libel action against the *Sun* was scheduled for Wednesday 16 January. Oliver and Josephine arrived at the Strand court complex to be informed by his lawyer the newspaper was offering a five-figure sum as an out-of-court settlement, plus all the actor's legal costs. There would also be apologies from the *Sun*'s editor, Kelvin MacKenzie, and his News Group bosses. Accepting the last-minute deal, Oliver said, 'The money's not important, it was the full apology that matters. I'm only sad that Josephine's gran and my mother and uncle – all of whom have died over the last few months – did not live to hear it.'

As ever, Josephine's comment on the *Sun*'s wife-beating allegations was clipped and supportive: 'I've only had two black eyes in my life, when I was twelve years old and a horse kicked me. Oliver would never hurt me and he certainly wouldn't throw anything at me.'

The publicity surrounding Oliver's success, and his presence in London, was too good an opportunity to miss for the producers of Channel 4's discussion programme, *After Dark*. By coincidence the question for the following week's late-night forum was already decided: 'Do men have to be violent?' Oliver was invited to join the eight-strong panel, admits one member of the production staff, not simply on the back of the court case but on a 'promise' that he would liven things up. To the crew's astonishment the fifty-year-old actor arrived 'very quietly and very sober'.

Already dubbed a 'pretentious chatter-show' by the majority of critics, the show had its guests seated in soft, low armchairs and illuminated in a pool of light. In the shadows was a bar, which guests were allowed to visit while the discussion continued on camera. Oliver suffered the first fifteen minutes like some bemused court jester attempting to make sense of statements such as, 'If there is one single existential line . . .', before shuffling off into the darkness to pour himself another drink.

Off camera a microphone caught Oliver's husky voice: 'Oh shut up, you silly old fool.' Having staggered back to his seat, he continued to snipe: 'I've had more fights in pubs than you've had hot dinners, girl.' And he goaded: 'A woman's role in society depends on whether she wants to get shafted.' Most acted as though he did not exist.

In the control room the director and production staff were getting their money's worth. Oliver's apparently inebriated and foul-mouthed state was enough to generate a couple of hundred telephone protest calls, and certainly enough for a delighted press office to start dialling news desks across the capital. Oliver's stage-managed stunt, however, was about to take on a life of its own. A horrified telephonist suddenly found herself listening to someone demanding to know why the show was being allowed to go on – and sounding remarkably like the Channel 4 chief executive Michael Grade.

It was decided, without warning either the viewers or the participants, to pull the plug on the show while Grade's 'comments' were verified. To fill the gap the production staff apparently grabbed the first film on the library shelf, a black-and-white documentary entitled *The Importance of British Coal Mining in the Fifties*. Twenty minutes later, and convinced the Grade call was a hoax, the programme resumed. Oliver decided it was time to go into acting overdrive.

Fixing a gentlemanly, inoffensive and rather nervous psychoanalyst with a chilling stare, Oliver threw in his own argument: 'Why . . . should you forgive yourself if at some . . . Palaise de Dance . . . a Celt . . . a boy . . . falls before you?'

'I'm sorry,' said the man. 'I don't understand.'

Brushing the question aside with a string of obscenities, Oliver turned on a timid-looking military historian with glasses and a moustache. 'So what do you think about all this, Tash?' The laughter that echoed around the country failed to penetrate the studio and Oliver staggered off in search of the toilet.

His last victim was the wild-haired American feminist author, Kate Millett. Slumping into the chair beside her Oliver planted a sloppy kiss on her cheek and sat back grinning. 'Do I have to put up with this?' Millett pleaded. 'It's obnoxious and offensive.'

There was fifteen minutes of air time left. Oliver had broken the spell and knew it. 'Do you want me to go?' he asked, before finally disappearing in the gloom of the studio.

It was, arguably, the best performance of Oliver's career. It reminded one critic of 'a carriage full of people on a train, reading their papers and chatting amongst themselves, while a drunken loony raves away in the corner . . . superbly entertaining, nail biting adult television.' Others condemned Channel 4 for its feigned outrage: 'It's just like asking Dennis the Menace to a little girl's birthday party and then throwing up your hands in horror when he jumps on the cake.'

To the viewing public – or at least those who bothered to stay up and watch the early-hours debate – Oliver, as ever, could do no wrong. Letters to national newspapers praising the actor outnumbered criticism nine to one. One Southampton woman asked, 'What a boring world this would be if we were all on our best behaviour and only said what others wanted to hear.' While a Penzance fan demanded that television chiefs 'let Oliver Reed have his own chat show. He was a joy to watch, debunking all those feminist, sexist and utterly boring types.'

For Oliver's immediate family his *After Dark* exhibition was proof that the actor was finally out of control. What had started with a 'drunken and excruciating' appearance on *Aspel and Friends* had degenerated into a cruel and well-publicised long-running farce. Within weeks of his London Weekend Television appearance he reportedly caused havoc on a flight home by dropping his trousers and demanding the flight attendants judge a prettiest-boy competition.

In 1987, he once again appeared drunk on television, this time it was *Des O'Connor Tonight*, and Oliver was only just restrained from producing his penis. Even his off-screen existence seemed to be hitting the headlines: he enraged drinkers at a workingmen's club by slapping a £50 note on the bar and shouting, 'Get all the working-class pigs a drink', and a near riot in a Gwent pub was defused only when Oliver poured a pint of beer over his own head.

Publicly, at least, father and brothers remained united behind Oliver. As his agent, David Reed continued to defend his 'client' with noncommittal statements: 'Oliver's drinking habits are much the same as ever.' Simon Reed, as his one-time press agent, was acutely aware of the damage being inflicted on his brother's career. Peter Reed, by now almost eighty, admitted to a former colleague he was 'disappointed and ashamed'.

Something had to be done. With Peter Reed in Surrey, Simon travelling the world as a sports journalist and David living on his yacht in the Mediterranean, a family conference was out of the question. The trio discussed tactics by telephone, eventually deciding to write and sign a joint letter to Oliver in Guernsey. 'We wanted to inform him how unacceptable and embarrassing his behaviour had become,' recalls Simon.

Oliver's response was both characteristic and predictable. 'We never got a reply,' says Simon. 'He just went silent for a bit. But we knew, reading between the lines, what he was thinking. You don't understand me. You've missed the point. Calm down. Don't take life so fucking seriously.'

To Oliver his family had not only missed the point, they had also missed the plot. He was an actor and he was doing what he was being paid to do – act drunk. His inebriated escapades, at least on television, were nothing more than elaborate – and highly secret – stunts, arranged on a one-to-one basis and always with the show's director and host kept in the dark.

'When I was filmed in secret for *The Word*, I was shown alone in my dressing room staggering around swigging vodka from a bottle,' admitted Oliver. 'What the viewers didn't realise was that the whole thing was a set-up. I knew all about the "secret" camera and the vodka was water.' It was the same, he says, for the Aspel show. 'I staggered on with a jug in my hand. Viewers thought it was vodka and orange. In fact it was just orange.'

Oliver's confession has, for the first time, been anonymously corroborated by a researcher on one of those late-eighties shows. Still working in British television as a producer, she described her first meeting with the star. 'I went to meet him at a London hotel. He had already been booked to appear and it was my job to prepare some questions. Before I left my office I was taken aside by my producer, who suggested I persuade Oliver to "liven things up a bit". I didn't need to. The first thing he said to me was, "I suppose you want me to fall over?" '

When he arrived at the studios Oliver was sober and very relaxed, she recalls. 'In the green room he asked for apple juice and I started to get a bit worried. The next time I saw him was on the monitor and he was plastered, absolutely legless. In two minutes he had turned into a legless drunk. He emerged from the set with this great, stupid boyish grin on his face. He was sober again.'

As he left Oliver took the researcher's hand and, in a low serious voice, asked, 'Do you think I overdid it a bit?'

Another equally convincing performance took place on the networked American chat show *Late Night with David Letterman*. Oliver was sober throughout. Reading the transcript reproduced below – in which he mispronounces names and deliberately misinterprets questions – only underlines his affinity with his intoxicated alter ego.

It began inauspiciously when Letterman stood to shake hands with Oliver. The actor responded by pulling the interviewer forward, making him lose his balance. 'That's cute,' said Letterman. Once seated Oliver adopted an American tough-guy accent, aggressively pointing at the camera and warning he had come to the States to 'get Sly Stallone'.

Letterman brought the conversation round to Lee Marvin, with whom Oliver had worked on the pseudo western, *The Great Scout and Cathouse Thursday*.

Reed: He's [Marvin] one of the few actors I admire
           very much. Along with, how much time do you
           got?
Letterman: We have all the time you want.

Reed: Rock Hudson, Rod Steiger, uh Lee Marvin, Rod
             Steiger, Lee uh (snapping his fingers) Marvin.

Letterman: Now, uh, so you and Lee Marvin went drinking.
             And you had a contest to see who could drink
             the most.

Reed: Ya, first off, your researcher was told already
             that I don't want to talk about drink,
             understand? So let's cool that one. Let's get on
             another subject. I love trees and boats.

Letterman: So, it's true you and Lee Marvin had a tree
             climbing contest?

Reed: That's right. And we got to the top of this great
             fir tree. It was in the redwoods and a couple of
             pipers were over there. Can I tell you how they
             go? They put there, over here and (he puts his
             finger on his nose and imitates bagpipes) and
             then Lee Marvin came up, climbing this big fir
             tree. And I got into the boat at the top of the tree
             and sailed away.

Letterman: Wait a minute. Do you still drink? And I'll get off
             this in just a minute. I just want to, I mean, it's
             behind you, you don't drink anymore. So what
             we're trying to do is recall a colourful anecdote
             from your past.

Reed: (back in American tough guy voice) Ya, so what
             you got to do man, is understand I'm taking a
             high quantity, high porcelain diet. I drink a lot of
             cups, coffee cups. I eat a lot of plates. And then
             leave the hashbrowns and everything aside. And
             I eat the plates so that's why I am (adjusts his tie
             and looks into the camera) after you Sly.

Letterman: (looking into the audience) Is there anybody up
             there who would like to host the show tonight?
             (pauses for laugh to die down) Tell me about
             where you live?

Reed: I live in Guernsey.

Letterman: Where is Guernsey?

Reed: Guernsey is one of the Channel Islands, which is
             a little set of islands in between France and
             England. Near the 'nathe caste' of paste.

Letterman: The north coast of?
Reed: Paste.
Letterman: And what is life there like?
Reed: (replies in German)
Letterman: So, so you stopped drinking because you were afraid you might be doing permanent damage to your nervous system, I guess. Uh.
Reed: I thought this was the Johnny Carson show. I was going to be intellectual. But as I said, I live there because I wanted to become a fisherman.
Letterman: You wanted to become a fisherman? Okay, we'll get to that in just a second. (pause) You would like to turn my lights out, wouldn't you?
Reed: No sir.
Letterman: Boom! And I'm gone. Okay, (getting ready to pause for commercial break). Did you see this (Letterman shows off a giant Swiss army knife prop that is focused on, as they break, but Reed starts shouting and Letterman says with fear) Oh brother, we'll be right back.

During the commercial break – and off microphone – the two men continued to chat and apparently made up. But as the on-air light came up one of the microphones picked up a noise that sounded remarkably like someone breaking wind. Oliver jokingly asked his host if he had farted. Letterman shrugged off the question by admitting it was his gas. To which Oliver responded:

Reed: Hang on! I've got some digests (he reaches into his pocket and hands Letterman the tablets).
Letterman: Oh great, thank you very much.
Reed: That wasn't rehearsed.
Letterman: Ya. Have you been taking these? (Reed nods yes) Well then, I'll wait until a little later. Um anyway, so you were being a fisherman?
Reed: Ya, I came into a fisherman's village once. And, uh, they said to me, what you gotta, you a fisherman boy? Are you a fisherman? So I

thought I've got to wear a boat in order to wear the hats on my head. And wear the boots in my ears.

Letterman: You have a boat too?

Reed: No. I am lying about the wench.

Letterman: I see. I see. Well now we're really getting . . .

Reed: (interrupts) Yes, I have a boat and it has a wench. And I'm a fisherman. And I live over there. And it's wonderful. And I drank 106 pints. And I screwed Lee Marvin at drinking. And I. And we got that out. And that's your research. And jolly good (he angrily claps). Are you going to be bright now?

Letterman: No, I . . . I . . . no, no.

Reed: I thought we were going to talk about movies this stretch?

Letterman: You want to talk about movies?

Reed: I want to talk about *Castaway*.

Letterman: But now you're pissed off, right?

Reed: No, I'm off.

Letterman: OK, so tell me about *Castaway*. You know the woman who wrote the book was actually here. The woman who lived the story was here. (long pause, Reed says nothing) And at the time, I thought it would make a darn good movie. How did it, did it turn out OK?

Reed: Ya well that's for everybody that goes to see the movie to judge for themselves. A lot of people make the mistake of um messing up Lucy Erwin, who played . . .

Letterman: She was the Amanda Donahoe . . .

Reed: That's right. She played Lucy Erwin. And Amanda Donahoe played the part. And myself, Gerald Kingson [sic]. A lot of people mix us up, especially women's libbers. I can't talk for myself. I thought it was, uh, she's got a great body.

Letterman: Uh huh. And briefly the story is, a gentleman wants to . . .

Reed: No, he's no gentleman.

Letterman: Alright, a guy wants to retire to an island. I guess in the South Pacific, off the coast of Australia or New Zealand, or something, roughly?

Reed: Ya, ya.

Letterman: And he runs an ad for a female companion. Isn't that the story?

Reed: Thank you for filling me in.

Letterman: I wasn't filling you in. I was trying to educate the . . . (starts to say audience but Reed cuts him off)

Reed: Oh, it didn't hurt.

Letterman: Well, considering your condition, maybe it wouldn't hurt.

(At this point, Reed pushes his nose so it looks flat like David Letterman's)

Reed: Tell me what my condition's about then?

Letterman: No, it's just a joke.

Reed: No, what's my condition? C'mon.

Letterman: No. No, it's just a joke.

Reed: Oh, a joke is it?

Letterman: Only a joke. And not much of a joke, I'll grant you that. Believe me, I didn't even think it was (he breaks off and looks to his band leader Paul Shaffer). Paul, get over here. (Shaffer puts his hands in the air to show he is passive. Reed takes off his glasses and stares down Letterman). No, no, c'mon no, uh. We have soda and snacks in the green room. And you can have what you want.

Reed: I thought they were there.

Letterman: Alright, so the movie comes out soon. Briefly, shortly, soon?

Reed: Yes, it comes out in New York in, uh. I've got to say all these things and I'm sure that I'm right. It comes out in the beginning of September in New York. And the rest of America, in the end of September. (pause) Can I thank you for being so erudite.

Letterman: Thank you very much, I appreciate your patience here.

If Oliver Reed was the master of his acting he was certainly incapable of controlling his mouth. There was, in Oliver, an almost childlike urge to be the centre of attention. It was the engine behind his talent. For more than twenty years he had done everything possible to cultivate the image of a chauvinistic oaf and almost nothing to dispel it.

Interviewed by a male journalist, Oliver would go to almost any lengths – and frequently beyond – to further his image as the wild man of British cinema. Confronted by a female writer, he would unveil an antediluvian philosophy of marriage and women: 'I believe that my woman shouldn't work outside the home. When I come home and I'm tired from filming all day, I expect her to be there and make sure everything is cooked for me. You know, like drawing my bath and helping me into bed. That's the kind of job she should have and, in return, she can bear my children. And if any man talks bad to her, I'll hit him.' He never believed it, but he convinced anyone listening that he did.

As always there were directors around who remembered Oliver Reed from the old days and were willing to gamble on his reputation and professionalism. Sixteen years after the actor had worked – briefly – for Ken Russell on *Lisztomania* the director approached Oliver with the offer of a part in a film he was making for cable television. It was called *Prisoner of Honor* and Oliver played General Boisdeffre. Watching his old friend on the set, Russell soon noticed that the spark, the erotic promise in Oliver's eyes, had gone out. 'There was always an animal lurking under the surface and the animal had either been tamed or driven out of him,' reflected Russell. 'It wasn't the same Oliver. He was a different man.'

For those who knew Oliver Reed personally – or were astute enough to detect the mischief hidden deep in his pale-blue eyes – it was, quite evidentially, an act. 'I give them what they want,' Oliver admitted. 'I am a professional entertainer. That is what I do to the best of my ability and I give them what they want.'

'They' could be anyone from the owner of a bar or restaurant eager to cash in on Oliver's reflected notoriety or a journalist or photographer willing to embellish the facts for a good headline or freelance cheque.

Confronted by a photographer while enjoying a drink with friends, Oliver could switch from sober to legless without missing a beat. When the slurred banter and spilled drinks were over and the photographer had left he would return to his friends as if the impromptu press call had been nothing more than a trip to the gents'. 'In some perverse way Ollie considered it a duty,' one friend attempts to explain. 'It was as if this shy man had somehow fashioned this grotesque mask and was forced to put it on and act out this drunken fantasy whenever the press or public demanded.'

There were times when the Peter Pan in Oliver – 'I'm stuck somewhere between ten and fifteen' – was not averse to tweaking the nose of a news editor or two. After one quiet lunch with friends Oliver noticed the restaurant manager, who had obviously recognised the actor, talking excitedly into the telephone. 'Watch this,' whispered Oliver. Passing an empty table, he 'accidentally' caught it with his hand, sending the chairs and place settings flying. The next day Britain's biggest tabloid announced, DRUNKEN OLLIE WRECKS RESTAURANT.

'Even if I wanted to make myself seem like a normal human being, I couldn't,' Oliver said philosophically. 'Because that's not what people want me to be. They want a baddy or a carouser or a rake.

'In the movies, it is the person who comes from behind the tree in a mask and a black hat who is really interesting, not the knight in white shining armour. You know he's going to slay the dragon, ride up to the castle, kiss the princess and run away with her.

'I have cultivated the image of a baddy, which is what I will pursue if that is what people wish. That's why, if I go on a chat show, I give them the very thing they want, and sometimes I go over the top.'

Away from Guernsey the Reeds were quickly developing signs of homesickness: Josephine missed the peace and solitude of Petit Houmet and Oliver yearned for his cliff-top walks with the dogs. Each day they would ring the Halls to be reassured and diverted with trivialities and news of the garden, which Richard Hall was digging and replanting. Stopovers in London were always punctuated with interviews and television appearances.

Each week *This Is Your Life* paid tribute to a personality or celebrity. This week the thirty-minute programme was honouring Ron Moody. Among the actor's friends and colleagues, Mark Lester and Oliver Reed, who Lester hadn't seen for more than fifteen years, were invited to reminisce about the making of the Oscar-winning *Oliver!*. As the pair delivered their tribute and took their seats on the stage the 33-year-old Lester was suddenly aware of a 'giant negative wave' from the other guests. 'It was quite obvious nobody wanted to sit next to Oliver.'

After a successful recording the Thames Television hospitality suite should have buzzed with excitement and evaporated adrenaline. Instead the only sound of celebration came from a group of men and women standing near the bar. Mark Lester found the atmosphere slightly unnerving. For several minutes the one-time child star tried to locate the apparent target for his fellow guests' animosity. Oliver, who had quite obviously been drinking in the green room before the show, was left to continue sipping his double brandy alone. It was a situation that reminded Lester of a rowdy and rebellious schoolboy whose antics had become so boring that his classmates wanted nothing to do with him. 'More significantly,' adds Lester, 'he appeared quite content with the situation and wanted nothing to do with them. He had become his own repelling magnet.'

Lester, who had become good friends with Oliver Reed, crossed the room and shook hands with his former co-star. They chatted for about half an hour. Oliver was relaxed and spoke enthusiastically about his Channel Islands home and seemed genuinely interested in Lester's new career as an osteopath – 'he was a perfect gentleman'.

Attempts to ensnare Oliver Reed as a subject in his own right were fraught with danger and ultimately ended in failure, for once not of the actor's doing.

Because *This Is Your Life* was transmitted live on a weekday evening, the biggest problem facing the programme executives was ensuring Oliver was sober. Their only hope was a double bluff. Oliver was asked to make a brief appearance as a guest on a show highlighting the life of Michael Winner. 'The theory was that, as it was me, and we had been friends for so long, he might just stay off the booze,' recalls the director. However Oliver and Winner and the other guests finally arrived at the studio only to be told the programme had been scrapped because of an electricians' strike.

Back on Guernsey, Ivy Hall was preparing for the couple's return with a batch of Oliver's favourite pasties. Her husband was putting the finishing touches to the garden and had still found no trace of Josephine's missing jewellery, lost some time before. After a particularly heated late-night row Oliver had grabbed a spade and, in the pitch black, buried the expensive collection of bracelets, necklaces and rings. The next morning, sober and full of remorse, he could not remember where the hole was.

The garden surrounding Petit Houmet covered several acres. Beyond the lawn at the back of the house and hidden by trees was a second, rougher, pasture and a pond fed by rockface waterfalls, beside which stood a nine-foot wrought-iron 'bird cage'. Oliver would tell friends, 'That's where Josephine goes when she's naughty.' Richard Hall had spent the time tidying this hidden garden, planting shrubs and laying new borders. Oliver took one look at his week's work and announced, 'No, no, I don't want it like that. There are too many straight lines. It's like a bloody parade ground.'

Oliver had been a committed and competitive vegetable grower since his first Wimbledon house, and his horticultural ideas were always unconventional. At Broome Hall he had ordered the destruction of a lawn and prize rose beds occupying a site he considered ideal for potatoes. And at the front of Petit Houmet, on a plot expected to welcome new visitors, he dumped four tons of steaming manure to grow his exhibition marrows.

Unlike the gentry and nouveau riche of Surrey, the Guernsey islanders were far less forgiving. Oliver's initial approach to buy an adjoining lake received tacit approval from the neighbours. When word got out he wanted to build a bar in the middle and ferry guests across in a boat the sale was swiftly vetoed.

In many ways Oliver remained supremely naïve to fallout from his lifetime of hellraising. Two decades after his exploits first hit the headlines, and ignoring his recent press as a gentler married man, many top London hotels and restaurants still operated a polite but firm ban.

Visiting London on their way home from filming, the Reeds checked into the Washington Hotel. That afternoon the telephone rang in Stephen Ford's Gloucester Place apartment. 'Steve, tonight I want to go to a restaurant. A good restaurant.'

'OK, Oliver,' said Ford. 'Where do you want to go?'

'The Savoy,' announced Oliver.

'Right,' said Ford, already dubious of the outcome. 'You make the booking and call me back.'

A few minutes later the telephone rang again. 'Steve, it's Monday night and they were full. I can't believe it, they're full.'

'That's unfortunate,' said Ford. 'What's your second choice, Oliver?'

Oliver thought for a moment and then suggested the Connaught. The phone rang a third time. 'Bloody amazing,' grumbled Oliver. 'They're full up too. Well where do you want to go?'

Ford suggested Harvey's, an exclusive Wandsworth restaurant where the chef-patron was Marco Pierre White. 'Oh yes,' said Oliver with enthusiasm, 'he's the guy who plays football on the common with his staff. Brilliant idea, we'll go there.'

This time Ford, who knew how difficult it was for anyone to get a reservation at the Bellevue Road establishment, coached his friend on tactics. Oliver telephoned the restaurant. 'This is a well-known actor who would like to speak to a well-known chef,' he said to the maître d'. A few seconds later Pierre White came on the line to be informed: 'Oliver Reed here, I'm coming to dinner tonight.'

'Sorry, Mr Reed,' said the startled chef. 'We are booked for six months.'

'Don't give me that PR shit,' countered a well-rehearsed Reed. 'We're coming, right?'

Silence. 'What time are you coming and how many of you?'

'There will be four of us and we'll arrive by taxi at nine,' said Oliver, ominously adding, 'Don't let us down.'

As they stepped out of the cab, Pierre White greeted them with a magnum of champagne. His restaurant did not escape entirely undamaged. As Oliver plunged himself into an armchair the legs snapped, sending him somersaulting into a floral display.

The meal arrived accompanied by several bottles of very expensive wine – 'it doesn't matter how much, Lou Grade is paying' – and Oliver took a few indifferent mouthfuls. It was too much for the chef to stand. 'What's wrong with it? What's wrong with it?' he demanded.

'Nothing,' said Oliver.

'Don't you like it?'

'Yes,' said Oliver.

'Well, people don't leave my food.'

'I do,' said Oliver.

The evening ended with Pierre White's amazed clientele watching one of Britain's top chefs arm wrestling one of the country's equally famous actors.

Chapter Nineteen

'I like everything I'm not. I like gentle people and puppies. I like softness because life is so hard.'

OLIVER'S SEVEN-YEAR SKIRMISH WITH REG PRINCE was coming to a head. During the second week in December 1993 he and Josephine flew from their Guernsey home to London. Two days later, on Monday 13 December, the actor stepped into the High Court witness box after rejecting a last-minute suggestion he deposit a six-figure sum prior to an out-of-court settlement. 'I insisted I wanted to fight this case to the very end,' said Oliver.

Prince arrived at the High Court claiming the back injuries he suffered during the Seychelles incident had made him dependent on a walking stick and forced him into retirement. Oliver, he alleged, had either been deliberate and reckless in his lack of care or, far worse, purposefully negligent.

The hearing lasted four days. Both men repeated their version of events. Asked how he thought his one-time friend may have suffered the spinal fractures, Oliver suggested it may have happened the night of the restaurant incident. Prince had gone to fetch a bottle of champagne. 'After about seven or eight minutes we heard the slapping noise of flesh on concrete and then a cry,' he told the court. 'Reg then came into the bungalow and said, "Cor, I think I have done my back in – but I've saved the champagne." '

Late on Thursday the judge, Mr Justice Owen, returned to dismiss Prince's claim for damages. After so much drink, and after so much time, he felt neither man could recall exactly what took place. 'It may be – as may be the case with Mr Reed

– that now, through the mists and vapours of drink, he [Prince] doesn't know what the truth is.'

The months of legal wrangling and four days in court cost Oliver more than £50,000. 'I'd like to think a reconciliation is possible,' said Oliver. 'But I don't know. A lot of mud has been slung.' Prince, too, admitted, 'I hold nothing against, Ollie. I believe he didn't realise when he tipped me up that he would damage my spine.' The pair never spoke again.

Josephine, who too often found herself in Prince's cross-fire, was less magnanimous. 'Reg Prince always used Oliver's image because he was a well-known figure and it was to Reg's advantage,' she said. 'The years running up to the court case were unpleasant and sad, but they didn't affect us as a couple.'

Oliver emerged from the court victorious, but with his honesty – at least his version of the truth – tarnished. That night, his face pocked and puffy, he held court in the bar of the Langham Hilton Hotel in Portland Place and said, 'I am the last of a dying breed – who is going to carry on after me?'

Two days later Dillie Keane, writing in the *Mail on Sunday*, answered his question. One of his more eloquent admirers, Keane reflected on the star's dissolute life:

Poor old Ollie: he appears before us like a monument to sozzlement, a Hogarthian example of debauchery's perils, a wasted talent and a waste of space.

And I, for one, love him for it. Yes, I love the binges, the brawls, and the ridiculous stories of his tattoo. I love the way he really doesn't care what the world thinks of him. I'm sorry for Reg Prince and his damaged back, but it doesn't stop me admiring Ollie, because he's absolutely and relentlessly his own man.

The world needs Oliver Reed. Well, he's the last great bad boy, a lone, shining beacon in the long dark night of political correctness. Richard Burton and John Bindon are dead, Richard Harris has had to reform to stay alive, Anthony Hopkins is a campaigner for Alcoholics Anonymous, Mel Gibson suffers horrible remorse, and Bruce Willis doesn't count. No, only Ollie still raises hell day in, day out.

The new heroes are self-denying ascetics who go to find themselves in Tibet, or victims of abuse who've fought through their difficulties with tremendous strength. New heroes are little fascists who preach against fox-hunting and smoking, and proselytise on behalf of veganism, teetotallism, 'outing' and therapy. I bet you Ollie's never had therapy. He'd give you a fat lip if you so much as suggested it. That's because Oliver Reed is the last mad musketeer in an increasingly prim and boring world, the only Cavalier in a mob of Roundheads.

He drinks, he swears, he often behaves badly, he undoubtedly eats raw steak and I'm sure he tells offensive jokes. And he's an old male chauvinist who loves rugby and boxing and other 'unacceptable' sports. But if he's sometimes a bore and a boor, he's probably very good fun quite a lot of the time.

I'd much rather get hung over with Ollie Reed than discuss cabinet-making with Harrison Ford, or be bored witless with Kevin Costner.

Oliver's reputation for drinking did not go unnoticed by advertisers. One lucrative contract that winter was a television commercial for Alka Seltzer, a proprietary hangover remedy he had made use of on more than one occasion. The following year the company would hire Oliver again, this time for a telephone hotline. 'A quick plink-plink-fizz will stop the reindeers dancing in your head,' he growled at callers.

Two decades earlier, Southsea pier was destroyed by fire during location shooting for *Tommy*. The owners of Blackpool Tower had no intention of losing one of Britain's most popular seaside landmarks to misadventures of a film crew. As part of the pre-filming negotiations the producers of *Funny Bones* were forced not only to take out multimillion pound damage and loss-of-earnings insurance on the structure, but also agree to have a fire appliance and crew on constant stand-by.

The Reeds arrived in Blackpool on the last Friday in April 1994. For the actor it was his first visit to the Lancashire resort – his only previous sortie north had been to the Lake District while filming with Ken Russell. 'I'm here for the fresh air and fish and chips and mushy peas,' Oliver announced to a waiting reporter. 'I'm the same as any other visitor – except I am working as well.'

For Oliver, whose filming schedule lasted just under a month, his conversations with the local press far outshone his dialogue. Punctuated by one-liners – 'But you gave them all the money?' – and crowd scenes, his time on screen totalled just 136 seconds. His screen credit, in order of appearance, was little better – 26th after Sniff the dog.

His role, as Dolly Hopkins, an effeminate but vicious funfair owner and mobster, gave the film a near-silent yet malevolent undercurrent. He was cast against type, but the director and co-writer, Peter Chelsom, explained, 'Oliver Reed has a tremendous presence and to cast him as this very precious, terribly neurotic character was taking him into an area as an actor that he had never played before.'

It was Oliver's second gay character of his career, but sporting long grey hair tied back in a ponytail and wearing a yellow kaftan it was a career and a half since Oliver flounced in and out of *The League of Gentlemen*. His attention to detail was still as acute – 'We toyed with the idea of a full pigtail, but settled on a ponytail, less sinister and more camp.'

While painters gave the metalwork above its first coat the Tower Circus was transformed into a film set. Shooting lasted a month. As ever Oliver remained sober and concentrated and made the local headlines only once – when the regulars of a Garstang pub complained he had drunk its entire stock of imported lager.

Finding yourself face to face with Oliver and his reputation could be a daunting – and revealing – experience. The first impression was how much older he seemed than in his pictures or television appearances. The second was that he was surprisingly nervous, not an unattractive trait because he hinted that he had never grown blasé by his celebrity.

Oliver Reed, like his grandfather, found it almost impossible to differentiate between dukes and dustmen, cabbies and counts – all deserved his equal attention. In her biography of Beerbohm Tree, Madeleine Bingham claims he was forever 'skeptical of appearances, and on that account had a penetrating insight into the real character of people . . . he was instantly able to sum up men and women.' A description just as appropriate to his grandson.

For Oliver every encounter with a stranger was a human occasion. It was not unusual for him to be seen helping the handyman wash the windows of a hotel in which he was paying for the most expensive suite, not through boredom, but simply because he was interested in the man and what he had to say.

There was a confusion in Oliver's personality which he could ground only through contact with other human beings – confiding some of his deepest thoughts and self-questioning doubts to complete strangers. 'I think he confused himself,' offers Simon Reed. 'His ego confused him, the ill-education, the dyslexia with intelligence, Ollie could never understand – or appreciate – how intelligent he really was. To most people he was incredibly intelligent, incredibly intuitive and incredibly sensitive.'

In 1963 Fiona Adams was a photographer taking celebrity pictures for some of Britain's biggest-selling magazines. One of her assignments that summer was to shoot Oliver Reed on the set of the Hammer swashbuckler, *The Scarlet Blade*. Thirty years later, and after a career travelling the world, Adams was commissioned to take some more pictures of the star – this time by Oliver himself.

Josephine telephoned Adams at her St Pierre du Bois studio to arrange a session. Aware of her subject's reputation, the photographer tactfully asked when Oliver would be at his most accommodating. 'Eleven o'clock in the morning is usually his best time,' said Josephine.

Adams drove across the island to Petit Houmet to find the actor charming and his house a photographer's nightmare. It was, she recalls, a mishmash of period styles and very dark, 'sinister in its own way, with great velvet curtains keeping the light out of the living room'. Oliver explained he was about to leave for Canada and needed a new set of informal publicity pictures. During the photo session, which progressed from the conservatory to the 'play room' above the garage, Oliver talked openly about his private life and marriage.

'I'm sorry,' said Adams, 'I've been abroad and there are some gaps in my knowledge of your career.'

'You know I have this very young wife?' Adams nodded. 'Well it has all worked out really well. Sometimes I don't know how she puts up with me, but she does, and I love her very much for it.'

The photo session, which Oliver mistakenly claimed was the first time he had ever commissioned his own publicity pictures, produced Josephine and the family's favourite portrait: slightly scruffy, hair too long and sporting designer stubble, the man of the photograph gives the impression of an independent yet still handsome Oliver. His eyes, still possessing the depth that made him a sex symbol, are fixed and in control.

Cutthroat Island was Renny Harlin's tenth film. As director-producer he had already cast his Oscar-winning wife, Geena Davis, to play the female lead in the seventeenth-century pirate adventure. Finding – and keeping – a leading man was harder work.

Harlin's first choice was Sean Connery. When the original Bond star was unavailable the Finnish-born director, whose previous blockbusters included *Nightmare on Elm Street 4* and *Die Hard 2*, continued his search for a 'bankable' British actor. When Harlin approached Oliver Reed with a six-figure deal the actor eagerly agreed to play Davis's screen uncle Mordachai.

Although the majority of the film would be shot in Hollywood, Harlin decided the sea and storm sequences should be staged in the giant tip-tanks at Malta's Rinella Film Studios, the same tanks in which Oliver made *Christopher Columbus* eleven years earlier.

Oliver flew into Malta's Luqa Airport on 12 November 1994. The following day, a Sunday, he spent lunchtime with Lino Cassar, a film critic and former managing director of the Rinella Studios. 'He was very excited about his latest film,' recalls Cassar. 'Very eager to give a good performance.' The pair arranged to meet for a formal interview later that evening after Oliver had had dinner with his fellow cast members and the film's executives. By the time the writer arrived at the St Julian's Bay hotel the dinner was still under way.

The next morning Oliver awoke to the sound of knocking on his hotel suite door. A bellboy handed him an envelope. He read one phrase over and over again '. . . inappropriate behaviour related to alcohol'. He had been sacked from *Cutthroat Island* for an incident he could barely remember.

Three hours later – just as Oliver should have been attending a costume fitting – he was ensconced in the executive lounge on the first floor of Luqa Airport awaiting a flight back to Britain. A Carolco spokesman, Peter Haas, was less reticent about meeting the press. Announcing the actor's departure he said, 'Oliver Reed was drunk and offensive. It was not a difficult decision to ask him to leave.'

By Wednesday the story had made the British and Irish newspapers. The *Sun* carried its own 'exclusive' version of the incident:

Outrageous Ollie stunned a posh restaurant by stripping down to baggy flannel underpants.

As guests choked on their champagne he was persuaded not to flash his willy, which sports an eagle's talons design.

Ollie – who revels in exhibiting his 'mighty mallet' – downed wine and vodka before throwing off his shirt and dropping his trousers.

One onlooker said: 'Everyone braced themselves for the worst. The men around him told Ollie he mustn't go any further and calmed him down.

'He sat their smirking at a table with baggy grey undies covering his bulging backside. He had a beard which made him look menacing. Virtually all the people left, including Geena [Davis] and her husband. They were clearly not impressed.'

The truth, according to Cassar, was very different – far less offensive than the *Achille Lauro* episode.

Keeping his appointment with Oliver, he had not been allowed into the function room. 'I sat and watched the dinner from the bar,' explains the sixty-year-old writer. 'Ollie, as ever, seemed very jovial and was drinking no more than anyone else. Toward the end of the meal he stood up and unbuttoned and removed his shirt. That was all. There was no commotion and no outrage. In fact most people took it as Ollie just being Ollie.'

Taking Oliver Reed for granted was becoming a habit with the majority of the world's press, and the British newspapers in particular. 'I don't resent them reporting me getting thrown out of restaurants, landing in jail or being smashed in the face by a jealous husband,' he would admit in a more thoughtful moment. 'What annoys me is that they often write about the violence and ignore any wit or charm. Some journalists deliberately misquote me, others make the whole thing up.'

In the autumn of 1993 Oliver was once again approached by Channel 4, this time to see if he would consider being a subject for its 'Obituary Show'. It was a risk for any personality. As the name suggested, not only was the victim expected to appraise his or her own life from an imaginary heaven, but a variety of guests would also pass judgement on the personal and professional life of the 'deceased'. Oliver, who had long since given up caring what people thought of him, readily agreed.

Screened as part of a *Without Walls* series, the programme opened with the first of more than thirty celebrity sound bites, each, in its own way, defining the compass points of Oliver's life.

Oliver Reed was the ham from Hammer who graduated to acting, rose like a sky rocket in about six movies, then fell very ignominiously to earth.

– Sue Heal

He was a drinking man's icon, he was a hellraiser par excellence and he will be remembered as such.

– Gary Bushell

When I heard that he had died I felt that we had lost a fine actor, but not a man who had done very much for relations between men and women.

– Helena Kennedy

Characters are not thick on the ground and he was one big character.

– Jack Tinker

By the end of the programme Oliver's life had taken some serious knocks, but the majority – nineteen for, thirteen against – regretted his demise. Far more chilling was the actor's prophesy of his own death: 'I died in a bar of a heart attack, full of laughter . . . And somebody made a bet with me that was so lewd that I took it on and he shook my hand and I laughed so much I was sick and died.' Six years later Oliver would collapse and die of a heart attack in a laughter-filled Maltese bar.

His wake and funeral – over which he did have more control – was equally accurate: 'It was wonderful and the only thing I regret about my funeral was the fact that I couldn't go to my own wake, because it was a wonderful party and every time I kept tapping somebody on the shoulder they didn't know I was there.'

The *Obituary Show* was broadcast on Tuesday, 22 February 1994, the week after Oliver's 56th birthday. To publicise the programme he agreed to a 'My Kind of Day' interview for the *Radio Times*. It is a brief and surprisingly honest account of how 'insular' the Reeds' life at Petit Houmet had become.

I will tell you my idea of a good evening. In bed by 6.30 p.m. with a cheese sandwich, my four dogs around me and Radio 4 on. I listen to the radio all the time, partly to block out the buzz of my tinnitus, the ringing in my ears and screaming in my head that I've suffered for years. The dogs don't sleep in the bedroom, but they crash in first thing. That's fine – except when I'm having an attack of gout and they leap on my feet.

I have places all over the world – Barbados, Ireland, Reykjavik, Zimbabwe, Scotland – but home is in Guernsey, 25 miles from St Peter Port. My wife Josephine and I have lived there for 14 years and I loved the place as soon as I saw it. I felt immediately that it was for me. It's an amazing island, so delicate. It has its own decency, its own literacy. It's like being back in 1942 – but without the war. I've found extraordinary peace there.

We're very insular. We live in a 1947 red-brick house with a large garden, a dovecote we built from old teak (we're trying to get two fantails into it), a swimming pool, the dogs and a marmalade cat. I've always had dogs and these four are my great, great friends – Tweeg the lurcher, Generali (an Italian truffle hound), a border terrier called Curlygirly and another little terrier, Bigsyboy from Biggleswade.

I take them for a walk on the beach every morning, then come back and make sure the gardener is looking after my medlar, a wonderful fruit tree that produces a fruit rather like a small brown apple and needs to be cosseted like a prima ballerina. Josephine will probably be doing something in the garden, too, and when we go in she'll cook lunch – venison if we're feeling posh and then pears in red wine. We seem to be besotted by that.

In the afternoon I'll take the dogs out again or get Josephine to turn on the sauna or cool the beer in the pub. I have my own bar which I've built over the garage. Members only. About three days a week I don't drink at all but, when I do drink, I drink. Lager, bitter, vodka, crème de menthe, whatever.

The *Sun* once reported that I had only two years to live but, as that was in 1987, I reckon I must be all right. The only thing that's different between my drinking and non-drinking days is that my dogs get confused: I'm faster when I'm not drinking.

I never read a book or a paper because I'm dyslexic. It's bad enough trying to learn a script. I just read it very slowly. But I'm a professional listener and, as the radio is on all day, I'm well up with the news. Exercise? Not much, apart from walking and taking out my lobster boat, the *Ollie Jo*. Nobody sane swims. I'd rather keep afloat.

In the evenings we eat in. We don't have enough posh friends in Guernsey to have roast potatoes but, luckily, I like working-class food and I can't wait for a squeak up – bubble and squeak is my favourite. If I cook, which isn't often, it's usually spaghetti bolognese with all the leftovers chucked in and plenty of garlic. I don't go for fancy wines, either. Something acidic, spiked up with a drop of something else, is fine by me.

My day ends when it gets dark – I really don't want to go out after dark. I put the TV on for Sky Sports – my brother Simon is a commentator for them, and I watch Katarina Witt and anything that England does, whatever the sport – and CNN. Then it's off to bed and the radio. I have the World Service on all through the night and never have any difficulty sleeping. Josephine has grown so used to it now that she can't sleep unless the radio is going. That's one of the niceties of love.

Painkillers had long since replaced alcohol to ensure Oliver a comfortable night. Sleep was something he could dip in and out of, catching the hourly repeats of the World Service news or snatches of obscure programmes. He rarely dreamed. When he did they were invariably twin nightmares he had suffered on and off for more than twenty years. Like the psychiatrist studying Oliver's youth, they provided intriguing material.

In the first there was a huge black fly crawling across the ceiling above his head. He would watch it grow – 'as big as your fist, and then as big as your head' – the buzz of its wings getting louder and louder. Suddenly it would drop. Before it reached him, Oliver would be awake. 'The fly never reaches me, but I know if it ever did I would die; smothered; dead.' When he eventually fell back to sleep the second nightmare would arrive. He would be studying a laboratory jar. As he got closer he could see two round objects preserved in the liquid. At first he would think they were peeled white onions. In a millisecond would come the realisation that he was inspecting his own testicles and with that the gasping shock would wake him. 'That is the real frightener,' admitted Oliver. 'That one puts the fear of God in me.'

By 1995 the obligatory pre-contract insurance medical demanded by producers had assumed their own significance in Oliver's life. Having received the all-clear for his guest appearance in *Russisch Roulette*, the actor telephoned his confidant Stephen Ford. 'You think I'm dying, don't you Ford?' There was no greeting, no preamble. 'You think I'm an old fart. Well, I've just had a medical and I'm much fitter than you: heart one hundred per cent; liver one hundred per cent; lungs one hundred per cent.' End of call.

For Oliver, who hated telephones, it was a typical conversation. When he finished talking, he finished the call, recalls

Ford. 'I wouldn't hear from him for weeks and then, out of the blue, boom, boom, boom, and he would put the phone down – whether you had finished speaking or not.'

A few months later on his return from Minsk, where filming had been taking place, the 57-year-old actor demonstrated his apparent health with equal zeal. Inviting Oliver to his fourth-floor apartment, Ford warned his friend that the front of the Gloucester Place property was encased in scaffolding while builders rectified a structural fault. 'Great,' said Oliver. 'Sounds like fun.'

Two hours later Oliver had still not arrived. Suddenly Ford was aware of someone knocking on his skylight. It was Oliver. Armed with an eight-pack of beer, which he distributed to the workmen on his way up, the actor had climbed eighty feet up the scaffolding and over the roof. For the next four days Oliver insisted they use his 'adventure playground' entrance to the flat, poo-pooing Ford's claims of vertigo and abject terror. On one ascent he stopped off to lay a course of sixty bricks.

By early 1995 the Reeds agreed it was time to quit Guernsey. Josephine, by now in her mid-thirties, had become a passionate and accomplished rider. A search of the south of England for a property with suitable stables and grazing proved unsuccessful. Oliver suggested Ireland, his 'spiritual home' since the late 1950s.

The move was clinched when the couple discovered Castle McCarthy, a former parish priest's home near Churchtown. The £200,000 asking price included eighteen acres of Cork countryside. 'It seemed to me that, before my wife got too old, she should be allowed to do what *she* liked to do,' admitted Oliver, who, dressed in waterproofs and green wellingtons, was equally at peace overseeing the maintenance of his new domain and touring the pubs of Churchtown and Mallow.

In Ireland, poorer and a good deal wiser than he had ever been, Oliver returned to playing the benevolent nineteenth-century squire, adopting animals and human friends with equal sincerity. When he sensed his horse was lonely he adopted Scratchy the donkey from a local sanctuary. For the second time in his life Oliver provided financial and moral support for a promising young professional boxer, this time Oliver O'Dea. And, when he heard a radio interview by the parents of a girl born with no arms or legs, Oliver pledged his support for a £90,000 fund to build her a specially adapted house. 'Ollie never wanted to wear a halo above his head,' admitted a neighbour. 'He simply believed that if you said thank you to someone just once a day you would not die screaming.'

Sarah Reed also noticed the change in her father: 'Ireland made him feel very happy because everyone took him at face value. They didn't give a hoot about who or what he was – he was Ollie and he was a little bit eccentric and because of that he fitted in perfectly.'

Meanwhile, Josephine cooked and baked, listened and laughed, as ever correcting her husband's exaggerations and keeping track of his business and their joint expenses. As her husband's manager and personal assistant, Josephine brought a quiet order and discipline to his life. It was her opinion he sought when a new script arrived, and it was left to Josephine to negotiate the contract and settle on a fee – one million dollars for *Gladiator* – and make all the travel arrangements. When they arrived on set Josephine ensured the dressing room and facilities were worthy of her star husband and kept him relaxed and happy between takes by reading passages to him from her favourite books.

It was on these trips away from Castle McCarthy, and on open view to friends and journalists, that Oliver's dependence on his wife shone through. They were – the man in his late fifties and the woman in her early thirties – more than just a married couple. Each, in his or her own way, relied totally on the other: one to give and one to take.

Unfamiliar doors and cupboards needed to be opened and, in strange hotel bedrooms, it was Josephine who would switch on the television or retune the radio. On a rare occasion when Oliver travelled alone he telephoned Josephine at home in Ireland to ask how the video in his Californian hotel suite worked. Studying a menu, Oliver would instinctively hand his long-focus glasses to his wife, who would have his reading glasses open and ready. Ollie was always an impressive orderer, but a picky eater, so it was Josephine who secretly wrapped his leftovers in a napkin and slid them into her handbag; upsetting the chef had become a long-running neurosis.

When Oliver held court it was Josephine who hinted at looming boredom by flapping a hand over an exaggerated yawn or gently corrected an obvious error in her sensible, quiet way.

'What?' he would ask. 'May I speak?'

'Well you were going on a bit,' she would say.

'I can behave myself,' Oliver would counter. 'I can shut up. I can shut up for hours at a time.'

'Of course you can,' his wife would agree, smiling sweetly. 'Of course you can.'

The horror of reading a script, at least in rehearsal, never left Oliver. Studios or dubbing booths, where he was surrounded by fellow actors and technicians with whom he could laugh and joke, were only slightly less nerve-racking. Three decades earlier he had found the experience of narrating *Always on Sunday* a 'very painful and embarrassing way to earn a fee'. Now Ken Russell wanted him to do it again. Oliver remained hesitant but finally, with Josephine's encouragement, agreed to take the part of Aleister Crowley for the BBC Radio 3 premiere in 1995 of Russell's play, *The Death of Alexander Scriabin*. It was, at least for Oliver, his first time in a radio drama and a 'new and exciting' experience and proved that his fear of script reading was, in part, unfounded. The play was broadcast on Sunday, 18 June, while Oliver was in Scotland filming *The Bruce*.

On Friday, 9 May 1997 a telephone call informed Oliver that his father was dead. Since moving to Guernsey and then Ireland, Oliver had telephoned Peter almost weekly. Sometimes the calls would last less than five minutes, sometimes almost an hour. If there was a horse running that interested Oliver he would ask his father's opinion, quizzing him on bloodlines and staying power and track conditions. In a perverse way the increasing physical distance between them was bringing father and son closer together. Several times over the weekend Oliver told friends about the last time he had seen his father. He had arrived unannounced at Peter's home with several friends. As they were leaving Peter took his son aside and said that if he came round again could he make sure he was sober and would he not bring his drunken friends? 'I brought them because I'm proud of you,' said Oliver. His father shook his head and turned away.

The following Monday the *Sporting Life* noted his passing with a brief page-seven news story:

Peter Reed, the former racing journalist, has died at 85.

He was formerly Groom of the *Greyhound Express* and contributed to the *Evening News, The Sporting Life Guide* and *Sporting Chronicle Handicap Book*.

Reed, who died last Friday, was the father of actor Oliver Reed and broadcaster Simon, and was also the brother of the late film director, Sir Carol Reed.

Oliver's only English-released film of 1998 was *Parting Shots*, a light-hearted comedy produced and directed by Michael Winner. It was 34 years since the pair had first worked together. In that time they had made six films and spent more than three hundred hours facing each other across the camera.

'*Parting Shots* had been on my mind for some time,' Winner recalls. 'An affair with a girl had ended and she behaved particularly badly. I thought I would like to kill her! From this we developed the idea that it would be quite funny to tell a story about someone who was unlikely to live very long and decided to take the opportunity to kill five or six of the people who most annoyed and hurt them during their life.'

Winner collaborated on the script with Nick Mead and turned down a Hollywood offer to take over the project. To fill the cast list he turned to his friends. The composer and singer Chris Rea was recruited to play the dying wedding photographer, Harry Sterndale. Other leads went to Felicity Kendal, John Cleese, Bob Hoskins, Diana Rigg, Ben Kingsley, Joanna Lumley and Gareth Hunt.

When Sterndale – who has already added his school bully and his grasping ex-wife to his hit list – discovers he can boost his life-insurance payout by dying a violent death he hires a professional killer to end his life. Winner's masterstroke was using Oliver as the ageing hit man Jamie Campbell-Stewart.

Filming for *Parting Shots* started in August 1997 and lasted two-and-a-half months. Before sending Oliver his contract, Winner telephoned the actor at his Irish home. 'This is a nice movie. Everybody involved is very sweet,' Winner explained. Visions of Oliver's *Big Sleep* drunkenness and his Chorley Wood indecent exposure were still fresh in the director's mind.

'Oliver, I am sixty-four years old. I have had heart trouble,' he said. 'I can't take the strain of you being drunk on the set. If you feel this is a problem, you must not do the movie, because we have a perfect relationship and the one thing I don't want to do is sour it after so many years.' Oliver, who seemed genuinely remorseful, promised to keep his drinking to a minimum. Overweight and out of condition, yet supremely confident, he kept his promise and delivered his scenes with sinister menace.

The duration of Oliver Reed's fellowship with Winner followed a distinct and disintegrating pattern. Between films – and there had been six – there was silence. As shooting got closer, the actor would telephone – always in working hours – to query a detail or something in the script. Once the film was made, the calls became drunken and erratic, trailing off over a few months as if Oliver's attention had shifted to another plain.

With *Parting Shots* in postproduction, Oliver had taken to calling Winner late in the evening, and once or twice at three in the morning. The conversations always started the same: 'I love you, Michael. I really think you're wonderful,' Oliver would slur into the telephone.

'That's very nice, Oliver,' Winner would say. 'Is Josephine there?'

The handset would then be passed to the actor's wife and Winner and Josephine would chat for a few minutes, with the drunken Oliver shouting thoughts and messages in the background. Suddenly, from four hundred miles away in Ireland, Winner could hear the dull thud of his friend hitting the floor. 'I've got to go,' Josephine would say. 'Oliver needs me.'

* * *

Christmas 1998 was happy and relaxed. By January a strange fatalism had settled over Oliver's life. Some of his closest friends and associates sensed a change they had never noticed before: he seemed eager to rebuild broken bridges. In one bar the landlord caught him clutching his chest, bent almost double with the pain. 'Indigestion,' said Oliver. 'Just indigestion.' When the moment was right, and away from Josephine, he would ask his closest friends, 'Do you get these pains in your chest?'

In February of the following year Oliver heard the news that his one-time agent Dennis Selinger had died and flew to England to attend the funeral. It was an ideal opportunity, Michael Winner thought, to get the actor to tidy up some noisy *Parting Shots* lines. An air-conditioning unit in one pub scene could just be heard behind the actor's voice; it was almost unnoticeable, but to the perfectionist Winner it had an irritating rough edge. Winner arranged for Oliver to call at his house and speak the lines into a tape recorder; they would then be dubbed on to the film soundtrack.

On the morning of Oliver's visit, Winner telephoned the actor's Hampstead hotel. 'I'm sorry,' said the receptionist. 'Mr Reed did not stay here last night. He arrived, but went out and got blind drunk and got himself arrested. He never came back.'

Winner telephoned Hampstead police station. 'I understand my friend Mr Reed spent the night with you,' he told the custody officer.

'We've just released him,' said the sergeant. 'He was arrested at ten o'clock for being drunk and disorderly, but we haven't charged him because he was so charming.'

A few minutes later, Oliver's taxi pulled up outside Winner's Knightsbridge house. He looked tired and repentant; his voice was rough and unusable. As he was leaving, Oliver turned to his friend and admitted, 'You know, I mustn't travel without Josephine. She looks after me.'

Rested by a holiday in Scotland, Oliver made the surprise announcement that he intended to retire. 'It is time to slow down and grow old gracefully,' he admitted. 'I would prefer to go out acting, buzzing like a bumble bee, instead of a rated has-been.' Unknown to Oliver, British television executives already had other ideas.

Within weeks Yorkshire Television issued a four-paragraph press release. It was headed OLIVER REED STARS IN NEW YTV DRAMA and read:

> Internationally renowned actor Oliver Reed is joining Yorkshire Television to head the cast of a new six-part drama, from the team that created the ratings-hit series *The Darling Buds of May*.
>
> *My Uncle Silas*, written by *Buds* creator HE Bates, is set in the summer of 1900 and centres around the exploits of Uncle Silas played by Reed.
>
> 'We are all excited about this new project and very much hope it will have some of the charm and enchant-ment of *The Darling Buds of May*,' says YTV's controller of comedy drama and features David Reynolds.
>
> *My Uncle Silas* is a Yorkshire Television production associated with Excelsior. The executive producers are David Reynolds, Philip Burley and Richard Bates, the eldest son of the story's creator.

It would be the first series Oliver had made for British television and the first time he had worked on a small-screen drama since the early sixties.[1]

---

[1] Following Oliver Reed's death Yorkshire Television shelved *My Uncle Silas*.

Chapter Twenty

'I've been to some fearsome wakes and I've had some fearsome hangovers burying the dead.'

T HE MALTESE WORDS FOR MADNESS (*genn*) and genius (*genju*) are confusingly similar. Arriving for his third visit to the Mediterranean island, Oliver Reed would prove the difference with fatal consequences.

In many ways the enclosing circle Oliver felt about his life was also true of his career. Several times before accepting the *Gladiator* contract he sought the reassurance of Michael Winner, the producer to whom he owed his first international success. 'I've got an interview with Ridley Scott and he wants me to read,' Oliver confessed to the producer-director on the telephone from Ireland.

'Oliver, read,' said Winner. 'You've got to capitalise on *Parting Shots*. If you have to read, do it.'

'It's an insult. I feel like a bit player.'

'Never mind all that shit, Oliver,' persisted Winner, 'if he wants you to read, read.' The conversation was repeated three times before Oliver agreed to meet the 62-year-old Scott and fly to England.

But Scott took an equal amount of persuading to employ Oliver Reed. During the autumn of 1998 he interviewed Oliver three times before satisfying himself the actor could not only deliver a good performance – 'something I was sure he was capable of' – but also stay out of trouble. In the end Oliver was offered the part of Proximo, an ageing former gladiator, and a million-dollar fee.

Gladiator is set in Rome in the year AD 180. Emperor Marcus Aurelius is dying a slow death and his one wish is that his true son, Commodus, should continue his dream of building a Roman Republic. When the ailing Aurelius realises his son is too consumed with the lust for power the emperor adopts his favourite general, Maximus, as a son and announces he will be crowned Caesar instead. When Commodus learns of his father's plans he plots to have Maximus sold into slavery. Still in captivity, the former soldier is spotted by the owner of a combat school called Proximo and, after extra tutorial attention, fights his way from provincial arenas to Rome's Colosseum.

The majority of the $120-million epic would be shot in Malta in 1999. Six months before the cast and crew arrived on the Mediterranean island a team of three hundred British and Maltese craftsmen started work on a near life-size replica of the Colosseum. Other sets included an authentic Roman palace, a forum and a gladiator school. The site chosen for the set was Fort Ricasoli, on the island's northeast coast, and just across the Grand Harbour from Valletta. Several scenes from *Raise the Titanic* were also shot in and around the seventeenth-century fortifications.

While Scott was directing the first *Gladiator* location shots in England – and not far from Broome Hall – his casting director was facing an equally mammoth task: auditioning 22,000 Maltese extras. Training and costume fitting began as Oliver joined the team for three weeks shooting in Morocco and North Africa. By the time Scott and the cast arrived in Malta on 22 March the thousands of part-time actors and actresses were ready to start filming.

Oliver and Josephine were booked into one of the Hotel Le Meridian Phoenicia's harbour-view suites. Set in its own private gardens, the five-star Phoenicia has, for decades, advertised itself as Malta's most luxurious and famous hotel. The opening paragraph of Nicholas Monsarrat's wartime novel, *The Kappillan of Malta*, was written in one of its rooms:

The man in the bar of the Phoenicia Hotel, by the main gate of Valletta, gave me more information, in the space of two hours, than even six gins and tonics could really satisfy. He was a fattish, pinkish man in bulging blue shorts; a man on a long lazy holiday, but discontented none the less.

Oliver's two previous visits had given him little time to explore the island, yet there was something about the Maltese character with which he readily identified: as a race they were energetic and industrious and wealthy; as a crowd, they were loud and proud and enthusiastic; as individuals, open and warm but basically shy. Traits that overlaid his own character almost exactly.

Among the international stars flying into Malta was David Hemmings, Oliver's co-star from *The System*. All the *Gladiator* cast were warned to expect studio calls any time between Monday and Saturday. By his second weekend in Malta Oliver had nosed out a small bar in Valletta he felt at home in and worked out a route to and from his Floriana hotel passing as many discreet drinking establishments as possible.

Three doors up from the Greek Church of Our Lady of Damascus in Valletta's Archbishop Street was a small single-room bar half the size of Oliver's Castle McCarthy kitchen. Above the door between the two mock-Victorian lanterns and written in Gothic script were the words: The Pub. The bar's owner, Paul Cremona, had recently returned from hospital after receiving treatment for cancer. 'Whenever it got busy, Oliver would offer to help behind the bar or give me a hand with the crates,' recalled Cremona. 'But mostly he sat quietly in the corner enjoying a drink and talking to the other customers.'

His bar bill seldom came to less than a hundred Maltese lira – more than £160 – and he never left The Pub sober. Around two on Sunday afternoons Oliver would continue west down Archbishop Street and across the end of Palace Square until he came to Straight Street, a narrow alley barely wide enough for a car, which ran uphill all the way to the city gates. Just around the corner was the Roy Bar, ten yards further on the Malta Lounge Bar and still further on, side by side, the New Life Lounge, Larry's Bar and the Tico-Tico. Untroubled and unrecognised by the tourists he could pick and choose his stops as he fancied. If Josephine was with him they would stop at the Labyrinth, an upmarket arts centre and restaurant.

On 16 April Josephine celebrated her 35th birthday. They had been together for twenty years. The following day Oliver slipped out of the Phoenicia Hotel and through the bus terminal. He was following the directions a manager at the hotel had given him. Just beyond the white-fronted Law Courts and next to Costa's Men's Wear he found Mallia Borg's jeweller's shop. Inside it was pleasantly cool.

'I've been told you're the best jeweller in Valletta,' Oliver said to the small man standing behind one of the display counters. Mallia Borg smiled modestly, not recognising his celebrity customer. 'I want you to design a very special bracelet. I want it to be like no other piece in the world,' he explained.

Examining samples of Borg's work, Oliver confessed that the bracelet was a special birthday present for his wife. 'I sometimes worry she doesn't realise how much she means to me,' he added. The work would take two weeks to complete; it would be ready on Friday, 30 April.

In the meantime he concentrated on his part. Each morning after breakfast in their harbour-view suite Oliver and Josephine walked through the Phoenicia's garden to the secluded swimming pool. They were seldom recognised or disturbed; if a fellow guest approached them Oliver chatted amicably or offered to buy them a drink. The poolside bar was tended by Stephen Attard, who thought Oliver was one of the hotel's 'less snobbish' residents. 'They were a very relaxed and happy couple,' recalls Attard, who kept his guests supplied with chilled apple juice. About mid-morning the house telephone would ring and Attard informed Oliver he was wanted by the studio.

On Sunday, 25 April, Lino Cassar – the writer who witnessed the *Cutthroat Island* fiasco six years earlier – arrived at the Phoenicia to interview Oliver and found him ensconced in a corner of the hotel's cocktail bar. As Cassar shook hands with Josephine, Oliver ordered another round of drinks. It was obvious the actor had been drinking for some time. 'He was not drunk,' says Cassar. 'Just very talkative and happy.'

To Cassar's surprise – 'I can't remember what prompted it' – Oliver began reciting part of the *Triple Echo* script, the film he made with Glenda Jackson 27 years earlier. For several minutes the Green Bar came to a standstill as fascinated guests and staff listened to Oliver voicing a scene from the movie, speaking the parts in turn and mimicking his female co-star perfectly.

In England Michael Winner had just finished speaking to the show-business editor of the *Daily Mail*. Aware of his long friendship with Oliver – and with *Parting Shots* due for release in less than two weeks – she asked the film's producer-director to arrange an interview with his most infamous star. It was Thursday afternoon. She wanted to fly out to see Oliver early the next week before returning to cover the Cannes Film Festival.

Winner picked up the telephone in the first-floor office of his luxury Kensington home and dialled 00-356, the Malta code, and then the number for the Phoenicia Hotel. Oliver sounded upbeat, excited, and said he was anxious to get back and start work on *My Uncle Silas*. 'I've never done a television series before,' he said. 'Do you think it will be all right?'

'I remember the film version,"[1] said Winner reassuringly. 'You'll be perfect, Oliver.'

Oliver's part in *Gladiator* was almost over. He had completed his last full week of shooting. On Friday evening Mallia Borg delivered the gold bracelet to the Reeds's hotel. It would be the last present Oliver would give his wife.

On Sunday, 2 May, Oliver and Josephine ate breakfast in their third-floor suite. The sky was blue and cloudless and from the balcony they could see across Marsamxet Harbour and beyond to the roofs of Sliema. The sound of traffic using Siege Road drifted upwards through the trees in the hotel garden.

By mid-morning the Phoenicia's lobby was still deserted. Joseph Borg, the hotel's senior concierge, tidied the tourist leaflets on his desk and wished he had more to do. Behind him the vault-roofed lounge was empty. Even the restaurant was quiet. 'Good morning.' Borg looked up to see Oliver standing beside the open front doors.

'Good morning,' replied Borg. Oliver could see he was nervous. 'Mr Reed, would you mind if I had my picture taken

---

[1] Winner was incorrectly thinking of *Uncle Silas*, the 1947 film adapted from the Sheridan Le Fanu novel by Ben Travers. The Yorkshire Television series was based on HE Bates's *My Uncle Silas*.

with you? I have a camera.' Oliver grinned and waved the concierge out from behind his desk. It was the last exposure on the roll and Borg hoped it would come out.

As they turned into Archbishop Street, Oliver and Josephine could see that the concertina metal grille across the front of The Pub had been pulled back. Inside it was cool and dark and Oliver desperately needed a drink.

Simon Reed switched on the television and settled himself for an afternoon of motor racing. His girlfriend, Claire, was away and their nanny was looking after the two children.

The hour-long preamble to the San Marino Grand Prix was over and the race itself was about to start. Surprisingly, Michael Schumacher was on the second row of the Imola grid behind Mika Hakkinen and David Coulthard. The telephone rang. Simon watched the cars clear the first corner before picking up the handset.

'You've got to come. You've got to help me.' It was Josephine's voice. 'He's gone, Simon. He's gone.'

A flicker of doubt stopped him answering. Over the last few months Oliver had made an effort to rebuild the lost relationship with his brother's family; after years of not speaking he had even telephoned and chatted to Claire while Simon was away. Maybe the pranks were also starting again.

'Please, Simon. I need your help.' The emotion in Josephine's voice was just too strong.

Warren Cremona had left The Pub early to return to his Valletta flat and watch the San Marino Grand Prix. Schumacher's red Ferrari was already in the lead and soaking up the cheers of the 90,000 near-hysterical Italian fans at Imola.

Outside the two-tones of an ambulance echoed down the city's narrow streets. Picking up the telephone he heard his mother's voice. 'Warren, come back quickly. Oliver is very sick.'

The Grand Prix coverage went to a commercial break. In London Stephen Ford got up from the sofa and poured himself another glass of wine. Standing with his back to the television, he didn't see the screen change to an ITN news flash. 'Oliver Reed has died in Malta. The sixty-one-year-old actor collapsed while drinking with friends in a Valletta bar. He died shortly afterwards in hospital.'

Ford's hands were shaking. The wineglass was shaking. Unsure of where Josephine might be, he telephoned Castle McCarthy. Jack Manning, the Reeds' house-sitter, picked up the phone. The Irishman had already heard the news. 'Look, if Josephine is there I don't want to talk to her,' said Ford. 'I just want her to know that when she's ready she can ring me back.'

Simon didn't need to look up the numbers. First he dialled Mark; his nephew was out walking. Then he dialled Sarah; she answered the phone in her car.

At the Phoenicia Hotel Joseph Borg finished his late lunch and returned to his desk in the front lobby. The British newspapers had arrived. After sorting the Sunday papers into neat piles Borg collected one of each and set off down the marbled corridor. As he passed the reception desk he noticed the clerks talking in a whispered huddle. It was unusual to see all three on duty at the same time.

Borg stopped outside Room 611. He could hear voices and what sounded like a woman crying. He knocked. The talking stopped and the door opened. The suite seemed full, almost crowded. Faces he knew, but suddenly could not put a name to. At the far end of the room, sitting on the edge of a chair, Borg could see Josephine Reed. Her face was white and wet with tears and she was twisting a white handkerchief in her hands. The man who had opened the door took the newspapers and nodded.

Back at his lobby desk Borg lifted his camera from its drawer. Somewhere inside was the last photograph anyone had taken of Oliver Reed.

Simon walked through the kitchen of his Walton-on-Thames house and into the back garden. He began picking up stones from the path and hurling them at the garden wall, just as his mother had done when Oliver frustrated her to distraction.

Now it was his turn.

Epilogue

O LIVER REED'S *Gladiator* character was to have ridden into the sunset at the end of the film. With just five days of shooting left, director Ridley Scott ordered a script rewrite to give Proximo a redeeming death – at a cost of two million dollars.

Two earlier scenes were adapted to allow Oliver's head to be computer grafted on to the body of an acting double and high-tech imaging was used to change his expression and add shadows and wrinkles to his face. Additional appearances, filmed weeks earlier, were clawed back from out-takes and already discarded sequences: one entire scene is a repeat of a previous one, but with Oliver in different clothes, against a different background and uttering different words.

Proximo's death, for reasons of tact, was shot carefully from behind.

Gladiator is dedicated to Oliver Reed. Reed's performance as Proximo earned him a 2001 BAFTA nomination for best actor in a supporting role.

Appendix 1: Filmography

All years given are film release dates and are no indication of the year in which the picture was made.

	Title	Credit/Role	Year
1	*Value for Money*	A Dancer	1955
2	*Hello London*	Photographer & Dancer	1958
3	*The Square Peg*	Extra	1958
4	*Life is a Circus*	Extra	1958
5	*The Four Just Men*	Extra	1958
6	*The Captain's Table*	Extra	1959
7	*Upstairs and Downstairs*	Extra	1959
8	*The Angry Silence*	Mick	1960
9	*The League of Gentlemen*	Camp Actor	1960
10	*Beat Girl* [US: *Wild for Kicks*]	Actor in Plaid Shirt	1960
11	*The Two Faces of Dr Jekyll* [*Dr Jekyll and Mr Hyde*] [*Jekyll's Inferno*] [US: *House of Fright*]	Nightclub Bouncer	1960
12	*The Sword of Sherwood Forest*	Melton	1960
13	*The Bulldog Breed*	Teddy Boy at cinema	1960
14	*His and Hers*	Poet	1960
15	*The Rebel* [US: *Call Me Genius*]	Artist	1960
16	*No Love for Johnnie*	Man at party [bucket on head]	1961
17	*The Curse of the Werewolf* [US: *The Curse of Siniestro*]	Leon	1961

18	*The Pirates of Blood River*	Brocaire	1961
19	*Captain Clegg*	Harry	1962
	[US: *Night Creatures*]		
20	*The Damned*	King	1962
	[US: *These are the Damned*]		
21	*Paranoiac*	Simon Ashby	1963
22	*The Scarlet Blade*	Captain Tom Sylvester	1963
	[US: *The Crimson Blade*]		
23	*The Party's Over*	Moise	1963
24	*The System*	Tinker	1964
	[US: *The Girl-Getters*]		
25	*The Brigand of Kandahar*	Eli Khan	1965
26	*The Trap*	Jean La Bete	1966
27	*The Jokers*	David Tremayne	1966
28	*The Shuttered Room*	Ethan	1967
	[US: *Blood Island*]		
29	*I'll Never Forget What's 'isname*	Andrew Quint	1967
30	*Oliver!*	Bill Sykes	1968
31	*Hannibal Brooks*	Hannibal Brooks	1969
32	*The Assassination Bureau*	Ivan Dragomiloff	1969
33	*Women in Love*	Gerald Crich	1969
34	*Take a Girl Like You*	Patrick Standish	1969
35	*The Lady in the Car with Glasses and a Gun*	Michael Caldwell	1970
	[FR: *La Dame Dans L'Auto Avec Des Lunettes Et Un Fusil*]		
36	*The Hunting Party*	Frank Calder	1971
37	*The Devils*	Father Urbain Grandier	1971
	[*The Devils of Loudun*]		
38	*Sitting Target*	Harry Lomart	1972
39	*Zero Population Growth*	Russ McNeil	1972
	[US: *Z.P.G.*]		
	[US: *Edict*]		
	[US: *The First of January*]		
40	*Age of Pisces*	Guest Appearance	1972
41	*The Triple Echo*	Sergeant	1972
	[US: *Soldier in Skirts*]		
42	*Bite and Run*	Guest Appearance	1973
	[*Mordi E Fuggi*]		
	[*Dirty Weekend*]		

43	*Fury* [*Il Giorno del Furore*] [*Days of Fury*] [*One Russian Summer*]	Palizyn	1973
44	*The Three Musketeers:* (*The Queen's Diamonds*) [ES: *Los Tres Mosqueteros*]	Athos	1973
45	*Mahler*	Train Conductor	1974
46	*Blue Blood*	Tom	1974
47	*Revolver* [*Death in the Streets*] [FR: *La Poursuite* *implacable*]	Vito Caprini	1974
48	*The Four Musketeers:* (*The Revenge of Milady*)	Athos	1974
49	*Tommy* [*Who's Tommy*]	Frank Hobbs	1975
50	*Royal Flash*	Otto von Bismark	1975
51	*Lisztomania*	Princess Carolyn's servant	1975
52	*And Then There Were None* [US: *Ten Little Indians*] [US: *Death in Persepolis*] [IT: *e poi non ne rimase* *nessuno*] [ES: *Diez negritos*] [GER: *Ein Undekannter* *rechnet ab*] [GER: *Zehn kleine* *Negerlein*]	Hugh Lombard	1975
53	*The Sellout* [*The Set-Up*]	Gabriel Lee	1976
54	*The Great Scout and* *Cathouse Thursday* [*Wildcat*]	Joe Knox	1976
55	*Burnt Offerings*	Ben Rolf	1976
56	*Maniac* [US: *Assault on Paradise*] [*Ransom*] [*The Town That Cried* *Terror*]	Nick McCormick	1976
57	*The Prince & The Pauper* [US: *Crossed Swords*]	Miles Hendon	1977
58	*Tomorrow Never Comes*	Detective Jim Wibon	1978

59	*The Big Sleep*	Eddie Mars	1978
60	*The Class of Miss McMichael*	Terence Sutton	1979
61	*No Secrets!* [*Touch of the Sun*]	Captain Donald Nelson	1979
62	*The Brood* [FR: *La Clinique de la terreur*]	Dr Hal Raglan	1979
63	*The Mad Trapper* [Never completed]	Guest Appearance	1979
64	*The Lion of the Desert* [*Omar Mukhtar: Lion of the Desert*]	General Rodolfo Granziani	1980
65	*Dr Heckyl and Mr Hype*	Dr Heckyl/Mr Hype	1980
66	*The Great Quest*	Colonel	1981
67	*Condorman*	Krokov	1981
68	*Venom*	Dave Connolly	1981
69	*Death Bite* [see television: *Spasms*]	Jason Kincaid	1982
70	*Al-Mas' Ala Al-Kubra* [GB: *Clash of Loyalties*]	Colonel Leachman	1982
71	*The Sting II*	Doyle Lonnegan	1983
72	*99 Women*	Guest Appearance	1983
73	*Frank and I*	Guest Appearance	1983
74	*Two of a Kind* [*Second Chance*]	Beazley	1983
75	*Fanny Hill (Memoirs of a Woman of Pleasure)* [GER: *Fanny Hill – Die Memoiren eines Freudenmachen*]	Mr Widdlecome	1983
76	*Captive* [*Heroine*]	Gregory Le Vay	1986
77	*The Last of the Templars*	Guest Appearance	1986
78	*Castaway*	Gerald Kingsland	1986
79	*Rage to Kill*	Guest Appearance	1987
80	*The Misfit Brigade* [*Wheels of Terror*]	The General	1988
81	*Skeleton Coast* [*Coast of Skeletons*]	Captain Simpson	1988
82	*The House of Usher*	Roderick Usher	1988
83	*Captive Rage*	General Belmondo	1988
84	*Gor*	Sarm	1989

85	*Damnation Express*	Guest Appearance	1989
86	*Hold My Hand, I'm Dying* [*Blind Justice*]	Reverend Ballinger	1989
87	*The Adventures of Baron Munchausen* [GER: *Die Abenteuer des Baron von Munchhausen*]	Vulcan	1989
88	*The Return of the Musketeers*	Athos	1989
89	*Treasure Island* [see television: *Treasure Island*]	Captain Billy Bones	1989
90	*The Revenger*	Jack Fisher	1990
91	*Panama Sugar and the Dog Thief* [*Panama zucchero*]	Guest Appearance	1990
92	*Severed Ties* [*Army*]	Dr Hans Vaughan	1991
93	*The Pit and the Pendulum*	Cardinal	1991
94	*Hired to Kill*	Michael Bartos	1991
95	*Blue in the Face*	Guest Appearance	1992
96	*Funny Bones*	Dolly Hopkins	1995
97	*Cutthroat Island* [Fired from film]	Mordachai	1995
98	*Luise Knackt Den Jackpot*	Mattias	1996
99	*Superbrain Der Bankraub Des Jahrhunderts*	Superbrain	1996
100	*The Bruce*	Bishop Robert Wisharton	1996
101	*Russisch Roulette* [*Russian Roulette*] [*The Moscow Connection*]	Guest Appearance	1996
102	*Mastermind*	Guest Appearance	1996
103	*The People vs Larry Flynt*	Governor Rhodes	1996
104	*Parting Shots*	Jamie Campbell-Stewart	1999
105	*Gladiator*	Proximo	2000

Appendix 2:
TV Appearances

Year	Title	Role/Appearance
1959	*The Golden Spur* (BBC TV)	Richard of Gloucester
1963	*The Saint: King of the Beggars* (ITV)	Joe Catelli
1963	*The Debussy Film* (BBC TV)	Debussy
1964	*R3* (Series 2)	Dr Richard Franklin
1964	*It's Dark Outside*	Sebastian
1964	*The Saint: Sophia* (ITV)	Artistides
1965	*Always on Sunday*	Narrator
1967	*Dante's Inferno* (BBC TV)	Dante Gabriel Rossetti
1973	*Cinema Now*	Interview guest talking on *Triple Echo*
1981	*Spasms* (Canadian cable) [see films: *Death Bite*]	Jason Kincaid
1984	*Black Arrow*	Sir Daniel
1985	*Cristoforo Colombo* (Italian TV)	Martin Pinzon, television mini-series
1985	*Twenty Years On*	Interview guest talking on 'Sexual Revolution'
1985	*All Star Secrets* (LWT)	Guest appearance
1987	*Newsnight* (BBC TV)	Interview guest talking on *Castaway*
1987	*The Max Headroom Show* (Ch 4), 20 January	Interview guest
1987	*Dragonard*	Guest appearance
1989	*Treasure Island* (TNT – America) [see films: *Treasure Island*]	Captain Billy Bones
1989	*Hot Air and Fantasy* (*The Adventures of Terry Gilliam*)	Guest appearance

Year	Title	Role
1990	*El Flecha Negra*	Guest appearance
1990	*Master of Dragonard Hill*	Guest appearance
1990	*Aspel & Company* (ITV), 5 May	Interview guest
1990	*This Week:* *The Last Picture Show*	Interview guest
1990	*Treasure Island*	Captain Billy Bones
1991	*The Lady and the Highwayman*	Sir Philip Gage
1991	*After Dark:* *Do Men Have to be Violent* (Ch 4)	Interview guest
1991	*The Pit and the Pendulum*	Cardinal
1991	*A Ghost of Monte Carlo*	The Rajah
1991	*Prisoner of Honor* (Cable TV)	General Boisdeffre
1993	*Return to Lonesome Dove* (TV Movie, USA)	Gregor Dunnegan
1993	*In the Hot Seat*	Interview guest
1994	*Without Walls:* *The Obituary Show* (Ch 4)	Programme subject
1994	*The World of Hammer:* *Peter Cushing*	Narrator
1994	*The World of Hammer:* *Dracula and the Undead*	Narrator
1994	*The World of Hammer:* *The Lands Before Time*	Narrator
1994	*The World of Hammer:* *The Vamps*	Narrator
1994	*The World of Hammer:* *Wicked Women*	Narrator
1994	*The World of Hammer:* *The War*	Narrator
1994	*The World of Hammer:* *Science Fiction*	Narrator
1994	*The World of Hammer:* *The Mummies, Werewolves* *and the Living Dead*	Narrator
1994	*The World of Hammer:* *The Thriller*	Narrator
1994	*The World of Hammer:* *Frankenstein's Monster*	Narrator
1994	*The World of Hammer:* *Christopher Lee*	Narrator
1994	*The World of Hammer:* *Hammer*	Narrator

1994	*The World of Hammer:* *The Costume Adventure*	Narrator
1995	*Die Tunnelgangster von Berlin*	Role: Prof Norbert Marcus
1996	*Orpheus & Eurydice*	Narrator
1996	*Freddie Starr Show* (ITV), 18 July	Guest appearance
1996	*Freddie Starr Show* (ITV), 5 September	Guest appearance
1997	*Marco Polo* *Marco Polo: Return to Xanadu*	Guest appearance
1998	*The Bible: Jeremiah*	Role: General Schafan
1998	*Before They Were Famous*	Guest appearance
1999	*My Uncle Silas* (YTV)	Uncle Silas Shelved after Oliver's death

Appendix 3:
Radio Broadcasts

Year	Title	Role/Appearance
1995	*The Death of Alexander Scriabin* (BBC Radio 3), 18 June	Aleister Crowley

Sources and Acknowledgements

This book would not have been written without the help I received from a great many people. It is impossible to measure their contributions. While some contributed part or all of a chapter others confirmed a date or provided a sentence. Others, through their expertise, helped me understand the complexities of Oliver Reed's life.

As ever a special thank-you to Sarah Berry, my secretary-cum-assistant-cum-researcher – but most of all friend. She knew when to bully and when to encourage and never lost faith. She allowed me to lose heart without ever losing hers. Also my agent, Jane Judd, for her endless loyalty and support and patience.

My gratitude and thanks must also go to Josephine Reed and Simon Reed – the former who tolerated my persistence through what must have been a sad and difficult time, and the latter who gave me his time and memories.

For his ceaseless enthusiasm, endless anecdotes and some hilarious meetings I must thank Stephen Ford. Also Squiffy the cat. I am also indebted to Michael Winner for his time and permission to use copyrighted pictures and material.

I must also thank Trevor Ermel, of Monochrome, Newcastle, who excercised care and enthusiasm when copying some very valuable material.

Extracts from *Winnie-the-Pooh* by AA Milne reproduced by permission of Curtis Brown Ltd, London, on behalf of the Trustees of the Pooh Properties.

Permission to use copyrighted material and photographs was kindly granted by *The Times*, Malta; the *Sunday Times*, Malta; Albert Moses; the *Gazette*, Blackpool; Richard and Ivy Hall; Joseph Borg; Stephen Ford; John Hogg and Fiona Adams.

Finally, I must show my indebtedness to the following authors, publishers, institutions, individuals and societies whose sources I have drawn upon and who gave their time and goodwill and helped in the creation of this book.

Principal printed material cited and quoted:

BOOKS

ANN-Margret. *My Story* (Orion, 1994).

BAXTER, John. *An Appalling Talent* (Michael Joseph Ltd, 1973).

BINGHAM, Madeleine. *The 'Great Lover': The Life & Art of Herbert Beerbohm Tree* (Hamish Hamilton Ltd, 1978).

BRYANT, Chris. *Glenda Jackson: The Biography* (HarperCollins Publishers, 1999).

CRAWFORD, Michael. *Parcel Arrived Safely: Tied With String* (Century, 1999).

DAVIES, Russell. *The Kenneth Williams Diaries* (HarperCollins Publishers, 1993).

FLETCHER, Tony. *Dear Boy: The Life of Keith Moon* (Omnibus Press, 1998).

FONDA, Peter. *Don't tell Dad: a memoir* (Simon & Schuster Ltd, 1998).

Kelly's Directory: Wimbledon, 1940.

HARDING, Bill. *The Films of Michael Winner* (Frederick Muller, 1978).

HAYWARD, Anthony. *Phantom: Michael Crawford Unmasked* (Weidenfeld & Nicolson, 1991).

LAWRENCE, DH *Women in Love* (unknown).

LEE, Christopher. *Tall, Dark and Gruesome* (WH Allen & Co. Ltd, 1997).

MILES, Sarah. *Bolt from the Blue* (Orion Books Ltd, 1996).

MILNE, AA *The Complete Winnie-the-Pooh* (Eyre Methuen Ltd).

MILNE, Christopher. *The Enchanted Places* (Eyre Methuen Ltd,1974).

MONSARRAT, Nicholas. *The Kappillan of Malta* (Pan Books, 1994).

Photoplay Film Year Book, 1976 (Illustrated Pulications Ltd).

REDGRAVE, Vanessa. *An Autobiography* (Hutchinson, 1991).

REED, Oliver. *Reed all About Me* (WH Allen & Co. Ltd, 1979).

RUSSELL, Ken. *A British Picture* (Heinemann, 1989).

SACHS, Bruce, and Russell Wall. *Greasepaint and Gore: The Hammer Monsters of Roy Ashton* (Tomahawk Press, 1998).

TREVELYAN, John. *What The Censor Saw* (Michael Joseph Ltd, 1973).

WALKER, John. *Halliwell's Film Guide 10th Edition* (HarperCollins Publishers, 1994).

WOODWARD, Ian. *Glenda Jackson: A Study in Fire and Ice* (Weidenfeld & Nicolson, 1983).

PERIODICALS AND NEWSPAPERS

ANON:

'And another fine mess . . .' (unknown).

'Boozy Ollie a TV turn-off'. *Sydney Daily Telegraph*, January 1991.

'Death of journalist Peter Reed'. *Sporting Life*, May 1997.

'Five-star boot for fighting actor'. The *Express & Star*, Wolverhampton, July 1973.

'Folly of putting on tragic Ollie' (unknown).

'From out-of-work film extra to £1,000-a-week star'. The *News*, Wimbledon, June 1967.

'Hellraiser Reed calls time on film world'. *Daily Mail*, February 1998.

'Hoax call got boozy Ollie blacked out!' (unknown).

'Legless Before Wicket'. *Daily Mirror*, July 1992.

'Mushy peas is now the high life for mellow Ollie'. The *Gazette*, Blackpool, April 1994.

'My schoolgirl love has tamed me'. The *Express & Star*, Wolverhampton, July 1981.

'Oliver Reed' obituary. The *Daily Telegraph*, May 1999.

'Oliver Reed' obituary. The *Independent*, May 1999.

'Oliver Reed scuffled story denied' (unknown).

'Ollie girl gets a ticking off'. The *Express & Star*, Wolverhampton, January 1981.

'Reed fined for drunken rumpus'. The *Express & Star*, Wolverhampton, August 1984.

'Reed hopes he will be reconciled with accuser' (unknown) December 1993.

'Reed lifts the spirits' (unknown).

'Sir Carol Reed: Obituary'. *The Times*, April 1976.

ALLEN, Paul. ' "Ollie was not drunk" says angry ex-wife' (unknown).

BENATTAR, Mark. 'Oliver a real gent'. The *Gazette*, Blackpool, April 1994.

BETTS, Ernest. 'Carol Reed makes his first musical film after a long wait'. *The Times*, September 1968.

CASSAR, Lino. 'No baths or showers for British extras in Gladiator'. the *Sunday Times*, February 1999.

CASSAR, Lino. 'Oliver Reed, the screen's fascinating carouser'. *The Times*, Malta, May 1999.

CINI, George & Jesmond Bonello. 'Oliver Reed dies after being taken ill in Valletta Pub'. *The Times*, Malta, May 1999.

DOBB, Vikram. 'Hellraiser with the hidden talent'. The *Guardian*, May 1999.

DUNN, Rosie. 'Ollie ... the beer departed'. *Sunday People*, May 1999.

ELLAM Dennis and Ted Oliver. 'Ollie star of life'. *Sunday Mirror*, May 1999.

FOSTER, Howard. 'Boozy Ollie's too scary' (unknown).

GALLAGHER, Jim. 'Ollie's Beer-ial Ground'. *Sunday People*, May 1999.

GILLARD, David. 'My Kind of Day'. *Radio Times*, February 1994.

HAYMAN, Ronald. 'Oliver Reed'. *The Times Saturday Review*, October 1970.

HOWARD, Philip. 'Enter Bill Sykes as rescuer'. *The Times*, April 1969.

HUGHES, Simon, and Justine Woods. 'Ollie's last orders'. The *Sun*, May 1999.

JORDAN, Hugh. 'Outrageous Ollie sails into town'. *Sunday World*.

KEANE, Dillie. 'Raise a glass, for 'tis the season to be Olly'. The *Mail on Sunday*, December 1993.

KING, Norman. 'Oliver Reed'. The *Guardian*, May 1999.

LEVINE, Ray. 'Ollie gets floored by a scouser' (unknown).

LUCAS, Tim. 'A toast to Mr England'. *Film Comment*, July/August 1999.

MARKFIELD, Alan. 'Ollie Reed: A tough guy in love'. *Woman*, July 1981.

MASSA, Ariadne. 'Hunt for 20,000 Maltese extras'. *The Times*, January 1999.

MASSA, Ariadne. '1,500 turn up for Gladiator roles'. *The Times*, February 1999.

MASSA, Ariadne. 'Four attempt to steal Lm80,000 from Gladiator building'. *The Times*, April 1999.

MASSA, Ariadne. 'Oliver Reed died of severe coronary heart disease'. *The Times*, May 1999.

MASSA, Ariadne. 'The Pub owners recall close friendship with Oliver Reed'. *The Times*, May 1999.

MASSA, Ariadne. 'Oliver Reed's haunt, the new attraction in Valletta'. *The Times*, June 1999.

MCGURRAN, Aidan. 'Pal Ollie broke my back with a drunken prank'. The *Sun*, December 1993.

MCGURRAN, Aidan. 'Ollie's off for night on kiss'. The *Sun*, December 1993.

MIDDLEHURST, Lester. 'How my marriage has triumphed against all odds'. *Daily Mail*, June 1995.

MIDGLEY, Carol. 'Hellraiser who went the way he wanted'. *The Times*, May 1999.

MOULAND, Bill. 'Victory hangover'. *Daily Mail*, December 1993.

MOULAND, Bill. 'Knife at my throat'. *Daily Mail*, December 1993.

OLIVER, Ted. 'Ollie's laughing all the way to the pub'. *Daily Mirror*, January 1991.

PARSONS, Jane. 'Awesome weekend with Ollie'. The *Bucks Herald*, May 1999.

POOK, Sally. 'Oliver Reed, hell-raising actor, dies after collapsing in Maltese bar'. The *Daily Telegraph*, May 1999.

RISSIK, Andrew. 'Devil of an actor'. The *Guardian*, May 1999.

ROBERTS, Glenys. 'Nothing broken about this Reed'. *The Times*, October 1976.

ROGERS, Susan. Untitled interview. The *Express & Star*, Wolverhampton, August 1971.

ROONEY, Ciara. 'Portaferry mourns hellraising actor who loved village'. *Down Recorder*, May 1999.

ROWE, David. 'I so much wanted to give Ollie a child, but I can't. Sadly, it's not to be'. *Sunday Mirror*, December 1993.

SMITH, Muriel-Jane. 'I'm no hellraiser' (unknown).

TAYLOR, Robert and Mydrim Jones. 'Alex Higgins drank my perfume!'. The *People*, September 1991.

VELLA, Alan. 'Don't chuck . . . just ciak!'. The *Sunday Times*, June 1999.

VINCENT, Sally. 'Portrait: Oliver Reed'. The *Guardian Weekend*, June 1995.

WHITTINGHAM, Stewart. 'Ollie Reed dies in pub'. The *Sun*, May 1999.

WILDE, Jon. 'Oliver Reed 1938–1999'. *Loaded*, May 1999.

WINNER, Michael. 'Untitled'. *Daily Mail*, May 1999.

Bulletins of the British Film Institute, 1961 to 1981.
Journal of The Tony Hancock Appreciation Society:
The Missing Page; August 1999.

INSTITUTIONS

I am grateful to the following curators, archivists and reference librarians who donated a great deal of time and enthusiasm.

Edwin Bowman, librarian with Allied Newspapers, Malta.

Carole Davies, librarian at the *Gazette*, Blackpool.

PJV Elliott, senior archivist at the Royal Air Force Museum, Hendon.

Simon Goodie, historian to the Amateur Rowing Association.

The Tony Hillman Collection.

W Siemaszko, E Farlow and S Andrew at Merton Libraries and Heritage Services.

Neil Somerville at British Broadcasting Corporation, Written Archive Centre, Caversham.

PH Staring at the Army Medical Services Museums, Aldershot.

Bill Torrens, local studies librarian with Buckinghamshire County Council.

ADVERTISING

Agamemnon Films-British Lion. *Treasure Island*, 1989.

Alpha Films. *The Brood*, 1979.

Associated British Picture Corporation. *The Brigand of Kandahar*, 1965.

Associated British Picture Corporation. *The Rebel*, 1960.

BLC Films Ltd. *The System*, 1964.

British Lion Films Ltd. *Life is a Circus*, 1958.

British Lion Films Ltd. *The Angry Silence*, 1960.

Columbia. *Oliver!*, 1968.

Columbia. *Take a Girl Like You*, 1969.

Columbia. *The Lady in the Car with Glasses and a Gun*, 1970.

Columbia. *The Pirates of Blood River*, 1962.

Columbia. *The Sword of Sherwood Forest*, 1960.

Columbia. *The Two Faces of Dr Jekyll*, 1960.

Columbia-Tri-Star. *The Adventures of Baron Munchausen*, 1989.

Columbia-Warner Pictures. *Lisztomania*, 1975.

Columbia-Warner Pictures. *The Devils*,1971.

Columbia-Warner. *The Sellout*, 1976.

EMI. *And Then There Were None*, 1975.

Entertainment Film Distributors Ltd. *The Return of the Musketeers*, 1989.

Fox-Rank. *The Four Musketeers: The Revenge of Milady*, 1974.

Fox-Rank. *The Three Musketeers: The Queen's Diamonds*, 1973.

Good Times Enterprises. *Mahler*, 1974.

Hand Made Films. *Venom*, 1981.

Hemdale International Films. *The Triple Echo*, 1972.

Hemdale International Films. *Tommy*, 1975.

Hollywood Pictures. *Funny Bones*, 1995.
ITC Entertainment. *The Big Sleep*, 1978.
Monarch Film Corporation. *The Party's Over*, 1963.
Paramount Pictures. *The Assassination Bureau*, 1969.
Rank Films. *Fury*, 1973.
Rank Films. *I'll Never Forget What's 'isname*, 1967.
Rank Films. *No Love for Johnnie*, 1961.
Rank Films. *The Bulldog Breed*, 1960.
Rank Films. *The Captain's Table*, 1959.
Rank Films. *The Jokers*, 1966.
Rank Films. *The League of Gentlemen*, 1960.
Rank Films. *The Square Peg*, 1958.
Rank Films. *The Trap*, 1966.
Rank Films. *Upstairs and Downstairs*, 1959.
Regal Films International. *Beat Girl*, 1960.
Regal Films International. *Hello London*, 1958.
Scotia-Barber Distributors. *Zero Population Growth*, 1982.
Seven Arts Productions. *The Shuttered Room*, 1967.
Twentieth Century-Fox. *The Prince & The Pauper*, 1977.
Twentieth Century-Fox. *Two of a Kind*, 1983.
United Artists. *Burnt Offerings*, 1976.
United Artists. *Hannibal Brooks*, 1969.
United Artists. *The Hunting Party*, 1971.
United Artists. *Women in Love*, 1969.
United International Pictures. *Parting Shots*, 1999.
Walt Disney. *Condorman*, 1981.

PERSONAL INTERVIEWS

I wish to thank the following people, whom I had the pleasure of interviewing or corresponding with during my research for this book.

Fiona Adams
Stephen Attard
David Ball, Producer at CF1 Limited
Joseph Borg
Norman Brown
Lino Cassar
Brian Clarke
Warren Cremona at The Pub, Valletta, Malta
Lawrence Edge
Freddie Francis

Johnny Goodman, former President of the Guild of Film Production Executives
Ann Harris
William Hobbs, swordmaster and fight arranger on the *Musketeer* films
John Hogg
Phil Kelly
Steve King
Mark Lester
Joan Mee
Albert Moses
John O'Connor Snr
Edward Orbell
Pat Parrans
Andy Potter at BBC Radio Derby
Bruce J Sachs at Tomahawk Press
Michiel Stevenson
Michael Winner

Finally to Michael Brown, whose endless research and enthusiasm for this, and my previous books, deserves special thanks.

For background material and insight into Oliver Reed's life I am also indebted to:

Barry Balmayne
Claire Berry
Maurice Blisson
Vera Crump
Howard F Gregg
Joanne Gunn at the *Racing Post*
Richard and Ivy Hall
William Hanover
Hoe Bridge School, Woking
Karen Jensen-Jones at Yorkshire Television
Paddy MacDee at BBC Radio Newcastle
Mick Monks
Derek Noonan
'The General'
Claudia Smith at *Woman*
BSK Turner, assistant head at Wimbledon Common Preparatory School

Every effort was made to trace and seek permission from those holding the copyright to material used in this book. My deepest apologies to anyone I may have inadvertently omitted. Any omissions or errors in the form of credit will be corrected in future printings.

Cliff Goodwin, 2000

Index